WORKING W...
TEACHING MET...
WHAT'S AT STAKE?

Earl W. Stevick

A TeacherSource Book

Donald Freeman
Series Editor

Heinle & Heinle Publishers
I(T)P An International Thomson Publishing Company

Pacific Grove • Albany • Bonn • Boston • Cincinnati • Detroit • London
Madrid • Melbourne • Mexico City • New York • Paris
San Francisco • Tokyo • Toronto • Washington

The publication of *Working with Teaching Methods: What's at Stake?*
was directed by members of the Newbury House ESL/EFL
Team at Heinle & Heinle:

Erik Gundersen, Editorial Director
Jonathan Boggs, Marketing Director
Kristin M. Thalheimer, Senior Production Services Coordinator
Thomas Healy, Developmental Editor
Stanley J. Galek, Vice President and Publisher/ESL

Also participating in the publication of this program were:

Project Management and Composition: Imageset
Designer: Jessica Robison
Manufacturing Coordinator: Mary Beth Hennebury
Associate Market Development Director: Mary Sutton
Cover Designer: Ha D. Nguyen

Heinle & Heinle is a division of International Thomson Publishing, Inc.

Manufactured in Canada

p. 8. "Their Lonely Betters" by W.H. Auden, copyright © 1951.
Reprinted by permission of Curtis Brown Ltd.

p. 6. Madeline E. Ehrman, Understanding Second Language Learning Difficulties,
pp 187-189, copyright © 1996. Reprinted by permission of Sage Publications, Inc.

pp. 116-122 Ted Swartz, from Newsletter of Educational Solutions, December 1976—
February 1977 issue, pp 14-16. Copyright © 1977. Used by permission of Shakti Gattegno.

ISBN 0-8384-7891-3

10 9 8 7 6 5 4 3 2 1

TABLE OF CONTENTS

Thank You

The series editor, authors and publisher would like to thank the following individuals who offered many helpful insights throughout the development of the **TeacherSource** series.

Linda Lonon Blanton	University of New Orleans
Tommie Brasel	New Mexico School for the Deaf
Jill Burton	University of South Australia
Margaret B. Cassidy	Brattleboro Union High School, Vermont
Florence Decker	University of Texas at El Paso
Silvia G. Diaz	Dade County Public Schools, Florida
Margo Downey	Boston University
Alvino Fantini	School for International Training
Sandra Fradd	University of Miami
Jerry Gebhard	Indiana University of Pennsylvania
Fred Genesee	University of California at Davis
Stacy Gildenston	Colorado State University
Jeannette Gordon	Illinois Resource Center
Else Hamayan	Illinois Resource Center
Sarah Hudelson	Arizona State University
Joan Jamieson	Northern Arizona University
Elliot L. Judd	University of Illinois at Chicago
Donald N. Larson	Bethel College, Minnesota (Emeritus)
Numa Markee	University of Illinois at Urbana Champaign
Denise E. Murray	San Jose State University
Meredith Pike-Baky	University of California at Berkeley
Sara L. Sanders	Coastal Carolina University
Lilia Savova	Indiana University of Pennsylvania
Donna Sievers	Garden Grove Unified School District, California
Ruth Spack	Tufts University
Leo van Lier	Monterey Institute of International Studies

To Betty Rae,
without whose love and support
I could not have become
who I am.

SERIES EDITOR'S PREFACE

As I was driving just south of White River Junction, the snow had started falling in earnest. The light was flat, although it was mid-morning, making it almost impossible to distinguish the highway in the gray-white swirling snow. I turned on the radio, partly as a distraction and partly to help me concentrate on the road ahead; the announcer was talking about the snow. "The state highway department advises motorists to use extreme caution and to drive with their headlights on to ensure maximum visibility." He went on, his tone shifting slightly, "Ray Burke, the state highway supervisor, just called to say that one of the plows almost hit a car just south of Exit 6 because the person driving hadn't turned on his lights. He really wants people to put their headlights on because it is very tough to see in this stuff." I checked, almost reflexively, to be sure that my headlights were on, as I drove into the churning snow.

How can information serve those who hear or read it in making sense of their own worlds? How can it enable them to reason about what they do and to take appropriate actions based on that reasoning? My experience with the radio in the snow storm illustrates two different ways of providing the same message: the need to use your headlights when you drive in heavy snow. The first offers dispassionate information; the second tells the same content in a personal, compelling story. The first disguises its point of view; the second explicitly grounds the general information in a particular time and place. Each means of giving information has its role, but I believe the second is ultimately more useful in helping people make sense of what they are doing. When I heard Ray Burke's story about the plow, I made sure my headlights were on.

In what is written about teaching, it is rare to find accounts in which the author's experience and point of view are central. A point of view is not simply an opinion; neither is it a whimsical or impressionistic claim. Rather, a point of view lays out what the author thinks and why; to borrow the phrase from writing teacher Natalie Goldberg, "it sets down the bones." The problem is that much of what is available in professional development in language-teacher education concentrates on telling rather than on point of view. The telling is prescriptive, like the radio announcer's first statement. It is emphasizes what is important to know and do, what is current in theory and research, and therefore what you—as a practicing teacher—should do. But this telling disguises the teller; it hides the point of view that can enable you to make sense of what is told.

The TeacherSource series offers you a point of view on second/foreign language teaching. Each author in this series has had to lay out what she or he believes is central to the topic, and how she or he has come to this understanding. So as a reader, you will find this book has a personality; it is not anonymous. It comes as a story, not as a directive, and it is meant to create a relationship with you rather than assume your attention. As a practitioner, its point of view can help you in your own work by providing a sounding board for your ideas and a metric for your own thinking. It can suggest courses of action and explain why these make sense to the author. You in turn can take from it what you will, and do with it what you can. This book will not tell you what to think; it is meant to help you make sense of what you do.

The point of view in **TeacherSource** is built out of three strands: **Teachers' Voices**, **Frameworks**, and **Investigations**. Each author draws together these strands uniquely, as suits his or her topic and more crucially his or her point of view. All materials in TeacherSource have these three strands. The **Teachers' Voices** are practicing language teachers from various settings who tell about their experience of the topic. The **Frameworks** lay out what the author believes is important to know about his or her topic and its key concepts and issues. These fundamentals define the area of language teaching and learning about which she or he is writing. The **Investigations** are meant to engage you, the reader, in relating the topic to your own teaching, students, and classroom. They are activities which you can do alone or with colleagues, to reflect on teaching and learning and/or try out ideas in practice.

Each strand offers a point of view on the book's topic. The **Teachers' Voices** relate the points of view of various practitioners; the **Frameworks** establish the point of view of the professional community; and the **Investigations** invite you to develop your own point of view, through experience with reference to your setting. Together these strands should serve in making sense of the topic.

In 1980, when Earl Stevick's *Teaching Languages: A Way and Ways* first appeared, the world was a different place, and so was language teaching. We were then in the midst of methods, in an era in which we expected pedagogy to address the major challenges of effective teaching. Against a backdrop of the relative sameness of grammar translation and the audio-lingual method several vastly differing conceptions of language teaching had bloomed, each rooted in its distinctive view of human learning. Earl Stevick captured three of these approaches—Gattegno's Silent Way, Curran's Counseling Learning, and Lozanov's Suggestopedia—in *A Way and Ways*, thus offering many language teachers their first acquaintance with what seemed then like exotic classroom practices. The uniqueness of Stevick's contribution was more than a catalogue of interesting pedagogies, however. It lay in the fact that he took seriously the far-reaching thinking about human learning proposed by these innovators. In so doing, Stevick saw what many of his contemporaries did not, namely that any classroom teaching is founded on beliefs as much as (or indeed more than) it is on facts. Teachers teach from what they believe to be true about learners, learning, and the nature of language as subject matter. To understand beliefs, we must take their proponents seriously in what they think and what they do in their actual classroom practice. In *A Way and Ways*, Stevick gave provisional belief to each innovator as he probed, elaborated, and interacted with their different views of learning.

Now, nearly two decades after that pioneering work, Earl Stevick returns to the central premise that beliefs animate teaching. In *Working with Teaching Methods: What's at Stake?* he examines fundamental questions of language teaching. These are not questions of material, procedure, or technique, but of principle and value. In replying to the question in his title, he writes that the three approaches—Silent Way, Counseling Learning, and Suggestopedia—share knowledge that freedom and learning can enhance and not interfere with each other. He then lays out the core consequences of the book: "Because this learning takes place in the human mind, and because this freedom is the freedom of human personhood, the possibilities for good are breathtaking, but so are the risks of ill. This must be truer in the field of education than in any other field." As a writer, Stevick's approach epitomizes the orientation of sense-making at the core of the TeacherSource project. His style is direct and personal as he shares both the certainties and the doubts he has gleaned from his experience. In so doing, he takes us to the questions that truly matter at the heart of teaching and learning.

There is a wonderful symmetry in these two books; indeed they are as closely allied as they are distinct from one another. It is as if the second finishes the conversation begun by the first. In *A Way and Ways*, Stevick was concerned with methods, and with the spectrum of approaches of learning that they captured. He sought to make clear the procedures of each approach as well as the beliefs and principles that underlie it. His aim was to fully investigate the cross-cutting nature of questions posed by the approaches. In *What's at Stake?*, the process is reversed. In this volume, we find a writer who is centrally engaged by questions of human learning, and who now uses the three approaches as ways to illuminate possible responses to those questions. This is a unique book, one which goes to the basics of who we are as learners and how we learn. As a teacher and a writer, Earl Stevick is a rare individual who seeks answers in both the realm of belief and the field of knowledge. He thus shows us a way to approach what's at stake in our own work, and he suggests how to move us along that road.

This book, like all elements of the TeacherSource series, is intended to serve you in understanding your work as a language teacher. It may lead you to thinking about what you do in different ways and/or to taking specific actions in your teaching. Or it may do neither. But we intend, through the variety of points of view presented in this fashion, to offer you access to choices in teaching that you may not have thought of before and thus to help your teaching make more sense.

—*Donald Freeman, Series Editor*

Prologue:
What You Need to Know Before We Begin

Some History

First of all, you should know that I got into language teaching for the worst of reasons. Three of the worst reasons, in fact. The first and most urgent was that in a very few months I'd be graduating from college and I needed a job. I was beginning to realize that the kind of work I thought I had been preparing myself for held no interest for me, and I was developing serious doubts that the prospect of my services would interest many prospective employers, either.

Then one day in early spring, someone asked me if I'd like to teach in an English Language program being run by a missionary organization in Warsaw. I'd have a few weeks of intensive training in the summer, then go right into the classroom as a practicing professional. Two thoughts quickly ran through my mind. One was that as a native speaker of English with a Bachelor's degree from a good college, I wouldn't need to spend a lot of time acquiring a new stock of things to teach. This was my second bad reason for going into language teaching. The third bad reason was that as a lifelong unassertive and nonforceful individual, I could count on teaching to give me a position in which I would at least to a small extent exert control over other people. I applied, was accepted, and went through the brief training. So far, so good.

That, however, was in 1948, and 1948 turned out to be the year of the Iron Curtain. More suddenly than it had appeared, my new job evaporated. What to do now?

I decided, with the support of the GI Bill, a working wife, and a teaching fellowship, to work for a master's degree in "Teaching English as a Foreign Language" under the same people who had conducted my summer training. It was an excellent program for its day. I enjoyed it immensely, and quickly realized that vocationally I had found my home. In due course, having apparently done a number of right things for a year and a half, I received the degree I had been pursuing for all those wrong reasons.

At that time, in June, 1950, I knew (or so I believed) approximately 97% of what anyone could ever need to know in order to be a fully prepared language teacher. The general conclusion I had reached was that success comes from a sound linguistic analysis applied through sound techniques: "sound analysis and techniques" (SAT for short). Three specific things I had learned stand out in my mind. One was that a language is a system of auditory and muscular habits, so that teaching a language means guiding people in forming new habits and breaking old ones. Today I see that as largely false.

A second main point was that the habits that made up a language were phonological and structural, with vocabulary in a minor and supporting role and everything else on the far periphery. Nothing was said about roles or functions or genres or anything of the kind. So this second point also was, if not false, at least dangerously inadequate. The third thing I learned was that people could indeed learn languages, and that I seemed to be able to help in the process. This I still believe to be true.

During the next fifteen years I worked in the teaching and learning of a wide range of languages besides English, and in several different settings. This enriched my experience and built my self-confidence, but it never challenged my basic SAT belief: All you need for a good language course is *a sound linguistic analysis presented by sound pedagogical techniques.* Then for a period of five years beginning in 1965 I was lent to the Peace Corps Language Office for a variety of chores, many of which involved visits to ongoing training programs.

During those years I kept finding that the two variables "linguistic analysis" and "pedagogical techniques" simply were not correlating with the success or failure of the training programs I observed. This repeated experience shook my SAT way of seeing things so deeply that I discarded it. Its replacement was a little rule of thumb that "success or failure in a language course depends less on linguistic analyses and pedagogical techniques, than on *what goes on inside and between the people in the classroom.*" I didn't mean this as a scientific hypothesis, but only as a suggestion about what to keep one's eye on as one designs or runs a language course. Call it my "inside and between maxim" (IBM).

This move from SAT to IBM, about 1970, left me with a satisfying intuition but with no documentation. The first edition of *Memory, Meaning & Method* (1976) is largely a record of my explorations of literature, much of it from outside language teaching, that would fill in details of "what goes on inside and between." Two points particularly caught my attention and the attention of many readers. One was the distinction between short-term memory (STM) and long-term memory (LTM); the other was the "dimension of cognitive and personal depth" in whatever is said or done in language study. The second of these points excited my interest still further, which led to the writing of *Teaching Languages: A Way and Ways* (1980). Later, a number of new developments within the cognitive sciences concerning both of these points led me to write a mostly new second edition of *Memory, Meaning & Method* (1996) in which I was able to turn readers' attention from short-term memory to working memory (WM), and to replace "depth" with the much broader concept of "affect."

And that was where I expected things to remain. I was therefore surprised two years ago when Donald Freeman, over breakfast in Brattleboro, raised the question of my doing a new edition of *A Way and Ways,* to be part of the new **TeacherSource** series he was editing. Yes, I said, I was interested. There would of course be certain conditions, he continued. The **TeacherSource** format, with its intertwining strands of framework, voice, and investigations, would need to be implemented in some fashion, and in any case the format allowed for only about half the number of words in my original. Both conditions actually pleased me because I saw immediately that the new format should be very lively to work with, and because almost from the beginning I had thought *A Way and Ways* was too long.

This leads to one frequently-asked question about this book: "How is *A Way and Ways* related to working with methodology?" The answer is that after I had worked on the "revision" of *A Way and Ways* for a few weeks, I realized I wasn't going to get the book short enough by just cutting out a few pages here and bidding a regretful farewell to a favorite chapter there. I was going to need a whole new perspective on the subject. If only for my guidance in writing, that perspective would have to be represented by a new title. That was where the subtitle *What's at Stake?* came in. For quite a while there was uncertainty on the part of the editors as to whether to keep simultaneously in print both the original *A Way and Ways* and the newer, shorter work. They, of course, were hardly in a position to decide until they saw what I actually produced, while for my part I was often uncertain which kind of book I was *trying* to produce. I'm therefore quite sympathetic with the readers of a prepublication typescript, all of whom complained that they found the relationship between the two obscure and confusing. The differences I see are:

- In 1980 I was mainly reporting on what I had found; now I'm telling what I want to keep.

- In 1980 I was mainly listing some fascinating items I had found; now I'm more concerned than I was with the relationships *among* those items. For example, this book includes frequent references from methodological details of the three "ways" (Community Language Learning, The Silent Way, and suggestopedia) back to features of the methodologically neutral treatment of learning and memory in Chapter 1.

- In 1980 I was explaining what each of the three "ways" can teach us if we adopt it; now, as one of the readers put it, I'm more interested in what each "way" will not allow us to ignore no matter what approach we finally adopt, and in what help it can offer in adapting other kinds of methods and materials.

- For this reason, some of the Tasks invite readers to make applications to methods, approaches, and specific materials that they themselves are using or are considering for use in their own classes.

Another question frequently asked not only about *A Way and Ways* but about some of my other writings has been, *"Why these three approaches instead of others?"* When I was writing *A Way and Ways,* the answer to that question would have been "Just because these are approaches that I'm finding exciting but that are not widely understood." What excited me was not merely that they were unconventional; it was that each of the three was in one respect or another concerned with a concept whose importance I had begun to discover as I worked on the first edition of *Memory, Meaning & Method*

(1976), the concept of cognitive and personal "depth." In 1980, I was spreading news of some promising practical approaches to applying the depth concept in the learning and teaching of languages.

"Then what is it that has kept you thinking and occasionally writing about these same three approaches all these intervening years?" some friends have asked. Of course I've been exposed to many, many other approaches over the last five decades, all of which had their strong points and some of which worked very well indeed. Just imagine we discover a means of reliably and validly quantifying the average quality of the outcomes of an approach and the average amount of the same outcomes. Then imagine we multiply those two figures together, and multiply that by the number of people who have studied under that approach, and finally divide the product by the amount of time, money, and effort expended. It might turn out that one or more other approaches would show a higher total score than any of the three I have chosen. Or perhaps not. In either event, the other approaches seemed to me merely a set of brighter, perhaps better, ideas for modifying tradition, but not ideas for illuminating tradition or for replacing it.

In contrast to many, Community Language Learning, the Silent Way and suggestopedia have three qualities in common. Each is:

- **radical.** I mean this in the literal sense that each goes to the root of things to apply some single principle or set of related principles from the ground up.

- **fresh.** That is, each originated in thinking based outside the historical traditions, consensuses, and controversies of the language teaching profession.

- **exceptionally effective,** at least for some learners under at least some circumstances.

Think of the language learning process as a complex three-dimensional figure. To me, working with these three unconventional approaches is something like illuminating the figure with bright light from one after another of three widely separated point sources, in contrast to looking at it under some variant of familiar general illumination.

Finally, I'd like to assure readers that I didn't stop learning and reading after my last exposure to one of "the three ways." For example, I'm aware that much has been discovered in recent years about learning styles and personality differences that I have barely mentioned.

I'm also aware that the "way" and the three "ways" of this book all deal with the learner only as an individual or as a member of small collections of individuals, and not as a member of a larger society. If we look at language education on a broader scale than personal psychology and individual experiences, then we may encounter serious questions about its role in relation to the body politic. What we find there may in turn lead us to look for ways to let what happens in our classrooms both motivate and enable students to confront and deal effectively with whatever oppressive structures control the societies within which they live. This element is conspicuously lacking from all of the approaches I have described in this book (as it is from most others). In relation to it, the contrasts I have spent so much time studying among the three "ways" become much less urgent, something like the proverbial differences among possible arrangements of deck chairs on the Titanic. We will in fact find that each of the three "ways" does intend to transform society, but none of them through confrontation.

The preceding two paragraphs have mentioned certain important aspects of language education that my career happened not to require me to deal with. In this book I have thought it best to limit my discussion to that side of the profession that I came to know most directly. My intent here, then, is to finish up my harvest of the small corner of the field that was given me to tend, rather than to offer an account of the whole farm.

THE PEOPLE BEHIND THIS BOOK

As far as I am aware, no one who read *Teaching Languages: A Way and Ways* was neutral about it. I'd like to take this opportunity to thank all who have communicated their reactions to me, some with direct encouragement and others with indirect encouragement in the form of honest skepticism. In approximately chronological order, they have included James R. Frith, Carol and Nobuo Akiyama, Mark Clarke, Madeline Ehrman, Peter O'Connell, Pat Mills, Alan Maley, Christopher Brumfit, Ron and Ana Maria Schwartz, Jane Arnold, and Herbert Kufner.

For what has turned out to be this new book, Donald Freeman has added rich, unexpected and very welcome meanings to the role of Series Editor. Diane Larsen-Freeman, Mike Jerald and Kathleen Graves of the School for International Training in Brattleboro, VT, gave very helpful comments on drafts or partial drafts along the way. Jennybelle Rardin once again checked my account of Counseling-Learning, Shakti Gattegno did the same for the Silent Way, and Georgi Lozanov found time amid difficult circumstances to scan the new account of suggestopedia. Barbara Fujiwara provided invaluable multilevel help with the treatment of suggestopedia, and Jennifer Deacon and Kristin Newton also contributed important information for that chapter. Irene Dutra's original chapter on Counseling-Learning has magnificently passed the test of dissection and close scrutiny.

I thank Curtis Brown Ltd. for permission to quote the W. H. Auden poem at the beginning of Chapter 2, and Shakti Gattegno for permission to use materials out of the *Newsletter* published by Educational Solutions, Inc.

Most of all, I'm grateful to the staff and students of the Master of Arts in Teaching Program at the School for International Training, who have made serious use of *A Way and Ways* ever since it first appeared and who have taught me by what they found in it.

And Betty Rae, in addition to supporting and encouraging me as usual, has rescued me and the project from many a computer glitch.

1

A FRAMEWORK
FOR THE FRAMEWORKS

Throughout A Way and Ways, *I tried to keep my theoretical explorations in touch with reality by drawing on what in the TeacherSource series are called voice materials of two kinds. First was a series of accounts of classes taught by me or by other people telling what we did and why and how it worked. Reader response has led me to retain most of those accounts in this book. They are chronicles, not recipes; the reader is invited to learn vicariously from our experience, but not necessarily to copy what we did. A second type of voice material consists of excerpts, some of them anecdotal, from papers written by language teachers in courses I have taught. All quotations are used with permission. (Personal names in quotation marks are pseudonyms. For ease in locating them, I have assigned the pseudonyms in alphabetical order.)*

"Abigail": Four years ago I was looking for any kind of job I could find. I happened to get one teaching ESL to a class of six women from various parts of the world who spoke no English. I had never heard of ESL before. The salary was poor and I didn't know if I wanted to pursue a teaching career, therefore my approach was very casual and low pressure. My method usually consisted of thinking up a topic to talk about, introducing it, and encouraging each student to express her feelings.

In spite of my casual approach, the teaching job was extremely pleasant. I had a deep empathy for anyone who was facing a language barrier because I had just returned from a trip around the world alone as a monolingual. They all started speaking English fairly well after the first two weeks of class. I remember a woman from Colombia telling me she hadn't spoken English before because she was afraid of making mistakes. After being in class for a while, she spoke English and made mistakes but didn't care. I didn't attach much significance to the progress that the women made. I had no idea how long it took people to learn a language.

Gradually I became quite career-oriented, and made a conscious decision to try to be a top-notch ESL teacher. I had guilt feelings about the casual way in which I had taught those first six women, and my teaching evolved into the traditional authoritarian style with the textbook dominant. Over the years, it has gotten to where I feel frustrated if a student takes class time to relate a personal anecdote.

I can look back on these four years and see a gradual decline in the performance of my students. Until recently, I have been assuming that I needed to be more attentive to their mistakes in order to speed their progress. My present style of teaching bypasses the students' feelings and basic needs, and concentrates on method. I never see successes like those first six ladies.

Some riddles have no final answers.

A few answerless riddles are still worth asking. They are worth asking not for their answers, since they have none, but for what we do in struggling with them. We may come to notice what formerly we had overlooked because it was too small or too distant or too large or too close to us. We may see how pieces fit together within what we had always thought were units, indivisible.

WHY THIS BOOK? THEN AND NOW

Loren: Oh, and what do *you* do?

You: I'm a language teacher.

What is Loren's most likely immediate unspoken reaction?

Why do some language students succeed and others fail? Why, "Abigail" wonders, do some language teachers fail and others succeed? What may the learners and teachers of foreign languages hope to succeed at anyway? How broad, how deep, how wide may be the measure of their failure, or of their success?

These questions have come to hold a greater and greater place in my thinking during recent years. In the early 1970s, I began to find some partial answers to these questions, answers that helped me and helped some of my colleagues (and our students) to succeed more often, helped us also to succeed in ways that went beyond mere learning of structures, sounds, and words. So I wrote a book titled *Memory, Meaning & Method* about what I was discovering. One of its two recurring themes was the operation of human memory. The other, intimately related to the first, was the personal "meaning," the "depth" of the learning experience.

I found considerable satisfaction in writing that book. One thing I liked about it was the numerous bibliographical references, which covered eight whole pages of small type, and the fact that the book itself contained hundreds of footnotes. I felt this showed that I had taken into account the work of many other people, and that I had checked my own thinking against theirs.

I was therefore surprised by one letter my publisher received from an anonymous person who appeared to have read my book with some care. This person seemed to like the book very much, but was impatient with the footnotes. She wrote, "I would like to see a book in which he speaks for himself entirely, instead of being spokesman for others. He should write a book that is firmly and unequivocally himself." Another friendly critic wanted more "detailed descriptions of what the students actually do."

I cannot write a book just to please critics. Nevertheless, I hope these two will feel that their suggestions have borne fruit in this one. The ideas that were growing in the writing of that first edition of *Memory, Meaning & Method* have been with me for these additional years. I have watched them develop with many additional language classes. I have worked through them with groups of language teachers from many parts of the world. As a result, these ideas are now more fully integrated within me; they are more truly mine. Footnotes thus become less necessary, and less appropriate. This is not to say I have originated all of this, however. The influence of Charles A. Curran permeates the book, and Chapters 2 and 3 draw heavily on Ernest Becker and W. Timothy Gallwey. The thinking of Caleb Gattegno and of Georgi Lozanov and Evelyna Gateva is conspicuous in the chapters devoted to their work.

As these ideas have matured, their roots have gone deeper into whatever it is that lies underneath the process, the experience, of learning and teaching a foreign language. *Teaching Languages: A Way and Ways* (1980) was in fact a further exploration of the "depth dimension" I had described in the first edition of *Memory, Meaning & Method*. Twenty years later others have written on the subject, most notably Madeline Ehrman in her book, *Understanding Second Language Learning Difficulties*. The second edition of *Memory, Meaning & Method* (1996) itself contains much new material about memory, but my conclusions about the *relationship* between memory and meaning remain much the same.

The present book started out to be an updating and abridgment of *A Way and Ways*, but I soon found myself carried along by an unexpected stream of thinking.

> First of all, abridgment required me to find criteria for what to keep.
>
> This search for criteria of inclusion revealed to me the large components of advocacy and excessive illustration in *A Way and Ways*.
>
> Removing those elements clarified for me why I am writing this new treatment of what is on the surface old subject matter.

My central goal now, I began to realize, is neither to expound nor to promote the three "ways" or any other approaches or methods. But it also is not to offer a comprehensive treatment of methodology. It is rather, I think, to identify for myself (as Gattegno might have put it) which "awarenesses, and awarenesses of awarenesses," I now bring to my reactions to any approach or any method, whether old or new, and whether on or off the beaten path. The provisional subtitle that guided me through the processes of abridgment and reformulation was eventually accepted as subtitle for the published book: *What's at Stake?*

There are of course many "ways" in language teaching other than the three I chose for my 1980 book, all of which were unconventional and relatively obscure. I did not mean to say that other methods are not equally worthy of attention. I did and do think the conclusions reached in this book apply to the other methods, or at least to the methods with which I am familiar. But as I said above, my purpose here was not then and is not now to write a full treatise on methods. Neither is it to present the definitive solution to the complex issues of language teaching. What I hope my readers will find in this book is not a key or compass, but only a little light. I will therefore leave readers to decide how to apply the ideas I present here to the Reading Method, the Grammar-Translation Method, the Audiolingual Method, Total Physical Response, the Natural Approach, and other methods that have come along since 1980 or will come in the future.

These first four chapters will outline one way of looking at the learning and teaching of languages, a way that is my own. In Chapters 5 to 10, I shall describe the work of three people who have influenced me. Then in Chapters 11 and 12 I shall come back to a further development of my own point of view. Because this point of view has emerged out of those same influences and experiences that form the subject matter of the intervening chapters, themes that I will introduce in this opening chapter will recur, with further development, in a series of other contexts.

"Inside and Between": A Metaframework

page 2

No, there are no final answers to the riddle with which I began this chapter. My earlier conclusion was that success depends less on materials, techniques, or linguistic analyses, and more on what goes on inside and between the people in the classroom. Since that time I have not changed my mind about the fundamental importance of "what goes on inside and between," but I have been able to pursue this principle more deeply and at the same time to practice it more broadly than before. As a result I have begun to suspect that the most important aspect of "what goes on" is the presence or absence of harmony: it is the parts working with, or against, one another. How such a thing may happen within and among the people in a language course is the subject of this book as it was of *A Way and Ways*. A unifying feature of this present treatment will be frequent reference to a sketch of learning and memory found on pages 6-16 of this chapter.

"Between"

In 1933, Leonard Bloomfield illustrated "what happens between" language users in terms of a simple story. Bloomfield's interpretation of that story, an interpretation that I will not repeat here, later became one of the foundation stones for the well-known audiolingual approach to language teaching. Figure 1 represents the essence of Bloomfield's diagram. I have made a few visual but nonessential changes. Here is the story.

> Jack and Jill are walking down a lane. Jill is hungry. She sees an apple in a tree. She makes a noise with her larynx, tongue, and lips. Jack vaults the fence, climbs the tree, takes the apple, brings it to Jill, and places it in her hand. Jill eats the apple.

In my interpretation of Bloomfield's story, the S-arrows in Figure 1 stand first and foremost for all the kinds of Stuff that comes into Jill's or Jack's head through their Senses: the sight of an apple, or its fragrance or flavor, or its feel of crispness against the teeth, or the noise that accompanies the bite, or any combination of these. The same arrow may stand also for a very special kind of noise: the Sounds of Speech (as also the Signs of Sign Language are a very special kind of visual stimulus). The R-arrows represent Jack's or Jill's Reactions or Responses, not to the S-arrows directly, but to whatever the S-arrows have contributed to inside Jack's or Jill's head. Those reactions may consist of fence-vaulting or tree-climbing, or they may be in the form of language: "A nice apple would taste s-o-o good right now!"

We of course recognize here two stereotypes that were not often challenged in Bloomfield's day: Jill as the physically helpless woman who controls Jack through her skill with language, and Jack as the strong, gallant, but largely nonverbal male. These stereotypes will however not be relevant to my treatment of the story.

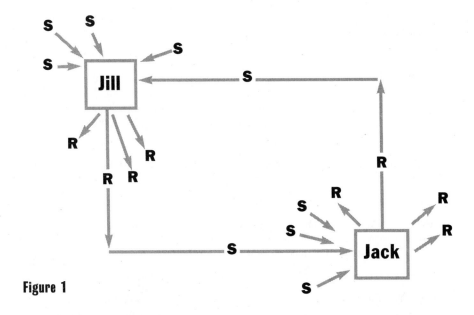

Figure 1

Of course, the R-arrows that originate with one person may become some of the S-arrows that enter into the head of another, and that's where things become interesting. Just for fun, let's pretend that Jill and Jack are not just names from a nursery rhyme. Instead let's suppose that Jack is a native speaker of the local language and that Jill is in the process of learning it. What Jill hopes for is that her own R-arrows will become for Jack S-arrows that will call forth from him some new R-arrows that will fit her own needs and purposes.

Everything turns on how Jill responds to what is coming into her head: the sight of the apple, the presence of Jack, and all the rest. Just how she can and will respond is influenced, enabled and limited, though not completely determined, by a set of inner resources she has built up over the years, resources that are located mainly in her central nervous system. These resources are based on Jill's earlier experiences, and are modified a bit with each new experience she has. So these resources, these enabling, influencing, and limiting resources, have both a lasting aspect and a changeable aspect. When we're thinking of their lasting aspect, we talk about Jill's "memory," and when we're focusing on their changeable aspect we talk about her "learning" something.

Under these circumstances the R-arrows that Jill puts out need to reflect not only what she knows about apples and fences, but also her past experiences with Jack personally and with his language. Only then will the new S-arrows that Jack receives from Jill call forth from him a kind of R-activity that Jill was hoping for. Just how Jack may react is in turn enabled, influenced, and limited but not completely determined by the resources inside his head, and Jack's resources like Jill's have been derived from his previous experiences not only with the inanimate world, but also with other people and their behavior. So while the locus of the *memories* is inside the heads of individuals, the learning is largely a result of interactions between and among them. It is in this sense that we talk about negotiation of meanings, and about learning as a social act. Compare

Freire's dictum that dialog is not just a technique used by teachers; more, it is "a way of knowing."

"Inside"

Much more is known today than in Bloomfield's day about the many kinds of data represented by the arrows, and about what happens inside Jack's or Jill's head. A large part of "what goes on inside" has to do with memory. This is apparent in Ehrman's interview with a student she calls "Beverly." (For the sake of alphabetical order, I have changed the pseudonym to "Aggie".)

(Ehrman 1996:187f)

"Aggie": I feel as if I'm falling behind. The teachers go so fast through the material, and I'm just running as hard as I can to keep up.

Interviewer: You'd like a pause to catch your breath.

Aggie: Yes! And furthermore, the presentation seems to leap around from topic to topic. Every hour the teacher starts something new, and it's not always related to what came before. I get so confused.

Interviewer: There seems to be no continuity for you to hold on to.

Aggie: Yes, I'm just accumulating a lot of material, but it isn't sticking very well. I don't really feel I understand it, and I really need some review. I just had a really frustrating week. We learned the negative imperative, and we didn't use it enough. Then we went on to the next lesson, and we went through that in two days. So then I got requests, which are complicated. I know a little about negative imperatives, and I know a little about requests, but I can't really use either one.

Interviewer: Sounds as though you feel you're [drowning].

Aggie: That's for sure. . . For one thing, I'd really like a written handout to go along with the book. It's hard to remember all the things that come up in class, and then I have to know them.

Interviewer: Part of that drowning feeling comes from the fact that you can't see all the new material?

Aggie: Yes, that's right. . . [emphasis added]

MY OWN "WAY" OF LOOKING AT "WHAT GOES ON INSIDE AND BETWEEN"

It's of course well known that no two brains work exactly alike. But in this book I will also leave out of account important kinds of differences, among them personality types and cognitive styles. The following summary is therefore only a partial sketch. I do however think it is generally accurate as far as it goes.

In describing my own "way" of looking at the learning of languages and discussing three unconventional "ways" to teach them, I'll be referring from time to time to certain ideas about learning and memory. I believe these ideas are just as relevant to whatever other method we are working with as they are to Counseling-Learning, the Silent Way, or suggestopedia. Let me summarize those ideas in the form of two answers to each of six questions: a traditional answer and a more contemporary answer.

I will of course provide a variety of examples as I present the summary, both from the language classroom and from life outside it. In order to unify my presentation, however, I'd like also to build up one single example as we go along. For that purpose I'll be using the learning and remembering of telephone numbers.

1. "How are 'learning' and 'memory' related to each other?"

Traditional: How we react to things is determined by our memory of what we've learned by experience.

Contemporary: As I said in the previous section, how we react to things is largely "enabled, influenced, and limited but not completely determined" by inner resources in the brain. These inner resources reflect answers to the question "What has gone with what in the past?"[2] Again, when we're thinking about the lasting nature of those inner resources, we talk about **memory**, and when we're thinking about their changeability, we talk about **learning**.

I have two friends, H and J, whom I telephone with just about equal frequency. If I want to call H, I simply go to the phone and punch in the seven digits. I can do that because something about my brain supplies the number when I need it. That something about my brain has supplied the number several times in the past, and I expect it will continue to do so. This is what I mean when I say I have H's phone number "in my memory."

If I want to call J, my brain doesn't help me, so I have to use the phone book. I say I "don't **remember** the number," or that I don't have it "in my memory." If I want to have J's number in my memory, I'll have to **learn** it in one way or another.

2. "What sizes of things go with what?"

Traditional: **Whole** words or structures are paired with **whole** meanings. For example, in English the word "lamb" goes with a certain kind of animal. Each language also has its own special grammatical structures. Each time a student meets an instance of a whole construction like Spanish *a mí me gusta,* which means "I like," the combination leaves a "trace" in the student's memory. The oftener this happens, the deeper the trace and the more likely the trace will be to lead to the desired result next time.

Contemporary: What is stored in the brain is not whole words or objects, but their **components**, which are later recombined. Some of the components of the **word** "lamb," for example, are "single syllable," "consonant-vowel-consonant structure," "contains a nasal consonant somewhere," and the like. Some components of the corresponding **meaning** are "offspring of sheep," "immature," "wool-bearing," "cute," and so forth. For anyone who has ever been around real lambs, there will also be components of sound, smell, touch, gait, and so forth. Components of the *a mí me gusta* construction include the facts that two pronouns (*mí* and *me*) referring to the same person occur side by side, that the verb is in third person, and that the preposition is *a* and not *para* or *de* or something else. All these fragments of information are joined into *networks* in the brain, and *the structure of those networks reflects an individual's past experience.*

In our local telephone directory, the number that goes with J's name consists of seven digits. One also finds a hyphen between the third and fourth digits, though

Actually, there are two questions here: "What went with what *at a particular time in the past?*" and "What has *usually* gone with what?" For details, see the discussion of "episodic" and "semantic" memory in Stevick, 1996.

the hyphen doesn't go with anything that has to be done in dialing the phone.

The first three of these seven numbers tell us the "exchange." Exchanges are loosely related to geographical areas, but two or more exchanges can overlap one another geographically, and in the last analysis they really have more to do with wiring patterns in the telephone lines than with boundaries on a map. On another scale, each spoken digit goes with one written digit and vice versa. In turn, unique combinations of spoken or written features go together to correspond to the digits.

3. "What kinds of components get stored?"

Traditional: Information comes in through five senses. People differ as to which sense is central for them. For some, the dominant modality is visual, while for others it is auditory or kinesthetic. (This three-way distinction is a conspicuous part of the *Neurolinguistic Programming* view.)

Contemporary: To begin with, there are more than five senses (Stevick 1996:5f). Cultures differ as to exactly how many they recognize, but even within the English-speaking world the number has varied. Certainly it is arbitrary to assign a headache and the warmth and the texture of a kitten's fur to the same "sense" just because none of the three comes in through the eyes, ears, nose, or tongue. But some essential kinds of information are not really sensory at all. One crucially important type of non-sensory information is the ability to keep track of autobiographical time, and so to know which sensory stimuli came in together and which did not. There are others, however.

I have already mentioned visual and auditory components of the written and spoken numerals respectively. But for me at least, successfully executing a phone number commonly draws on quite different sorts of visual and auditory components stored in my brain from past experience. One visual component that I notice myself using is where and in what directions my fingers moved the last time I called the number, and this kind of information is of course closely tied to parallel kinesthetic data about what I feel my fingers doing. Similarly the general pattern of pitches I hear from a touch-tone phone as I dial can confirm or fail to confirm what I have just done with my hand. These are simple examples of networking as the brain enables us to call a number without looking it up. As for "autobiographical time," we find that illustrated in our ability to have some idea of when and how frequently we have called a particular number.

4. "What else besides sizes and kinds?"

Traditional: What else is there?

Contemporary: What gets stored in memory is more than just whole pictures and other kinds of images, or even whole experiences—more complex even than those wholes simply broken up into parts of various kinds. This complexity exists in several dimensions. Most obviously, memories are more or less **abstract**. A lamb is not just a source of physical stimuli. It is also an example of many categories: young things, smelly things, and so forth. So the sight of a lamb tends to activate in memory not only certain physical characteristics. To some extent it also activates the categories that those characteristics represent, and other members of the same categories: human children and fledgling birds, or pigs and potting soil. We experience this activation in the form of conscious or non-conscious **reminding**. Among its other functions, reminding provides us with a basis for metaphors and other figures of speech.

Examples of written features are straight (as in 1, 2, 3, 4, 5, 7) vs. curved (as in 2, 3, 5, 6, 8, 9, 0), and closed curve (as in 6, 8, 9, 0) vs. open curve (as in 2, 3, 5).

Another kind of thing that gets remembered is **mental activity**. In a research-based example, if I am presented with something like S_U_R_EL and from it come up with SQUIRREL, I may form memories of *what I did* in order to complete the word. There are likely to be various levels of abstraction:

This example is derived from work by Rabinowitz discussed in Stevick 1996.

- The first blank needed a Q, the second blank an I, and so forth.

- I had to supply both vowels and consonants.

- This was a task that required the filling in of blanks.

- This task had to do with words.

- This was something I found pleasant, frustrating, or boring.

In a comparable example from language use, M and N are conversing. (This specific example is original with me, but the discussion is based on de Bot 1996.)

M: . . .and then we creeped. . .

N (looking confused): You did what?

M: We, er, we crept. . .

N (seems to understand): Oh.

Again, M may take away from this exchange memories that are more or less abstract:

- "Creeped" was not usable here, at least not with N.

- While I was saying "er," I went back and thought of another form of the same verb ("creep") and then asked myself what contexts I had found it in, what collocations it had been part of, and so on. Then I asked what past tense verbs I had found in the same contexts with the same collocations. This gave me a verb form ("crept") that turned out to be accepted by N.

- I can correct and improve my language through internal work, without depending on a teacher or someone else to supply me with new models.

Combinations of things remembered, together with the remindings that take place among them, produce interactions of various kinds. When we encounter just some of the elements in a network, we tend to prepare ourselves to find other elements of the same network. If I am in a large room filled with small tables surrounded by straight-backed chairs and with the smell of food, I look around for a menu and someone who is ready to take my order. If I run across a new verb in Turkish, I expect to find that the same verb has dozens of other forms which differ among themselves with regard to their combinations of suffixes; if it had been a Swahili verb, on the other hand, I would have looked for hundreds and hundreds of possible combinations of prefixes. If I enroll in a new language course, I anticipate (depending on my previous experience) a textbook, videotapes, entertainment, drudgery, friendliness, criticism, dependence on a teacher-figure, or self-expression. A term often applied to the results of such interactions is **schema**. Each person's schema for a given concept is a little different from everyone else's. On the other hand, it must also have a lot in common with theirs, at least with members of the same culture.

For me at least, **abstractions** are among my most frequent helps in reconstructing a phone number from what's in my memory. A few examples based on actual numbers I have learned are:

- 724-8659. The numbers for the exchange (724) are the same as the street number of our house when I was 12 years old.
- 257-3416. This number consists of the number 7 plus three other ways of expressing the same quantity. In each two-digit equivalent for 7, the smaller number comes before the larger.

These two phone numbers also provide examples of remembered mental activity. Along with some of the sensory components of the number, I may recall:

- that the prefix reminded me of a particular address;
- that I retrieved the address from memory;
- that I then used that number as the start of the number I'm trying to remember, and that those digits in turn helped to trigger the last four digits of the number I'm after.

In my country, the schema for telephone numbers is as I described it above: a three-digit exchange followed by four other digits. If one is working with numbers within one's local area, there are only a few exchanges, so that the exchange portion is likely to be familiar from other numbers one has used. At least until recently, the exchange number could not contain either a 0 or a 1 as its initial or its middle digit, and the combination 555 was also excluded for exchanges. The last four digits, by contrast, may occur in any combination.

5. "How long does memory last?"

Traditional: The duration of memory is a continuum.

More recent: I can remember my home phone number of ten years ago, but not my office number for the same period. I can remember our home phone numbers of ten years ago and 42 years ago, but not the one we had 37 years ago. This much is a common experience, and no surprise to the traditional view of memory duration. Either a memory is there or it's not there.

But now consider a second common experience. If someone tells us a phone number while we are busy addressing an envelope, we can often go ahead and finish writing the address, and then "play back" the spoken telephone number in our heads a few seconds later without difficulty. But if too many seconds elapse between our hearing the number and our attempt to play it back, we are much less likely to be able to do it.

Experimental studies of this difference in likelihood of availability have turned up three facts that would be surprising to the traditional view of memory duration.

(1) The likelihood of retaining the number doesn't just decline gradually and evenly. Instead, the ability to do so seems to disappear fairly suddenly after about 20 seconds. The name the investigators gave to this

special ability was "short-term memory" (STM). That left "long-term memory" (LTM) as the name for all the rest of memory in general, whether two minutes later or two days later or two years later.

(2) They also found that the STM kind of retention can be disrupted even within the 20 second period by a number of influences, one of which is electroconvulsive shock, while the same is not true of LTM. From findings such as this one, the investigators concluded that there is a fundamental physical difference between STM and LTM.

(3) Whether or not a new fact will "get into" LTM (i.e., be available from LTM to contribute to memory after the STM period has expired for it, two minutes or days or years later) will depend to a large extent on what did or did not happen to that fact during the STM period, and particularly on whether the person thought about the fact or processed it in some way during STM.

This view pictured the memory process in terms of a unidirectional flow starting from the senses, with some of this sensory input registering in STM, and then some of that material eventually going on to LTM. STM itself has no permanent contents. This is a more recent view of memory duration. A simplified graphic representation of this view is:

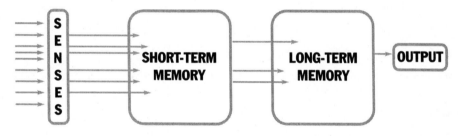

Figure 2

The pedagogical conclusion was that we need to find out how to select the short-term memory items we're interested in—phone numbers as in the above example, but also the sounds, words and structures of a new language—and then devise effective techniques for converting those items into long-term memories.

Contemporary: A careful reading of the examples I offered in explaining the more recent view of memory duration raises two questions that that view does not answer:

(a) When I was processing the phone number 724-8659 (above), where did the idea of using the former street address in processing 724-8659 (above) come from? Similarly in the example of 257-3416, where did the idea of reference to the number 7, or to "larger" and "smaller" numbers within the phone number as a whole come from?

(b) The processing I did definitely helped me to come up with the desired phone numbers when I needed them later on. Why so?

Just the raw acoustic representation of "724," or just the lines and angles on paper of the written form of that number could hardly have triggered memory of a place where I lived so many years ago. The noises or the marks on paper came in through my senses, all right, but they were immediately subjected to preliminary processing that gave them numerical meaning. Then *that meaning in turn* triggered the association with the street address. In other words, I **processed** what had just come in through my senses.

If I had never learned numbers or learned to read, or if I had never lived at that particular address, the result would have been quite different. The result was unique to me. Since STM has no permanent contents of its own that would have made such processing possible, *the preliminary processing must have been done by action that took place within the networks of my LTM.* This was processing that "just happened." It took place automatically, rapidly, and neither needing nor accepting any conscious guidance from me.

In a similar way, my time in second-grade arithmetic had built into my LTM a set of associations between "7" and "3,4," "2,5" and so forth, which were activated by the rest of the processing. This produced a number of abstract items. In order of decreasing abstractness, some of them were:

- A former address will help with this phone number.

- The part it will help with is the exchange.

- The address was on Range Line.

A set of abstractions for 257-3416 is:

- There's a key number for this phone number.

- Getting from the actual number to the key number involves repetition of the same arithmetical operation.

- That operation is addition.

- In each pair of numbers to be added, the second is larger than the first.

- The key number is 7.

[Let me emphasize that the above is not just idle speculation on my part. It is quite typical of what I commonly observe in my consciousness as I process phone numbers. Moreover, it is similar to how I have found myself processing words and structures in my learning or use of various languages. I do however recognize that others' minds may work a little differently from mine.]

These abstractions along with less abstract items from processing by LTM then *become available to the proprietor of the brain in a special state called working memory (WM).* Some things to know about WM are:

- Unlike the STM concept of the recent view, WM stands for a state into and out of which items move freely in two-way traffic, and not for some stage through which data pass like salmon struggling upstream toward the hoped-for spawning grounds of LTM.

- WM is physiologically distinct from LTM. That is, it makes use of special parts of the brain different from the parts used for LTM.

- Unlike LTM, the total capacity of WM is very small—just a relatively few items at a time.

- Unlike LTM, material stays in WM for only a short time unless it is reintroduced.

- Unlike what is in LTM, material in WM is subject to observation and manipulation by the proprietor.

Products of manipulation in WM, such as my observations about the internal structure of phone numbers, may move on from the WM worktable and *enter storage in LTM, where they will be able to contribute toward the processing of future inputs.* In a sense, then, WM has served as a kind of worktable on which the proprietor may place items drawn from storage in LTM, observe them, select from them, rearrange them, and send new configurations back to storage. Figure 3 is a simplified picture of this more contemporary view.

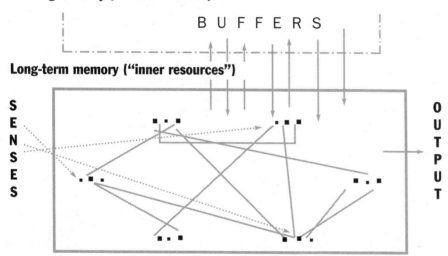

Working memory ("the worktable")

BUFFERS

Long-term memory ("inner resources")

Figure 3

The LTM-WM distinction of the contemporary view, like the LTM-STM distinction before it, is based on research conducted by people who were outside the field of language teaching. We shouldn't be surprised, therefore, that they missed one further distinction that is very important to us. Going back to my principal illustration, I suppose we've all had the experience of memorizing a phone number that we were going to need an hour later or a day later, producing the number as needed, and then when we needed it unexpectedly a week or two later, having to look it up all over again. Coming closer to home, we've all sat through demonstrations of snappy techniques for getting foreign language vocabulary into LTM, and sure enough the students were able to come out with the words five or ten minutes or an hour after they had learned them, so that by either the recent or the contemporary view they were "in LTM." A month or so later, however, the words had in effect evaporated. By contrast, other words learned at about the same time may prove to be available months, years, even decades later. This difference is of course crucially important in our work, so it needs a name. I have suggested the terms permanent memory (PM) and holding memory (HM). Two points about this contrast:

- There are, as we have seen, qualitative physical differences between LTM and STM, and between LTM and WM. I know of no such difference between PM and HM. Rather, they stand for two ends of a continuum.

- When a new item of information comes into LTM, it may be closer to one or the other end of the PM-HM continuum. We in language education would be immensely interested in knowing what makes the difference. An even more practical question is how we can move a given item of information closer to the PM end. This brings us to the sixth question.

6. "What is the role of purpose and emotion?"

Traditional: Memory is a self-contained psychological or neurological process. Purpose may play some role in choosing what to apply this process to, and success or failure of the memory process may lead to some kind of emotions, but otherwise purpose and emotion are unrelated to memory.

Contemporary: I shall use the word **affect** to stand for purposes plus emotions. This pairing together of purposes and emotions is not arbitrary. What we call "emotions" are actually sets of changes in the body proper and in the brain itself. Many of these changes take place as responses to how our needs, motivations, and purposes are or are not being met at the moment. "Feelings," in turn, are our perception of those changes, and in this way they act as "sensors for the match or lack thereof between nature and circumstance" (Damasio 1994, p. xv).

The relationship between affect and memory is intimate and complex.

- Most fundamentally, data about purposes and emotions are stored along with visual, auditory, and other sensory data. In her trip *Through the Looking-Glass,* Alice found that the chess pieces had come to life, and that the White King had fallen to the floor. When she picked him up and set him back on the table, he exclaimed, "The horror of that moment I will never forget!" In the terminology we were using above, he would have said that not only the physical experience but also the feeling of horror that accompanied it had entered his permanent memory. (Hearing this, his wife the White Queen huffed that unless he made a written memorandum of it, even the feeling wouldn't get past his holding memory, but perhaps she was just venting accumulated exasperation left over in her own LTM from earlier experiences with her husband.)

- Second, affective elements may produce extraneous imagery that acts as clutter in the limited capacity of working memory. If my mind is busy visualizing possible long-term effects of a diagnosis the doctor has just given me, I am less likely to retain details of other things the doctor is trying to convey to me. Evidence for this "clutter" effect comes from a wide variety of sources including social, clinical, and experimental psychology.

- Third, these elements *participate in the associative networks* that make recall/retrieval/reconstruction possible. Perhaps most important, they are in fact central to the organization of such networks. Again, support for this assertion is broad, coming from psycholinguistics and cognitive science as well as from neurology and psychoanalysis. In this centrality, I think we have an important part of the answer to the question (above) about what it is that places a new word or structure at one point or another along the PM-HM continuum.

At this point, the reader may well exclaim, "Aha! That must account for why you recall H's phone number easily but have to look J's up! Your basic feelings about your two friends must be somehow different!" That is certainly a plausible guess, and quite consistent with this third aspect of the influence of affect. In this instance, however, the reason goes back to what I said earlier about the role of abstractions (and introduces a fact I didn't mention before): I know that J's number is entirely different from mine, while H's differs in only the fourth digit.

- A fourth influence of affect on learning is that there is also the matter of playing back or reviewing material we have seen or heard. To the extent this experience is voluntary, affect certainly exerts an influence on what we choose to play back and when. Even where playback is involuntary, however, the so-called "din in the head" effect modifies our reactions to what the playback has brought into working memory.

- Finally, affect can also *interfere* with one's ability to draw on and make use of material *already well established* in memory. We find this most vividly in stage fright, but as we will see in Chapter 2, it may also play a role in the learning and use of foreign languages.

SUMMARY OF A CONTEMPORARY PERSPECTIVE ON MEMORY

If we string the contemporary answers together, we can say that learning involves changes in long term memory, whether in the permanent memory end or in the holding memory end or in both. The goal in a language course is to get the learners to modify their permanent memory resources to reflect what new forms usually go with what meanings (simple, complex, or abstract), and also with what other forms and expectations. Permanent memory is organized around affective data. Changes in permanent memory resources are products both of what comes in through the senses, much of which has its source in other people, and of what happens in working memory. Holding memory can be a valuable source of content for working memory, and this content can contribute to the shaping of permanent memory, but changes in holding memory are no substitute for changes in permanent memory.

The distinctive feature of this synthesis is its further development of the complex and all-pervasive role of "affect," of needs, purposes, and feelings. This is the kind of thing I meant in the first edition of *Memory, Meaning & Method* by "depth." Nowadays I think of it more as what's at stake when we invest time, effort and money in learning or teaching a new language.

Chapters 2 and 3 will explore this point of view generally as it applies to the learner and to the teacher. But this same point of view is also the one from which I have rewritten the chapters on specific approaches, each of which illuminates one or another aspect of what's at stake. It is true that a few teachers whom I respect highly have told me that *A Way and Ways* led them to adopt one or another of the approaches I described there. My primary intention in covering them here is however not to propagate them. It is not to offer some dramatic new release from the week-in-and-week-out labor of teaching Somalis in North Dakota or forty assorted adults in the inner city or indifferently motivated adolescents in their home country. What I hope most of all is not to open readers' minds to the new, but to throw new light on the familiar, not so much to provide escape from our daily lot as to help readers develop their own fuller understanding of how to deal with some of its inescapables.

My overall goal in this book as in my other books is to help language teachers to understand better what they are doing. The first step toward understanding one's work is to understand oneself. A number of the investigative tasks I propose will therefore require a certain amount of introspection and personal recollection.

Actually, to me the word "investigations" sounds a bit bureaucratic, and "tasks" reminds me of mopping the corridor, so I've been working with an acronym in mind:

T-hink for yourself.

A-sk a few colleagues.

S-ee what you can find.

K-eep open to new developments.

I hope that in working through these tasks readers won't try to give right answers or reach correct solutions, or to avoid wrong ones. The goal is not to do things right, but to do things better, and one of the factors in what is good or better or even possible for you as a teacher is who you are—your own combination of inborn abilities and past experiences. In making progress toward something better you can only start from where you are, and in order to start from where you are you must first see where you are.

But self-understanding is not an entirely solitary undertaking, either; it also requires a certain amount of seeing oneself in relation to one's peers. I therefore urge readers, if at all possible, to do even the introspective and recollective tasks in the company of colleagues. Most obviously, this will provide a wider range of data. Just as important, however, it will be a constant reminder that there are many dimensions along which such data vary.

---

1 *Think about these questions:*

- What kinds of things is "Aggie" having most conspicuous trouble in retaining?

- What kinds of abstractions are mentioned in the interview with Aggie?

- What figures of speech do Aggie and the interviewer use? Which shared components of meaning do these figures of speech depend on?

- How is the contrast between "holding" memory and "permanent" memory exemplified in Aggie's account?

- How does the relationship between purposes, needs and motivations on the one hand, and emotions and feelings on the other, show up in what Aggie says?

- How would Aggie describe the relationship between learning and memory?

- How might one apply the "contemporary" definitions of learning and memory to what Aggie has said?

---

2 *Answer the questions from Task 1 with regard to an experience of your own, or with regard to what someone else in your work group has told you about hers or his.*

---

3 *For the purpose of this and certain other Investigative tasks in this book, the reader is invited to select a textbook or other set of course materials that he or she either has used or is considering for use. I will refer to these as the reader's "comparison materials."*

Describe a schema for a typical lesson or unit in your comparison materials. Specifically:

- What tangible objects does it include? Textbook? Lecture pad? Toy houses or other "realia?" Other?

- What pictures or other sources of imagery and meanings?

- What audio recordings, printed stories, or other models of linguistic forms?

- What kinds of tasks? Repetition? Interpretation? Translation? Other?

- What number and groupings of people?

- What occasions for generating positive or negative feelings?

If you are working alone, answer these questions for two different comparison materials.

If you are working with one or more colleagues, compare your findings with regard to whatever comparison materials each person chose.

If two or more people are working with reference to the same comparison materials, did everyone agree on all the answers?

2

A VIEW
OF THE LEARNER

Their Lonely Betters

As I listened from a beach chair in the shade
To all the noises that my garden made,
It seemed to me only proper that words
Should be withheld from vegetables and birds.

A robin with no Christian name ran through
The Robin-Anthem which was all it knew;
And rustling flowers for some third party waited,
To say which pairs, if any, should get mated.

Not one of them was capable of lying,
There was not one which knew that it was dying
Or could have, with a rhythm or a rhyme
Assumed responsibility for time.

Let them leave language to their lonely betters,
Who count some days and long for certain letters;
We, too, make noises when we laugh or weep,
Words are for those with promises to keep.

W. H. Auden

FACING AN OBSCENE PARADOX

Only people use words.

We use words to stand for things that are absent, as well as for things that are present. Furthermore, we have a unique ability to put together highly complex strings of word-symbols so as to communicate with one another in detailed and subtle ways. (The ways in which we do all this make up the subject matter for the science of linguistics.) Because we are able to echo back and forth to one another both what we see now and what we remember—even what we hope for—we come to know that none of us is exactly like any other.

This is one gift from language. We feel in ourselves uniqueness ("I am one of a kind.") not only in our bodies but in the way we use our symbols. And with this uniqueness, beauty: beauty around us but also inside us, beauty and irreplaceableness, therefore a kind of miracle. Each of us can say to ourselves, "Like everyone else, I can realize that, out of a few resources, the human race has learned to make infinite uses, that because the possibilities are beyond counting, the choices I have made among them are my own, like no one else's. Uniqueness, beauty, choice, and power—I am a being like a god!"

There is of course another way in which our race is different from all other animals: we know that some day we (or at least our bodies) will die. We learn this fact through words (a second gift of language). We learn it quite early, and the knowledge grows up alongside our experience of uniqueness and our sense of beauty. This is the Great Incongruity, "the obscene paradox" with which we struggle, which churns within us, as long as we live. Psychiatrist/anthropologist Ernest Becker told us that the unifying principle behind all that people do is not economic determinism, not sex, but finding ways to deal with this knowledge: in Becker's phrase, "the denial of death." This is among the deepest, most abstract of the memory items mentioned in Chapter 1. As such it pervades the operation of the networks of long-term memory and helps to shape their output.

We discover that physical death is something we all will come to some day. Our only possibility of escape, then seems to lie in identifying ourselves with something that is eternal—or at least, something that will last longer than we will—and that is universal—true for all people. The obvious examples are what we call the great religions of the world, and these examples are valid ones. But if religion were the only example of this reaction to the fact of death, there would be no point in bringing the matter up here. The struggle against death includes more than faith in life after death (or in "life after life"); it includes our identification with any value system—any set of choices —that we share with others, and that we and others mutually affirm to be true, right, good, and valid for all people. These may be patterns that run through our entire culture, or habits we share with people of our own age, schooling, or occupation, or precepts handed down to us by our parents. We therefore hold desperately to those patterns and those precepts. And/or we look for new parent figures, new peer groups, new objects of allegiance that will assure us that what we have committed ourselves to—even if it is agnosticism—is truly of validity beyond ourselves.

We will see shortly how this principle makes itself felt in the language classroom. But there is another, a short-range way as well by which we fend off death: we put as much space and as much time as possible between ourselves and it.

Part of this is simple prudence: taking care of our health, looking both ways before we cross the street, and so forth. But another part consists in accumulating feelings that others are closer to death than we ourselves. This may be relatively benign—noticing that our classmates at the reunion have aged so much more than we have, for example. But these feelings of relative distance may also be manufactured. One way is to injure another person and get away with it. Another is to sit, successfully, in judgment on what another person is or does (or says!). Death-distancing is also one, though by no means the only, reason for wanting to outdo another person in any sort of competition.

"An Object of Primary Value in a World of Meaningful Action"

So the fact that we inevitably know the world only through our own eyes—our own senses—coupled with our struggle against death, means that each of us has an ultimate need to feel that he or she is "an object of primary value in a world of meaningful action." (Becker quotes this phrase from Alfred Adler, and I have found it helpful.) This was beautifully and repeatedly illustrated in the movie *Siddhartha,* which I saw while I was writing the first draft of this chapter: both the search for what is finally worthwhile, and the demand to be primary. The protagonist was not happy when he found himself the center of what he judged was not of ultimate value; on the other hand, when he concluded that a non-self-centered, nonseeking existence free of attachment was best, he found it was virtually impossible not to attach himself to nonseeking.

Each of us, then, develops a self-image—a set of perceptions related to our body, but also to our personal style, to our actions, and to the values (the choices) that underlie them. But (and this is the key to much that goes on in the language classroom as well as outside it) if what reinforces your self-image contradicts or detracts from mine, then mine is threatened. The same is true in the opposite direction, of course. I believe today's highly processed and chemically treated foods are unwholesome and avoid them; you eat them freely. Each of us secretly hopes the other will fall ill, not because we bear each other any malice, but just because we'd like to see our own choices vindicated. When you are the last person to leave a room in which the lights are on, you generally forget to switch them off, and I suspect you of rejecting not only this one rule, but also all of the values I learned from my parents. One teacher believes in "accuracy before fluency," another in "communication" even at the expense of accuracy. What do they say about each other to parents, to students, to other teachers?

The preservation of the self-image is the first law of psychological survival. Therefore in any social encounter each person exposes for public scrutiny and public testing—possibly for intolerable undermining—the one thing he needs most, which is the self-perception that he has so laboriously fashioned. This means that the stakes in any social encounter are incredibly high. No such encounter, therefore, can be merely routine.

To what extent, and how, are teachers and students natural allies? Natural competitors? Natural enemies?

"Alice": My undergraduate major was French. I was even a member of the National French Honor Society. However, when someone approaches me in French, whether he or she is a native or a non-native speaker, I am unwilling (not incapable) to respond for the fear of making a mistake. This is true even though I usually understand what he or she is saying.

"Allen": Several years ago I had the opportunity to live in Japan for six months, with the sole purpose of studying Japanese. Before I went, I had assumed that as my ability to communicate progressed, my involvements with the Japanese people would naturally increase. And what I wanted to avoid was what I felt I had often observed in young Americans going to Japan—becoming enchanted with things Japanese to the point of rejecting what is not Japanese. As it turned out, I did avoid becoming so enchanted, and I avoided it by practically avoiding all Japanese people. I hid in the intellectual study of the language and kept postponing a deliberate effort to use Japanese because I couldn't hold my own in conversation with a native speaker. But why did I feel it was necessary to hold my own in a conversation? And what, in fact, did I mean by "holding my own"? I think self-image was an important part.

And so a language class is one arena in which a number of private universes intersect one another. Each person is at the center of his or her own universe of perceptions and values, and each is affected by what the others do. If the denial of either physical or psychological or social death requires submission to something eternal and universal, then the teacher needs to appear strong, and competent, and self-confident. The textbook, in contemporary Western-influenced culture at least, ought then to be the latest thing because the latest has had an opportunity to profit from the experience and the errors of all the others, so that it is presumably closest to the right method (immortal). If approval from one's parent-figures is an important reassurance, then it becomes urgent to please the teacher, and to have frequent tests, and to do well on those tests. On the other hand, it would be intolerable to find that our teacher, no matter how strong, self-confident, and apparently competent, used a style of teaching that contradicted values that we had retained from our parents or from earlier teachers— or from sources to which we had developed loyalty more recently, for that matter.

> To what extent, and how, are language students natural allies? Natural competitors? Natural enemies?

"Andy": Graduate training in special education and three years' experience of teaching in a public high school that emphasized the need for a warm, humanistic learning climate caused me to become strongly committed to giving students plenty of latitude within which to develop their own inner resources. I carried these ideas with me to Taiwan, where I spent a semester teaching freshman and sophomore English at a university noted for the high caliber of its students. Emphasis was on developing the students' speaking ability. Yet despite my efforts to create the desired climate, the students remained inhibited and fearful for the entire semester. The key seems to have been the overwhelming difference between the two educational systems, for my students were products of a tradition I did not understand—one in which the learner craves a paternal, assertive teacher. Though the students seemed to appreciate my "warmth, acceptance, and understanding," their needs were not being met.

If the denial of death draws support from those around us, then we will resist whatever there is in the course that asks us to violate the norms we share with our peers. So we may resist the language itself, just for its foreignness, in the same way we resisted the native language teacher who tried to get us to say "it doesn't" when all our friends said "it don't." Further, a particular language may carry with it an undesirable stereotype of its speakers as snobbish, lazy, dishonest, and so on. To become faithful to this foreign way of speaking would feel like being unfaithful to the group that nourished and supports us. The only time my father-in-law ever rebuked me was when he heard me pronouncing French too much like a Frenchman.

The need for support from those around us may also prevent us from achieving all that we could, just because we don't want to be regarded as the one who puts our classmates in a bad light.

"Armand": My second semester was in a different school, with a different textbook, and I was soon put into what was called "the slow group." In time we began to stick together. We found a sense of security and protection with each other. We also had a feeling of belonging. Even though we were "the dunce group," we were able to form a bond and find comfort in each other's French inadequacy.

"Bernice": Somehow, during the semester a pathological condition seems to have developed within the class. In a competitive recitation with another class, these students laughed at each others' every mistake, and as a group, they fell far short of the other class. The atmosphere in this class was the opposite of the warm acceptance which enables a student to perform confidently from the depth of personality. In this environment, students couldn't give it all they had, but filled their class' expectancy for a low level of performance. The laughter was a social mechanism for enforcing this expectancy.

There is a third aspect of our "world of meaningful action" that makes itself felt in our response to a language course. This aspect consists of intermediate and long-range goals, and the like. We know we have only a certain amount of time available to us. We therefore become impatient with something that is presented to us as a new, separate goal in its own right, if it does not contribute toward the achieving of other goals. Psychologically, we may react to it the same way our body reacts to a splinter of wood that gets into our finger. This may help to account for the popularity of language courses that are especially designed for people with particular occupational needs: English for airline pilots, German for organic chemists, or Chinese for engineers.

See the discussion of "Spill and Spell" in Chapter 7.

Our "world of meaningful action," then, draws on the power figures in our life, and on our peer groups, and on more or less tightly integrated sets of goals we have adopted for ourselves. Other things being equal, we will respond better to a language course that fits into that system and less well to a course that does not. But it also may happen that some language courses, for some people, turn out to have been integrating elements in their own right, around which a previously ill-organized set of values becomes clearer.

This is most likely to be true when the student's experience of the language is relatively deep. A "world of meaningful action" is not a flat, two-dimensional thing like a map. We saw in Chapter 1 that its structure has many dimensions, and that some of its parts lie much farther beneath the surface than others. If what a student says makes little or no difference to him or her, it has little "depth" in this sense. But some things he or she says or hears or reads make a difference to him or her in many ways. This kind of experience is relatively "deep." It draws more energy from the learner's "world of meaningful action," and in turn it helps to shape that world.

"Bill": While I was working for a large English school in Japan, the basic text used in the lower intermediate classes consisted of short dialogs followed by a great number of substitution and transformation drills. Many of the instructors were dissatisfied with these materials. We felt there was no meaningful communication taking place in the classroom. A committee was formed, and after eighteen months, we produced what we thought was a better program. We had developed a series of lifelike, situationally defined dialogs on topics of relevance for today's world, followed by exercises that we hoped would elicit language that had previously been focused on in the study of the dialogs. The emphasis was on meaningfulness and communication. We were satisfied with the new materials in all ways but one: the students' final test scores were no better, and their actual use of the language did not improve perceptibly.

Looking back, I think the trouble was that we did not recognize that a great amount of "communicative" activity does not necessarily lead to "depth." The new, more meaningful materials that we developed were used in the classroom just like the older, less communicative ones. The teachers' focus was still primarily on the language, and so the method was virtually the same. The learning process was aimed at the shallower levels.

"Bonnie": Several months ago, I decided to try to get my class of eight intermediate students involved in group debates. After explaining the mechanics of a debate, *I allowed them to choose their own topic and the side of the argument that they wished to take,* the only restriction being that there should be four persons on each side. They had a full week to prepare their arguments for each topic. I was to serve as referee, but I refused their request that I choose the winning team.

The results were even better than I had expected. The first few minutes of the debate, the students were reluctant to speak, and I had to choose the first ones. In a very short time, however, they got into the spirit of it, and it was hard to get them to talk just one at a time. The students seemed to get lost in the debate and in their strong feelings about the topic, and to forget that they were speaking other than their native language. *The heat of the debate seemed to unlock capabilities they weren't aware they had.* They seemed to learn more during the Friday debates than they had in the previous four days. [Emphasis added.]

Compare Lozanov's intervention in Fujiwara's class (Chapter 10).

But as Siddhartha found out, we crave more than a "world of meaningful action"; we also demand a feeling of primacy, or at least strength, within that world. Hence the need for attention from the teacher and from fellow students. Hence also the desire to compete, not only in order to draw out our own full potential, but also, often, to have someone to look down on—someone who is closer to academic "death" than we are. On a more positive note, there is also the need for a steady series of short-term successes and long-term achievements. "Depth" in a language course contributes to this sense of "primacy," at the same time as it enhances the meaningfulness of the action.

In addition (and this is true for other academic courses, not just for foreign languages), there is the fact that new information is being imposed on us from outside ourselves. At best, this requires us to do the intellectual and emotional work of integrating the new into what we already had. Worse, it implies that what we already had was in some way inadequate. Worst of all, we find ourselves in the power of the person who is imposing the new information and evaluating our mastery of it. We find ourselves in the position of being ignorant, powerless, and constantly evaluated—a clear denial of our primacy! This can become a constant source of "clutter" on our "worktable." For any or all of these reasons, we may feel more or less of general resistance just to the idea of being taught. This is true even when the teacher is tactful and kind, but with other kinds of teachers it can become traumatic.

"Carl": Eventually, I perceived the incessant corrections as an adverse attitude on the part of the all-powerful "mother." [I felt] fear of an unexpected [homicidal impulse on the part of the teacher], pain, anxiety, depression, and desire to withdraw. In the class of one pleasant female teacher, [I] experienced her implacable and incessant corrections so adversely that [I] was unable to converse with her, or even approach her either in or out of the classroom.

Foreignness, shallowness, irrelevance, and the subordinate position of the student all may be obstacles to a learner's feeling of "primacy in a world of meaningful action." All of these originate outside of the learner. But there is another obstacle that originates inside the learner, and that may be even more troublesome than any of the external ones. This is the "divided self," which has been commented on by many writers over the years. Curran mentions it, Gallwey builds his "inner game of tennis" around this concept, and even the Apostle Paul complained that, "I do not do the good I want, but the evil I do not want is what I do."

This distinction seems to have resonated with many readers of *A Way and Ways*. It will come up several more times in this chapter, and figures also in Chapters 3 and 9.

The first of these selves is the Critical Self. This self tends to be calculating and verbal, and to impose its expectations on the second, the Performing Self. When the Performing Self fails to perform as the Critical Self thinks it ought, the Critical Self typically puts further pressure on it, or punishes it in some way: "I[Critical Self] don't know what's the matter with me [Performing Self] today." "I [Critical Self] keep telling myself [Performing Self] to try harder." Or the heel of the dominant hand comes up and smites the Body on the forehead. The trouble is that this kind of interaction between the selves usually produces additional anxiety, greater tension, and poorer performance.

One may guess that the expectations that the Critical Self lays on the Performing Self were acquired originally from parents and from early teachers, and so represent an attempt to identify with the powerful and the apparently eternal figures in the learner's early life. But these standards—or at least, such ways of using these standards—are counterproductive for a situation that demands learning and performing. (This is especially true for speaking, where performance has to be rapid and spontaneous.) So the learner is put into a self-defeating bind.

Up to this point, I have listed a wide range of feelings that may have their origin in the struggle against physical or symbolic death, and I have tried to suggest how those feelings may make themselves visible in a language classroom. It goes without saying that individual students differ among themselves in the relative strength of these feelings and in the configurations that the feelings assume within each personality. I do believe, however, that this view of the language student is more comprehensive and more down-to-earth practical than a view that sees him or her only as a combination of language aptitude, learning style, vocational goals, and so on. The picture I am proposing is one into which these others can be fitted, however, and I think it is particularly helpful in exploring what goes on inside and between the people in the classroom.

Clearly this view accounts for/predicts a great deal of conflict: between student and teacher, between student and student, and also within the student herself. It also accounts for/predicts a great deal of aloneness—of alienation between student and teacher, between student and student, and even within the student. In general, the student cannot live up to the conflicting demands she places on herself and the ones she allows others to place upon her: "I want to achieve, *but* I mustn't offend my classmates"; "I shouldn't dislike the teacher, *but* he constantly leaves me feeling stupid"; and so on. To the extent that the student cannot meet demands she recognizes as valid, her feelings of conflict and aloneness are capped by feelings of guilt.

Feelings about feelings play a large and complex role in life. See especially Chapters 1, 5 and 7.

REACTIONS TO LOSS OF MEANING OR VALUE

So instead of a student who is learning as a whole person, with body, mind, and emotions in harmony with one another, we have arrived at a quite different picture. We have a human being who started out to stave off physical or symbolic death but who winds up more or less conflicted, more or less alone, and more or less guilty— surely a sickness unto death! In defending himself from these feelings, the student may try to get away from what seems to be causing them: by dropping the course if he can, or by letting his mind wander, or by doing as little work as he dares. When he reacts in these ways, he only makes matters worse: his performance falls off, guilt and/or aloneness increase, and conflict between performance and expectation may become so unbearable that he lowers his expectation of himself.

> **"Caroline":** In a loud voice, we had to call out our failing grades for everyone to hear. We eventually became defensive against this humiliation by taking it as a joke and laughing it off.

> **"Clay":** Having had a number of unsuccessful (or at least unsatisfying) encounters with language learning, I determined to take an introductory course in German. It was a "good" conventional class, replete with irrelevant textbook dialogs and irrelevant workbook exercises and irrelevant classroom drills. As the teacher went around the room, calling on student after student to recite, I would be in near panic by the time she got to me. Because of my status outside the class, I had to perform well. And of course there were those inevitable "language whizzes" in the class to compare myself with. Well, whether I had programmed myself for it in advance I can't say, but the upshot was that I dropped out after a while—too busy to continue just now—and added another language learning failure to my record.

Or the student may react, not by withdrawing from the source of discomfort, but by striking out at it. She may come to hate all speakers of the language, or she may become very critical of the course and everything associated with it, or she may engage in disruptive behavior in the classroom, or she may mutilate books and equipment. Here again, of course, the result is poorer performance, increased conflict, and deepened alienation—a self-defeating reaction.

> **"Corinne":** One of my classmates seemed to take perverse delight in asking the teacher questions that she might not be able to answer about the grammar. Whenever he did this, the work of the class ground to a halt. I sometimes thought I saw a self-satisfied gleam in his eye.

> **"Dan":** For the inexperienced teacher, it is sometimes appealingly tempting and secure to adopt an authoritarian approach, particularly with docile students. On the basis of my experience as a student of Korean, however, I can say that while the obedient learner may seem to thrive in such an

environment, the less tractable individual is likely to become disruptive, at least socially, or psychologically. Thus, there were frequent complaints concerning the nature of the drills, particularly those on tape. These complaints arose even though we were free to draw on whatever resources were available, and to make creative use of them. In addition, coffee breaks became protracted.

A third reaction is that of the good student, who tries harder, gets the right answers more of the time, pleases the teacher, and learns something. Depending on which particular pattern of feelings the student started out with, this kind of reaction may in fact go far toward reducing the conflict and/or alienation and/or guilt we have been talking about. But there are two things to remember about this kind of reaction. First, it is possible only for students who already possess a fair amount of internal strength and harmony, as well as native aptitude for languages. Second, the "learning" that results is likely to be a piecemeal, intellectual variety that disappears soon after the examination is over. It may leave behind it a large amount of discomfort in the presence of the language, and even distaste for it.

Such "learning" probably takes place mostly in "Holding Memory" (Chapter 1).

"Debbie": All through my schooling, I have had a tendency to be a teacher-worshipper, doing my best to please my instructors. Ethnic reasons excluded me from social acceptance among my peers at an early age, and for this reason my need and desire to be accepted by my teachers was doubly strong. I excelled scholastically and received praise from my teachers in course after course. I graduated with many high honors. Yet an overwhelming feeling of inadequacy as a student has bothered me for years—and still does.

"Desmond": A couple of years ago, I was teaching English to engineers in the Persian Gulf. Most of the men had had English in high school, and used English grammar with some pleasant competence. But here, their careers were at least half conducted in colloquial English, at which they had no skill. Being inexperienced and eager to please, I taught to their strengths in grammar. Some of the students were quite ingenious at transformation exercises. They soon became my star performers. But conversation in class remained stilted and hesitant.

Outside of class, I saw a different social system forming among the engineers, and a happier one, in which one of my poorest, most reluctant students figured strongly. I did not know then that his spoken English was effective and rich, but delivered in a grammar so barely serviceable that after the first few days he had been shamed into barely opening his mouth in class. Eventually I found that I should talk less in class, look less keenly for learners' errors, and wonder a little at what my students really were. And this hitherto poor student began speaking. Impeded less and less by corrections, he brought out his conversational genius, and imparted a real spark to the class. He finally learnt considerable grammar, more from his classmates than from me.

THE LEARNING TURTLE

When I was growing up, we sometimes played with box turtles. These little animals, five or six inches long as I remember them, could make amazingly good time as they moved along on their stubby legs, head fully extended from the shell. What we liked to do, of course, was to find one of them earnestly marching along toward somewhere, and touch it ever so lightly on the back. It would immediately retract its head and its legs into its shell, and remain motionless. Then we would pick it up and set it down again wherever we liked. (I have sometimes wondered whether, after it had recovered from its alarm and set out again, it headed for its original destination, or whether it had lost its bearings and had to devise an entirely new trip.)

I think we often see something like that happening in language classes. The engineer in "Desmond's" narrative, for one, seems to have behaved in that way. Any student can arrive at a correct response in either of two ways: by using his own existing internal resources and deciding what to do next, or by complying with the teacher's skillful lesson plan. If he does what he does on his own, and in conformity with his own timing and his own purposes, then he knows where he is, and why, and how he got there. If he merely lets himself be carried along by the lesson plan, then what he does will not be truly a part of him, and it may be lost all too quickly. The resources of long-term memory, as described in Chapter 1, are shaped and reshaped by *everything that went on* inside the learner's head to produce a particular audible or visible response to a given audible or visible stimulus, *not just by the stimuli and responses themselves.*

An interesting quick litmus test of an approach or a method is to ask how these sentences do or don't fit with it.

The analogy breaks down, of course. In a language class, it is possible for the student to travel by both means at the same time: lesson plans provide opportunities for students to propel themselves along within the overall guidance of the teacher. What is unfortunate is that many lesson plans are based on the belief that we should get the turtle to the destination we have chosen for it as expeditiously as possible, even if we have to take it off its feet. Equally unfortunate, though less common, is the opposite extreme: "humanistic" techniques that place a premium on student initiative and student contributions sometimes fall flat. When this happens, it usually means that the turtle is being asked to come out of its shell in an environment which for some reason it finds alarming. Yet success in getting a new language, and especially in "acquiring" it, requires the turtle's head and legs to be as far out of its shell as possible. For any method, but especially for the "humanistic" ones, there needs to be harmony between the two "selves" of each student, and a minimum of irrelevant tension among the people in the classroom.

These points are conspicuous in the thinking that underlies Counseling-Learning/Community Language Learning and suggestopedia (Chapters 5-7 and 10).

The following account is typical of a dozen I have heard from people who are language students and/or tennis players. It illustrates the effect of the relationship between the Critical Self and the Performing Self.

> **"Elmer":** I have been playing tennis for about four years. When I rallied with my friends, my hits were smooth, swift, and natural. But when I played a game, I usually tightened up. The goal of winning posed a threat to me, and games really "psyched me out." After reading *The Inner Game of Tennis*, I decided to put into practice the idea of "letting it happen." I relaxed and let my whole being flow. I did not concentrate hard or think of the many things that I should or should not do. . . and it really worked! My shots were smooth and well-placed. Nothing could have gone better! I have never played so well. I had a great feeling of inner satisfaction.

The turtle may retreat into its shell outside of the classroom also. The following is by a Japanese-American.

> **"Emiko":** In the past, I have usually been successful at whatever I set out to do. Although I welcome challenges, I tend to avoid situations which make me feel incompetent or inferior. In my many opportunities to interact with Japanese

people, I have always been amazed at how my fluency in Japanese is affected by the other person's proficiency in English. I know two Japanese who can speak English fluently without any trace of an accent. I have generally used English in speaking with them. On several occasions when I did attempt to use Japanese, I found myself feeling uncomfortable and awkward, groping for words that I would ordinarily have been able to produce very easily. On the other hand, when talking with those who can speak little or no English, I am able to speak Japanese with great ease and fluency. I often surprise myself by coming out with words which I never realized I had in my vocabulary.

In this chapter, we have looked briefly at some of the anxieties that keep the Learning-Turtle's head back in its shell so much of the time—the attachments that preoccupy the prudent Critical Self and interfere with the potential of the Performing Self. They may contribute to a downward spiral in which learning is severely reduced.

> **"Evan":** I recall my first experience at learning a foreign language. I was in a private school for boys. The teacher faced his seventh-graders with an over-sized paddle propped against his desk. He called it his "whacker," and he said he would use it on each of us sooner or later. The Latin declensions, conjugations, eventually whole passages, were assigned, memorized, recited on command. An incorrect answer brought the humiliation of at least the teacher's scowl; enough correct answers brought only a good grade. However, no one doubted the teacher's skill at Latin, or his ability to get students to [absorb] vocabulary and structures.
>
> Well, midway through the ninth grade, my family moved to another continent and at last I left that teacher's classroom forever. Today I remember him down to the necktie he wore on the first day of class. But when after a month or so in my new home I looked again at my Latin books, I discovered (to my residual terror) that my Latin had washed off me entirely.

What we hope, of course, is that language study will become an upward spiral, and not a downward one—an affirmation of life and not just a relatively successful "denial of (or dealing with the prospect of) physical or symbolic death." Who, then, is to break, or to reverse, the spiral? Clearly the student herself or himself must assume some of the responsibility. Parents, friends, and academic counselors of various kinds may also be of some help. In the next chapter, however, we shall look at the role of the teacher. We shall do so for two reasons: First, this is a book for teachers, and the teacher is the only person over whom the teacher has direct control. Second, the teacher is the central and the most powerful figure in the classroom.

---

1 *Which "life and death" issues may have been active for "Andy's" students in Taiwan? Which may "Andy" himself have been facing in the experience he describes?*

---

2 *Of all the voices quoted in this chapter ("Alice" through "Evan"), with which do you think most language students would find it easiest to identify? Why?*

- With which would they find it hardest to identify? Why?

- What about yourself? Do you personally react to these voices the way you've predicted most language students would? Why, or why not?

---

3 *Here is some wisdom from an unfamiliar source: three Swahili proverbs.*

Jogoo wa shamba hawiki mjini.

rooster of countryside does not crow in city

Ukikaa na simba vaa ngozi ya mamba.

if you dwell with lion wear skin of crocodile

Heshima heshima si utumwa.

respect [is] respect it is not slavery

How do these proverbs fit, or how do they contrast with, what you have read in Chapter 2?

---

4 *The sixteenth-century book* Utopia *("good place") was Thomas More's description of an imaginary ideal country. Here's what he had to say about children at mealtime. The scene is a community dining hall.*

Among the nurses sit all the children that be under the age of five years. All the other children of both kinds, as well boys as girls, that be under the age of marriage, do either serve at tables, or else if they be too young thereto, yet they stand by with marvellous silence. That which is given them from the table they eat, and other several [*sic*] dinner-time they have none.

- Whose point of view, or whose interests, does this description represent?

- What would a modern idealized picture of children at mealtime in your culture look like? Whose point of view, or whose interests, would it represent?

- What may your first language teacher's idealized picture of language students have looked like?

- What would an idealized picture of students in your program, or in a program based on your comparison materials, look like? Whose point of view, or whose interests, does this picture represent?

3

ONE VIEW OF TEACHING

*Teaching is part of life or part of death, and learning is being born
or being stifled. It is gasping gladly for that next first breath, or
being told, "Always breathe in and never out."*

*Teaching and learning are two men sawing down a tree. One pulls,
and then the other. Neither pushes, and neither could work alone, but
cutting comes only when the blade is moving toward the learner.*

*At least that's how it should be. If the teacher pulls while the
learner is still pulling, they work against each other and waste their
strength. If, in zeal to help the learner, the teacher pushes, then the
blade will buckle, rhythm will be broken, both will become dis-
heartened. . .*

Anon.

TEACHING: SUBORDINATE BUT INDISPENSABLE

To what extent,
and how, are
teachers natural
allies of each
other? Natural
competitors?
Natural enemies?

Chapter 2 was about the classroom experience seen primarily from the point of
view of the learner. We like to talk about "learner-centered" instruction. As
Jakobovits and Gordon once pointed out, while we know that "learning" takes
place and that people can do it, we are much less sure about "teaching." There
can, after all, be "learning" without "teaching," but one cannot claim to have
"taught" unless someone else has learned. This is what has tempted us to play
down the importance of teaching. But. . .

There is an old story about a preacher in a revival meeting held in a big tent
on the edge of town. When the time came to pass the collection plate, a man in
the congregation stood up and shouted, "Hey, Brother! I thought you said salvation is as free as the rain from the heavens! Then why are you asking us for
money?" To which the preacher shot back, "Yes, Brother, salvation is as free as
the rain that falls from the heavens! But you have to pay to have it piped to you!"

Quite possibly many of our students, even our adult students, could learn
languages very well without us if they were dropped under the right conditions
into the right cultural and linguistic environment. With the world the way it
is, however, these conditions and this environment are extremely rare. We may
continue to affirm that the learner is in some ways "central" to what we do.
But we should at the same time remember that there are other functions for
which our society, and our students themselves, demand that we the teachers
stand steadfast at the center of language education. I can think of at least five
such functions:

1. Most obvious is the *cognitive* function: It is we teachers who possess the information that our students are seeking about the foreign culture and its language. To say the same thing more bluntly, we have what caused them to come—or to be sent—to the course in the first place.

2. Almost as obvious is the *classroom management* function: Our students, and the society in which both we and they live, expect us to take responsibility for how they use their time while they are with us. In placing this expectation on us they rely on our training and experience with materials, schedules, and techniques.

3. A third function has to do with *practical goals.* Our students, and society at large, have certain overall goals for language courses. Sometimes these goals are listed very explicitly, and sometimes they are only half-conscious, but they are still essential to the purposive side of "affect" as I used that term in Chapter 1. We teachers are supposed to take these long-range goals and translate them into goals that are weekly, daily, hourly.

4. The fourth function is *personal* or *interpersonal.* Because of our near-monopoly of information, procedures, and day-to-day goals, and because of the authority that society invests in the giver of the final grade, the teacher is by far the most powerful figure in the classroom. Therefore the teacher, more than anyone else, sets the tone for the *interpersonal atmosphere.* That atmosphere, in turn, may mean that the students' nonlinguistic, emotional needs are met, or are denied, during their time in the language classroom.

5. Related to this fourth function, but centered still more closely on the person of the teacher, the teacher may radiate *enthusiasm for the task* at hand, and conviction of its value, or may not. I am talking here not so much about what the teacher says explicitly as about what the students infer from the teacher's manner. This is more subtle than the other four ways in which the teacher is "central" to the course, yet it is perhaps the most indispensable of the five.

"Control" and "Initiative"

These, then, are five respects in which the teacher may rightfully demand, and must rightly accept, the center of the stage in language instruction. Here I agree with Freire's insistence that we should not abdicate the role of teacher in favor of becoming just some kind of "facilitator." So, the question now becomes, how can we reconcile the centrality of the teacher with the centrality of the learner? Do these two ideas not conflict? I think we have in fact often assumed, implicitly if not explicitly, that such a conflict does exist. We have sometimes talked and written as though an increase in the learner's initiative necessarily requires some reduction in the degree of control that the teacher exercises, and vice versa. We have therefore concluded that all we can do is try for an appropriate balance, or trade-off, between control by the teacher and initiative by the student. In recent years, however, I have come to believe that this is not so. I believe there is a way to define "control" and "initiative," not widely inconsistent with everyday usage, which allow the teacher to keep nearly 100 percent of the "control" while at the same time the learner is exercising nearly 100 percent of the "initiative." This distinction has proved to be one of the more useful ideas that I have run across.

Some kind of "control" is necessary for the success of human undertaking. As far as I can see, "control" by the teacher is legitimate even in "progressive," or in "humanistic" education. As I am using the term, "control" consists of only two essential elements. The first element is the structuring of classroom activity: What are we supposed to be doing? When is the time to stop what we are doing and start something else? In tennis, the teaching professional provides the court, explains the rules, provides suitable models, and sets appropriate goals. This part of the "control" function is tied in with the first three of the ways in which I have said the teacher is "central" to a language class.

The other essential element of "control" consists in making it easy for the learners to know how what they have done or said compares with what an established speaker would have said or done. In tennis, even novices can generally see for themselves whether or not the ball hit inside the line. In a foreign language, new learners are not immediately equipped to know these things for themselves. The second half of "control" is most commonly exercised through what we call "correction of errors," though the customary kind of correction is usually unnecessary and frequently undesirable. We will talk about some alternatives in Chapters 5–10 and elsewhere.

In this connection, readers may enjoy Ernest Hemingway's story "A Clean, Well-Lighted Place."

Seen in this way, "control" is clearly a teacher function, at least in the early part of any course. It is the teacher's necessary contribution toward making this new and bewildering corner of the students' "world of meaningful action" into a stable, clean and well-lighted place in which to work (or play!). As time goes on, students may become able to assume some of the responsibility for the first (the "structuring," or "steering") aspect of control. Certain of my colleagues have been quite successful doing this in their classes, using a daily "chairmanship" that rotates among the students, and this can be very productive. But I would repeat that students need to feel that this sharing of "control" is voluntary on the part of the teacher, and fits within his or her overall plan. (They also need to accept it.) Otherwise, they will begin to feel that this corner of their world is not so stable after all. Furthermore, control in the hands of students must not be allowed to lead to much loss in the smoothness or effectiveness of the activity. If it does, it will damage the students' feeling of adequacy within their world.

I once witnessed a dramatic example of masterly delegation of this first element of control within the overall guidance of the responsible authority. In the summer of 1976, I was with a group of language teachers who were returning to the United States from Victoria, British Columbia, on the Washington State Ferry. It was nighttime and foggy as the huge boat twisted its way among the hundreds of small islands in Juan de Fuca Strait. Some of us commented that under these conditions, we were glad the captain and all the boat's navigational aids were hard at work on our behalf. A minute or two later, one of the men in the group was paged and asked to come to the bridge. When he arrived there, he found that the person at the wheel was his own five-year-old son. The captain was standing several feet away, giving directions orally.

I don't know how far the boat was from the nearest island while all this was going on. I do know, if I had been the captain, it would not have occurred to me to invite a small child to carry that responsibility under those conditions. In any event, this incident shows what can be done by someone who has an exquisitely detailed knowledge of the external medium (whether geography or language), and of the learner's skills and readinesses.

Some teachers are in a great hurry to share responsibility with their students. They may do so because they take some kind of delight in seeing what they have enabled their students to do in this area (and/or having their students and their colleagues see it). I myself tend to be this kind of teacher. Or they may rush to transfer the "structuring" aspect of control because someone has persuaded them that Being Nondirective Is a Good Thing To Do. Whatever the reason, it is dangerous to turn this responsibility over to the students prematurely.

I said above that the second half of "control" in this sense consists of making sure that the student is not in the dark concerning her or his use of the target language: "Where is what I have said (or written, or understood) consistent with what a competent speaker would have said (or written, or understood) under the same circumstances, and where is it inconsistent?" This half of control is also a teacher function, at least in the beginning. It rests, of course, on the cognitive centrality of the teacher. It is the light, or the radar, by which the student begins to make out the shapes of unfamiliar objects that lie in his or her path. When the light is dim or intermittent, the student understandably becomes anxious, frustrated, and eventually hostile, thereby throwing "clutter" onto the "worktable." If, on the other hand, this light glares too harshly, the student may be blinded by it and flutter helplessly to the ground. We have seen in Chapter 2 "Evan's" firsthand account of how that can happen.

The second half of "control," like the first, can be shared. In fact, looked at from one point of view, a primary purpose of any language course is to make the student independent of the teacher in knowing what can be said and what cannot. When this happens, the student may rightfully feel that he or she has become an adequate center in the universe of the new language and can therefore accept the language itself as a part of his or her own personal universe. On the other hand, if this half of control is never adequately shared, the student is likely to wander through the big world outside the classroom permanently dependent on teachers and people whom he or she can treat as teachers, a perpetual alien in someone else's "world of meaningful action." But in the beginning, the second component of "control," like the first, is necessarily in the hands of the teacher.

"Initiative," as I am using the word here, refers to decisions about who says what to whom and when. These decisions consist of choices among a narrow or very broad range of possibilities provided by whoever is exercising "control." Seen in this way, "initiative" and "control" are not merely two directions along a single dimension. That is to say, "control" on the part of the teacher does not interfere with "initiative" on the part of the student: when the teacher tightens her "control" of what is going on, she need not cut into the student's "initiative"; often, in fact, she will actually increase it. Similarly, insufficient "control" by the teacher may reduce or paralyze the "initiative" of the student.

The box turtle, which I mentioned near the end of Chapter 2, may help to show why this is so. When the student displays "initiative" in this sense, he is beginning to play an active, central, self-validating role in a "world of meaningful action." But if the "world of meaningful action" that the teacher has provided is unclear, or half-formed, then the turtle will keep its head in its shell; that is, the learner will stick to simple choices and safe alternatives.

Another metaphor is the "jungle gym" found on many playgrounds. The apparatus consists of lengths of iron pipe connected so as to form a set of hollow cubes. The bars quite strictly determine when a child may and may not go, but leave to the child endless choices of where to start from, where to go, and how to get there.

Exercising clear and firm "control" is not the only way in which the teacher can help the learner to take strong and satisfying "initiatives," however. As I said above, the teacher is central for setting the interpersonal atmosphere in the class, and for conveying enthusiasm and conviction. These influence the turtle and its readiness to venture from behind its defense system even more than clear structuring can. We should remember also that clear structuring in an uncongenial atmosphere will produce only limited "initiative": limited involvement of the purposes and emotions central to the organization of memories. As we saw in Chapter 1, the resources of long-term memory will therefore remain underutilized.

"Fabian": Using a set of sequentially arranged pictures, I was eliciting a story about them from the class. The students were expected to limit themselves to English that they could fully control. In this, I was following the theory that incorrect usages would establish themselves as habits. The story was well rehearsed orally, and then used as a dictation exercise. One student, however, flatly refused to follow this procedure. He would have nothing to do with the rather ho-hum little narrative that the rest of us were laboring over. I sensed that if I insisted that he participate, it would lead to class disruption far out of proportion to "John and Mary's Beach Picnic." So I suggested that he create his own story. The effect was amazing. His attitude shifted from withdrawal to intense involvement, which resulted in an imaginative, spicy version of the story that amused all of us.

This incident illustrates dramatically the different degrees and qualities of "initiative" that may be available from any one student at any given time. At the same time, it also illustrates how a change in the teacher's exercise of "control" can restrict or release a student's "initiative." "Fabian" concludes his narrative by saying, "The experience was helpful to me as a teacher, though it was unnerving to be so directly challenged. I began encouraging this type of productivity and found the results beneficial to class community, and [therefore? EWS] to individual students' acquisition of English."

In exercising "control," then, the teacher is lending some kind of order or structure to the learning space of the student. In encouraging the student to take "initiative," the teacher is allowing her or him to work and to grow within that space. The trick for the teacher is not only to preserve this distinction; it is also to provide just the right *amount* of learning space. If there is too little, the student will be stifled. If there is too much, the student will feel the teacher has abandoned him or her. Consider the spark plug that releases the power of the fuel in an engine: if the contacts are touching one another, there is a short circuit and hence no spark. But if the contacts are too far apart the spark, electricity cannot jump the gap, and again there is no spark.

What so often happens, of course, is that the teacher, in the name of "exercising control," also monopolizes initiative, telling the student which line of the drill to produce, which question to ask (or how to answer it), whom to talk with, or so on. The student knows she or he has perhaps three to five seconds in which to respond before the teacher reasserts initiative by repeating the question, giving a hint, prompting, or calling on someone else. To avoid this requires skill and balance and maturity on the part of the teacher. It requires the teacher to become aware of and to control his or her own personal needs.

The Teacher's Own "Denial of Death"

Earlier in this chapter I said that the teacher is "central" with regard to the cognitive content, the structuring of time, the articulation of goals, the setting of climate, and the final human validation of the whole undertaking. But the teacher's own urge to become "an object of primacy in a world of meaningful action" can lead her or him to carry any of these five legitimate functions to undesirable excess. Cognitive primacy may become an assertion of infallibility; the responsibility for structuring time may lead to a demand for a monopoly on power and also to excessive defining of goals. Together these are the principal ingredients of the evaluative manner that is so effective in stifling the initiative of students. Here again is the teacher as god-figure: an omniscient, omnipotent judge!

> **"Fatima":** I remember I was always reluctant to go to English class, in which the teacher was always asking us, hour after hour, to "repeat after me." One time while she was doing pronunciation practice, she had us repeat the word "pupil," first in chorus, then in rows, then individually. When I was called on, I repeated the sound I thought I heard, but she kept telling me to repeat, without giving me any explanation. Some of my classmates began to giggle, and I couldn't bring myself to look at them. Finally, I learned the sound that had been wrong, but after the embarrassing moment I was afraid to pronounce English in class. . .
>
> Timid as I was in the English class, I felt quite at home with my Sunday School teacher, and could talk with her freely. In contrast with the regular school, Sunday School was free from the teacher's evaluation of the students.

The teacher's responsibility for keeping track of goals may similarly turn into an urgent need to see results, and therefore to a preempting of initiative.

> **"Felicia":** One day I had an opportunity to observe a teacher in an adult Basic English class of six people. I believe this teacher entered the class with a set image of herself to be presented to the students: she was the teacher whose goal was to teach the completing of the simplest income tax form. As she began explaining how to fill in the different blanks on the form, it was apparent that the students were not understanding much. It seemed that her teacher-image was being threatened; so, sensing this, she set about to defend herself from this

threat. For one thing, she did more talking and the talk became louder, perhaps with the notion that in this way the material would sink into the students' heads. Second, the teacher (in rapid English) told the students to write down what she said in the appropriate blanks without the students' really knowing why. Finally, after the students filled in the blanks with figures they did not understand, the teacher praised them with the classic "very good."

The teacher's concern to maintain a certain climate within the classroom may lead him or her to be uncomfortable and defensive when that particular climate is disrupted for any reason. Similarly her commitment to the language and the course, which is so essential to the appearance of final validity for the whole undertaking, can lead to great loneliness if the class does not respond in the desired way. There is also a potential for loneliness in the very act of committing oneself to transmitting a *foreign* culture and its language. Here again are "clutter on the worktable" and underutilization of valuable resources, and these can feed into each other to create a downward (or inward) spiral. (The good news: To the extent that the above conditions are reversed, the spiral can reverse itself and move upward and outward!)

> **"Ginny":** I gave up teaching English composition [to natives], and began teaching literature. This was a little more satisfying, for I love it. But I am not very articulate, and any attempt to conduct lecture-style classes was a personal disaster. I felt very keenly the loneliness and vulnerability of the teacher. My tendency was to present the material as a given. When I was not accepted with gratitude, I felt rejected.

So the language classroom can be a place of alienation for student and teacher alike. Becker says that what any person needs is, first, an overall view of how everything fits together and, second, possibilities of action within that view. He defines "alienation" as the absence of that combination, and says that "the human self-contradiction is not a medical or a narrowly biological problem, but is always and at heart a social problem—a problem of what society will allow people *to know and to do*" [emphasis in original]. Becker, of course, was talking about human existence in general. Is it possible that within the confines of our profession, the two essentials he is talking about are very close to what we have been calling "control" and "initiative"?

But, Becker says, no one human being can establish and maintain his own meaning, in a convincing manner, all by himself. And "the problem of conviction. . . is one of trying to get into contact with the full mystery and vitality of being." Quoting Martin Buber, Becker says that a human being can do this only in relation to another human self, even if the other self is just as limited and just as conditioned as she or he is. If we bring ourselves down now from the comprehensive viewpoint of these two philosophies, and into the relatively narrow back yard of the language teacher, we come again to the statement that what is really important is what goes on inside and between the people in the classroom.

Breaking Downward Spirals

What, then, can we as teachers contribute toward breaking the cycle of internal and external conflict, of alienation, of guilt, which accompanies so much of the academic experience that we call "language-learning"? Let's begin with three things I think we should *not* do.

First of all, as I said earlier in this chapter, we must avoid letting the classroom become a power vacuum. I begin with this point because of widespread misunderstandings about some of the "humanistic" approaches that try to take into account the whole person of the learner. The silence of the Silent Way teacher does not mean his or her hand is straying from the steering wheel. The patient, understanding, sometimes self-effacing teacher of Counseling-Learning does not "let the students do just whatever they want," in spite of the impression many people carry away from their first experience with it. And the one most basic principle of suggestopedia is the authority of the teacher. In the light of what I said earlier, we can see why this is so: A weak teacher would deprive the students of that stable arena for meaningful action they so desperately crave. This is not to say that the teacher should never give the students freedom of choice in some areas. In fact, I think this should be done often—much more often than many teachers would imagine. But the student needs to feel that those choices, no matter how broad, are granted within the teacher's overall plan, by the teacher's own free will, and not out of weakness.

> **"Girard":** In graduate school, I have met a few professors who promote equality while still providing strong guidance.
>
> By being treated as a colleague, I feel free to call upon their superior experience in ways which I never could have otherwise. But in all of my experience before graduate school, I never saw a successful example of the "liberté, égalité, fraternité" model. Teachers who tried it were generally using it to cover up their inadequacies, or their disinterest in teaching.

Next, I think we should not fill the power vacuum in the usual way. Most traditional classroom activity, in any culture I know anything about, follows the Evaluation Paradigm, which consists of variations on a single formula. In this formula, the teacher says to the student—cynically or warmly, threateningly or reassuringly—"*Now try to do this so I can tell you how you did.*" Mistakes are pointed out—harshly or gently, immediately or after some delay—and the student's response to the task is evaluated. The student generally comes away feeling that she herself has been evaluated—negatively or positively—along with her product. We may be offering to the student a "world of meaningful action," but by our evaluation we deny her primacy in it. If our evaluation is negative, we also cast doubt on her adequacy within that world. At the time, our Critical Self calls her Critical Self into action, and together we harass her Performing Self.

Most teachers are willing to agree that negative evaluation may sometimes be harmful to the student, but I have found few who are ready to see that *positive* evaluation is almost as dangerous a tool. It seems to be the evaluative *climate,* more than the content of the evaluation, that does the damage. Consider the following, an account by a middle-aged man.

> **"Gowan":** I learnt French in high school and in college. Outside the classroom I found numerous opportunities to use the language in valid social situations. The language flowed forth with a steadily increasing fluency. After a gap in usage from 1960 to 1975, I took an intensive advanced French course taught by a Frenchman, with success. Again the French flowed fluently forth and increased. Immediately following this intensive course, I returned to my home city, where a friend who was a native Parisian said, "Let's speak French now.

I want to hear how well you do it." My heart did a Highland fling, the cold sweat poured off me, goose pimples sprang out, breathing became hard, and the French section of my brain shut down with a bang. I could only answer (in English), "What do you want to test me for?" This friend and I have conversed quite satisfactorily on subsequent occasions, but not then.

I have had smaller-scale but quite analogous experiences myself with speakers of German. With one, we had just finished what I had thought was a reasonably fluent, *and mutually interesting,* conversation, when she said, "Oh, I like talking with you. You use such correct grammar [compared with most foreigners]." I avoided all further opportunities to speak German with this person, because just the memory of this remark would create an evaluative climate for me. Yet before and since, with other speakers, I have thoroughly enjoyed using the same language.

> **"Grace":** Languages which I have enjoyed studying are, of course, more available to me than those that were not enjoyable. Nevertheless, my ability to use even the former depends significantly on the cues received from native speakers. In a situation where some specific communication is the goal, I used Japanese fairly fluently, but in big cities, the reaction to a sentence from me in Japanese was often, "Oh, do you speak Japanese?" followed by a rather awkward exchange in English or Japanese. In a communicative situation, I am seldom at a loss for words, but if someone urges me, "Say something in Japanese," I tend to stick to formulas. Similarly, "I hear that you speak Japanese very well" is less satisfactory in eliciting a Japanese response than any non-evaluative conversational utterance in that language would be.

Gallwey, the tennis coach, tells us that if your opponent's forehand is giving you trouble, you may find it to your advantage to compliment him or her on it, saying, "Wow! Your forehand is really hot today! What are you doing?" This frequently has the effect, says Gallwey, of activating the other person's Critical Self, which immediately sets about interfering with his or her performing Self.

I used the first draft of this chapter as the basis for lectures to a larger class at the University of Hawaii. One of the requirements of the course was the writing of a pair of short papers. When the first few came in, I was so delighted with them that, thinking to encourage the class as a whole, I mentioned my pleasure at the next session. Although reaction to my announcement was mixed, it was overwhelmingly negative. Besides setting up an evaluative atmosphere, the students told me, I had given the rest of them the idea that they had a tough standard to *compete against.* Even those whose papers had been read and declared excellent felt that my public statement put them under extra pressure to *continue to perform.* What I had said left everyone feeling that I was *laying my own expectations on them.* Nothing I was able to say had much effect in reducing their uneasiness.

This experience fits in with numerous other occasions on which I have tried to praise individual students, in as noncondescending a way as I knew how, only to have their performance drop off. I am not saying one should never praise students, just as I would not say a surgeon should never use a scalpel. But praise is two-edged and very sharp, with more potential for damage than many teachers realize. Perhaps the beneficial elements in praise are the information it carries (comparable to a tennis player's seeing that the ball hit inside the line) and the feeling that one has given pleasure to another human being (in this case the teacher). The negative elements are self-consciousness and the expectation that the pleasure-giving performance ought to continue. The trick is to convey the positive without the negative, but this is a very subtle matter.

Finally, I am doubtful about the wisdom of trying to fill the vacuum by enclosing the student in too much linguistic security. A few systems of instruction seem to have aimed at keeping the student's activity as risk-free, and his or her language as error-free, as possible throughout the length of the course. Some early programmed courses appeared to pursue this dream. This has generally proved to be too enormous a task for even the best-financed materials writers. Even if it were not so large an undertaking, however, full-time wall-to-wall insurance against error would still run contrary to what I have been talking about, because it fails to call forth the student's full powers, and constricts the world within which she or he is permitted to take "meaningful action." It also gives "primacy" to the materials rather than to the student.

This is not to say that people do not get any benefit at all from the traditional evaluative system, or from the super-secure methods devised in the past. I do question, however, whether much informal "acquisition" of the soaking-up variety takes place. I'm not even sure most people do formal point-by-point "learning" as fast that way. Both styles of teaching provide the student's Critical Self with plenty of ammunition for keeping his or her Performing Self under a steady barrage of criticism. At the same time, they provide external Critical Selves to complete whatever the student's own Critical Self may have left undone.

PROMOTING UPWARD SPIRALS

On the positive side, I can see at least seven steps a teacher might take in order to work consistently with what we have been talking about. They both recapitulate what I have already said and point forward to features of the three approaches to be described in Chapters 5-10. I will list the steps in order of increasing demands that they make on the teacher. This is *not* a chronological order!

At the base of all else, the teacher may look closely, and steadily, at her or his own students in the light of what was outlined in Chapter 2. I am not saying that we are to psychoanalyze our students or even that we can hope to gain a detailed knowledge of what each one is up against inside and outside of class. That would clearly be out of the question. But I do believe we can be alert to this information as it becomes available. I also believe we can try to tie it together with a relatively comprehensive and relatively deep framework like that of Chapter 2: What attitudes do the students have toward speakers of the target language, toward language study, or toward study in general? How are they reacting to the course as it progresses? What general, and what specific, pressures do these students feel from their parents or from their employers, from us, from one another, and from themselves? Some of the answers to these questions will relate to individual students, while others will apply to whole groups.

Anyone who has ever seen an infrared photograph can understand what I mean here. The same terrain, photographed at the same time and from the same spot, looks quite different in infrared and in conventional color. It remains in some sense the same, yet features that are inconspicuous or invisible in the one become the most striking features of the other.

I would further urge that for the teacher to let his or her mind work in this way is not incompatible with any method, and that in itself it is not time-consuming. This first step, then, may be the only step that is open to all teachers.

This is not to say, however, that the first step is one that all teachers have taken. There may even be some who cannot take this step. A teacher may be so wrapped up in the academic substance of the course that she or he is oblivious to the other factors with which the student is dealing.

> **"Graham":** I am a teacher. I used to teach freshman composition and literature, but now I teach ESL. I stopped teaching composition because nothing in my B.A. or M.A. English programs had prepared me to cope with departmental regulations like 3 comma splices equals C or 3 comma splices plus 2 run-on sentences equals F. I didn't dispute the wisdom of such regulations. I didn't have the linguistic training which would have given me the confidence to reject prescriptive grammar, nor did I have the individual strength to encounter head-on my students' experiences or thinking. It was easier to add up comma splices, especially when the power of the whole English Department was behind me.

(This sounds very much like some of the teachers my own children have had.)

Another way of failing to take that first step is the opposite of the one I've just mentioned. The teacher may be aware of some of these nonacademic aspects of a student's experience, but use them as occasions to feel sorry for her, or to excuse her from meeting the subject matter of the course. Or finally, the teacher may see what is bothering the student, but shrug it off as something the student should resolutely put out of the way so that it will not interfere with the teacher's classroom responsibilities. In the second and third of these possibilities, the teacher's reaction is one of helplessness in the face of what he sees: a helplessness that leads either to destructive sympathy or to destructive callousness. These second and third possibilities are perhaps more pernicious than simple blindness to what the student is going through.

It is for this reason that we need to do more than just notice some of the forces that are at work in or on the student. We need also to relate our observations to some general framework comparable to the one sketched in Chapters 1 and 2. When we are able to do so, they cease to be capricious random bits of interference, and become parts of a comprehensible reality with which we are dealing. Walking through a darkened room, we stumble against the furniture. When the light is turned on, the furniture is still there, but our seeing it makes crossing the room easier, not harder.

A second step is also open to most of us. We can look at our lesson plans and at our actual classroom activities in terms of the "control" that we (or the students) are providing, and the "initiative" that the students (or we) are exercising. This distinction cuts across the distinctions among Hearing, Speaking, Reading, and Writing, or among Beginning, Intermediate, and Advanced, or among Mechanical, Meaningful, and Communicative—any and all of which are useful distinctions in their own right.

A third step is also available: The "control" provided by the teacher may lead the students to exercise their "initiatives" in ways that involve cooperation and mutual interdependence. This, in turn, improves the likelihood that a feeling of community will arise within the class. The "world of meaningful action" is thereby enriched. It no longer consists merely of me the student plus the more or less remote foreign culture, plus a teacher who is my social and linguistic superior. The things we do in class, and the things that we talk about, begin to draw their reality more widely and more deeply from the here and now. Becker, speaking in the most general terms, observed that "man must seek the maximum of uplift in his relationships to another concrete organism." The language class, transient and limited though it may be, is no exception.

> **"Greta":** My worst experience in teaching EFL was the year in which I taught first-year junior high school boys for five hours a week. At that time, I believed firmly that (1) language must be modeled and controlled by the teacher in order to avoid errors, and that (2) extensive oral practice was necessary to "set the language" into the students' heads. As the year wore on, I realized that my students were participating less and less in the artfully paced mix of oral drill activities that I had prepared for them. When I would say, "Turn to Chart 5," there would be little whines of "Mata ka?" ("Again??") I became very indignant at this lack of response and interest, especially since I felt that I had rescued these little ingrates through my modern techniques. Against this general background of frustration, I can remember one day on which things went well. I had given the students an assignment to work in twos and threes and write sentences about a picture in their book. That day, I walked around the classroom responding to questions, happily amazed at the transformation of my noisy, nonresponsive students into involved little workers.

At the same time, if I am the student, my place within the corner of my universe that is the classroom becomes more secure. The other centers (i.e., my fellow students), whose universes also include this classroom, no longer appear primarily as competing for status or for the teacher's attention. They now become welcome, even supportive, parts of this universe at the center of which I still sit. Then when I am able to be helpful to my fellow students, I gain feelings of satisfaction and of status which can themselves become powerful sources of reward and motivation.

A subtle fourth step is possible for many teachers. That is to give off what in recent years have been called "good vibes." These are indications of confidence in oneself and in the student, of acceptance of the student, and of pleasure in the encounter. But they are not overt statements of confidence, or pleasure, or approval. Such explicit messages do have their place, of course, but they are not part of what I mean by "vibes." "Vibes" are expressed in ways of which the students are not consciously aware, or of which they are only dimly aware. They take the form of facial expressions, body postures, tones of voice, and inferences that the students may draw for themselves from what the teacher says and how she or he says it. These messages are all the more credible, and therefore more effective, because the student does not perceive them as being con-

Frameworks

sciously directed at her or him by the teacher. In fact, an overt statement of "confidence" by the teacher may lead the students to infer, unconsciously and often correctly, that the teacher sees some reason why they, the students, should *not* be confident. They may also see in such a statement the teacher's way of imposing her or his own expectations on them. As we saw in Chapter 1, this sort of expectation may arouse resistance, anxiety at not being able to measure up, or both. We will talk more about "good vibes" later, especially in Chapter 10, which discusses the work of Lozanov and Gateva.

The extraordinary power of "vibes" lies in the fact that they sneak into the student's brain around the edges of awareness and so are not subjected to logical scrutiny. (This is an important part of the meaning of what Lozanov will be calling "suggestion" in Chapter 10.) They can therefore play an early and profound part in setting the climate for language study—in building the student's idea of what this corner of his or her universe is like. This is particularly true for the way he or she will perceive that central, powerful, and awesome personage, the teacher. We have already seen that the overt part of the teacher's feedback is the light by which the students keep track of their cognitive, their linguistic, progress. In the same way, the "vibes" accompanying that feedback are the light that tells the student where the teacher thinks he or she, the student, stands as a person within the universe.

This fourth step is one which a few teachers take by instinct, and which a very few are incapable of taking under any circumstances. Most of us can profit from watching ourselves on videotape, and from other help in becoming aware of how we come across to our students. And of course, none of this kind of teacher training is likely to help much unless our own genuine attitudes, which lie behind the "vibes," are wholesome and constructive.

A fifth possible step is to leave—to appear to leave—the Teacher role from time to time, and act the part of an Ordinary Person, a cordial, interested Fellow Human Being. There are many styles of enacting the Teacher role: demanding or gentle, sarcastic or constructive, calm or vigorous, and so on. Yet all of them convey to the student that "I am the *Teacher*, who is providing the 'control' for this course, and in whose presence you as *Students* are to *perform* certain tasks—tasks of an *academic* nature that will lead you, by the end of the course, to know the language better, and to make fewer **mistakes**." The words I have emphasized in the preceding sentence all contribute toward an atmosphere in which the student "learns" the language, rather than "acquires" it as I used those terms above. The activities carried on while the teacher is in the Teacher mode may be as cut and dried as dialog memorization or substitution drills. But they may also consist of virtually anything else, emphatically including student-initiated free conversation. The essential feature is that the students feel they are performing under the teacher's—the Teacher's—watchful eye.

Yet I have seen a few teachers who are able to come out from behind this Teacher mask, most notably during "free conversation." They have generally been among the best language teachers I have known. They escape the Teacher mask through changes in voice, posture, and facial expression. Their non-verbal behavior is the same behavior they might use at home in the living room talking with guests: animated, engaged, apparently intensely interested in the other speaker(s) and in what is being said. When wearing the Ordinary Person mask, the teacher appears to be speaking quite spontaneously, at normal conversational speed, and saying whatever comes to her mind. In fact, of course, she is filtering what she says through her awareness of what the students are likely to understand. If she supplies a word, she does so in a tone of voice that says, "This may be the word you're looking for. I'm giving it to you so that you may go on with this interesting thing you're saying." If she repeats something the student has said, it is in a manner that indicates a desire to verify the content, or simply to hear the phrase again because it has caught her interest.

This kind of mask-changing can be done at any time, from the first few hours of the beginning course all the way to the most advanced levels. It may last for a few seconds or for a whole hour. It may consume 5 percent of the total time or almost all of it. With beginners, this kind of conversation must be teacher-initiated, but later on the teacher may drop back and become just one of several participants.

I don't think most teachers would be able to—or should—wear the Ordinary Person mask all of the time. It is a supplement for the Teacher mask, not a replacement for it, and it is, after all, a mask. The requirement of play-acting within limits imposed by the students' ability may place this fifth step beyond the reach of some teachers.

See Chapter 6, p. 86 for an example.

Seen in the theoretical framework of these first three chapters, the "mask change" links the world inside the classroom with the world outside it; it can also give the student an exhilarating sense of adequacy within that world. Conversations conducted in this way may contribute to "acquisition," as contrasted with mere "learning" through "conversation practice." At the same time, these conversations draw on and are supported by what has been recently learned.

A sixth contribution a teacher can make is to provide the student with a model for his or her Critical Self—what Gallwey calls the "Self 1." Gallwey tells us that the best soaking up of skills, and the best performance, take place when the Conscious, Critical Self and the Performing Self are in a wholesome relationship with one another. In this relationship, the Critical Self notices what the Performing Self does, and how what the Performing Self has done compares with the goal; yet it notices without praising or blaming the Performing Self, or labeling what it has done as "good" or "bad." The Conscious Self also sets goals for the Performing Self and exposes the Performing Self to good models of the skill it has chosen to acquire. At the same time, however, it does not impose obligations on the Performing Self, or interfere with the Performing Self while it is performing by telling it *how* to perform.

This is an example of moving material from "Holding Memory" toward "Permanent Memory" (Chapter 1).

If Gallwey is right that the best learning (in the everyday, general sense of that word) and the best performance take place under these conditions, then it seems desirable that by the end of the course the student's Conscious, Critical Self should have learned to help, and not hinder, her or his Performing Self. This would be an additional goal, beyond (or before?) the linguistic goals. This is an example of an abstraction that is at the same time high-level and of great practical usefulness. In Silent Way terminology (see Chapter 8) it is a very special kind of "awareness."

How can the teacher contribute toward the realization of this goal? Perhaps the best way is through lending himself as a temporary Conscious Self, while at the same time serving as a model for how the student's own Conscious Self may eventually come to act. Bringing the Performing Self into contact with appropriate models, setting goals, and noticing results are, after all, parts of the "control" function discussed earlier. The trick is for the teacher to perform these services in ways that will not confuse or inhibit the student's Performing Self or throw it off its stride. How can a teacher get away from the evaluative, interfering style that is ingrained in academic traditions around the world?

One part of the answer lies in the area of technique: alternative ways of using familiar materials. These extra techniques can be helpful up to a point. But if they are to have their full effect, and if their effect is to last, then they must come from a teacher who really is relaxed and detached even while she is most vigorously active, most fully involved with the students and what they are saying—a teacher who really does see mistakes (or error-free utterances) for what they are, and not as occasions for generalization that leads to worry(or to congratulation). Much of the difference between this kind of teaching and the kind of teaching I have most often seen lies again, as with the "mask change," in the nonverbal signals that the teacher gives out. Most of us are not by nature this kind of teacher. (I know I am not!) So this sixth step may cost us a change in our own personal style—a price that may be too high for some.

In the seventh and final step that I would like to suggest, the students are free to talk openly about their reactions to the course and to the language; about what works for them and what doesn't; about what delights them and what bores them; about how they feel about the language and the people who speak it; about what their fears are, and their frustrations. The teacher listens with interest, occasionally saying whatever is needed to verify for herself and for the student that she is getting the same picture that the student has in mind. In this kind of listening, however, the teacher does not reply to the student, or disagree with him, or agree with him, or try to set him straight, or tell him he needn't feel the way he does. As the student hears his meanings being understood by the teacher, without the teacher's becoming defensive or evaluative, he typically becomes better able to deal with whatever feelings he may have, and their ability to interfere with his study subsides. His mind is then left clearer to work on whatever issues may have been raised. At the same time, the teacher may gain valuable information about how things are going with the class. (This kind of listening is a distinctive feature of Counseling-Learning and is not found in any of the other "ways" that I know. It will come up for further discussion in Chapters 5–7.)

This understanding can take place in regularly-scheduled teacher-student conferences. But if the teacher is alert, it can also happen when a student makes a chance remark, whether inside the classroom or outside it. Wherever this kind of understanding is found, it can go far toward reducing some of the kind of "alienation" we talked about in Chapter 2. Suppose, for example, that I as a student am having trouble in memorizing dialogs. If I cannot talk freely about this with my teacher, I am left feeling that I am cut off from her, and that I myself am in this respect inadequate. Around these two wounds, all sorts of secondary infections may grow up: tenseness and even poorer performance; feeling that my classmates resent me for holding the class back; dislike for the language and its speakers; lowered self-esteem; psychosomatic reactions, and so on. Bringing the difficulty out into the open and finding that the teacher sees but does not judge, tells me that I am not so unacceptable as I had feared. Insofar as my poor performance was due to anxiety and tension, even my classwork may improve.

The sort of thing described in the preceding paragraph sounds great—like something everyone ought to do. There are, however, three risks in taking this seventh step. One is that when the students' comments are negative or even hostile, the teacher may be thrown off balance and engage in some kind of defensive behavior. If this happens, alienation is increased and not reduced. The second is that as a result of what the students have said, the teacher may see that he needs to make some changes in what he has been doing. If he lacks the technical skills for making appropriate changes, both he and the class may be left with a new source of anxiety, even of guilt. On the other hand, and this is the third risk, he may accede too readily and too often to suggestions from the class. This can erode the feeling of firm "control" that is so essential to student morale.

Taking this seventh step and most demanding step, then, requires of the teacher both professional resourcefulness and personal resilience. It is not for every teacher, possibly not for every class. Yet without it there will always remain—more or less broad, more or less pernicious—unnecessary areas of alienation among the people in the classroom.

HAZARDS

The approach I have sketched in these first three chapters is one that nowadays would be called "humanistic." This label arouses uneasiness in some teachers, just as it is somehow attractive to others. Those who find themselves drawn to this kind of teaching may be interested in a list of seven hazards inherent in it. I classify this list as one of the "Teachers' Voices" because I have compiled it out of my own life and hard times, and have the scars to document each item.

1. In announcing that one is going to be "responsive" and "learner-centered," or that one is going to share "control," or invite the students' comments and suggestions, one may raise expectations that can't be fulfilled. After some initial euphoria, one may thus produce gripes that can't be dealt with. It is like throwing a paper airplane that is shaped wrong, so that it immediately rises sharply and then suddenly plunges to the floor. This is likely to happen unless the teacher has that combination of personal resilience and professional resourcefulness that we were talking about.

2. In a well-meaning desire to be "democratic" or "nonauthoritarian," one may abdicate responsibility for content and/or for technique. I have already mentioned this danger repeatedly, so there is no need to discuss it further here. It is the little boy in the progressive school saying, "Please, Miss Jones, do we have to do just whatever we want again *today*?" It is throwing an unfolded piece of paper instead of an airplane.

3. Trying to copy the surface structure—the concrete techniques—of someone else's method is a common temptation, particularly when one has just seen a brilliant "demonstration" by a prestigious personage endowed with charisma. This is like folding one kind of paper airplane and then using scissors to trim the wings into the shape of another style of plane. I have done this sort of

thing often enough myself. Maybe it is a necessary first step in learning from observation of master teachers. Nevertheless, it means that the teacher does not fully understand what he or she is doing and why; it does not grow organically out of his or her self and the present situation. Therefore, if things do not go as expected, the teacher may become confused, disappointed, and upset. Then teacher insecurity quickly translates itself into insecurity and restlessness on the part of the students.

4. A fourth hazard is that the teacher's verbal and nonverbal messages may conflict with one another. The teacher may say she invites the initiative of the student, but clearly show that she does not like what she gets. She may tell the students that she invites their comments and suggestions, yet appear threatened by ones they make. Again, confusion and general insecurity are the results.

5. The fifth hazard I have encountered is that there will not be a proper balance between the students' opportunities to contribute to the course and their opportunities to examine and work with what they have contributed. The most traditional kind of course goes to one extreme: the students spend almost all of their time examining and working with what the textbook and the teacher have set before them and are allowed to contribute almost nothing. At the opposite extreme, one kind of "humanistic" course may so load the students down with self-generated texts that they can't move. This is a paper airplane with one wing much broader than the other.

6. The teacher may use the course as a new way to show off his virtuosity with techniques, or to demonstrate to students and colleagues what amazing results he is capable of achieving in a short time. As I said earlier and as we will see all too clearly in Chapter 5, this is my own personal foible. But it is pernicious, for in this way the teacher is using the class for his own ego-needs instead of seeing where the class is and working with it. The result is like taking a well-designed paper airplane and throwing it much too hard.

7. At the same time that the teacher does focus on where the class is and on working with it, she must also focus on her own needs. This is quite different from being the puppet of her own needs, as in the preceding paragraph. It is in fact one way of escaping that kind of slavery. As we saw in Chapter 2, she too longs to feel that she is "the object of primacy in a world of meaningful action." Her world is confirmed when others commit themselves even partially and temporarily to the same foreignness that she has invested her career in, or when she sees her own cognitive style at work in other human beings. Her feeling of adequacy is strengthened when her students attend class regularly, behave themselves, learn well, and show personal respect/liking for her. All of these are normal needs, and legitimately pursued. My point is that the teacher needs to be able to see them for what they are, and to watch them in operation. Only to the extent that she is in full possession of herself can she give herself, in a nonexploitative way, to her students.

The first five of these seven hazards point out ways in which "control," as I have been using that word in this chapter, can be undermined. The fourth also indicates one of the most effective ways to erode "initiative." The last two move into fundamental issues relating to the need for focusing on the teacher as well as on the students.

If in our zeal to be "humanistic" we become too "learner-centered" with regard to "control," we undermine the learner's most basic need, which is for security. We may find we have imposed our own half-baked anarchy on the class. Absence of structure or of focus on the teacher may be all right in certain kinds of psychological training, but not in our classrooms. In a task-oriented group like a language class, the student's place is at the center of a space that the teacher has structured, with room left for the student to grow into. In this kind of relationship, there are two essentials for the teacher: faith that the student will in fact grow into that space, and understanding of where the student is in that space at any given moment. When both these ingredients are present, there is the possibility of true "humanism" in teaching.

And one last hazard: being so impressed with the first seven hazards that one becomes afraid to try!

> He that governs well leads the blind;
> he that teaches well gives him eyes.

> *South, quoted in Allibone 1875*

---

1 *Working if possible with colleagues, take turns describing one of your own favorite techniques for learning or teaching languages.*

- In a colleague's description, what examples or evidences do you find of "control" as that term was used in this chapter?

- What evidences of student "initiative"?

- Suggest ways in which, within the same basic technique, the relationship between control and initiative might be adjusted.

---

2 *Repeat the above task for one or more of the characteristic or most frequently used techniques found in your comparison materials.*

---

3 *With the sound turned off, watch a videotape of:*

- A sample lesson taught by a teacher trainer.

- Five minutes of one of your colleagues at work.

- Five minutes of yourself at work.

What "vibes" do you pick up? Try to identify the actual physical signs that carried those "vibes".

Now do the same thing with the sound turned on.

4

METHODS AND MATERIALS

Why talk about language teaching methods at all? In recent years, a number of writers have criticized the very concept of "method" in our field. "Let's just focus on learners and teachers and every-thing else will fall into place," they seem to suggest. Some say that teachers see methods as prescriptions for classroom behavior and follow them too closely, too inflexibly. By contrast, others argue that in planning their lessons, teachers don't really think about cod-ified methods at all. In the one view, methods and the prefabricated materials that embody them reduce teachers to mere technicians; in the other, teachers are mere improvisers in the here-and-now, with no use for general statements about how teaching acts may fit together. Either view should make any writer about methods and materials stop and think.

a. An excellent teacher can enhance the results from a mediocre set of materials.

b. An excellent set of materials can enhance the results from a mediocre teacher.

Both the above are true, but which needs the most emphasis these days?

Having stopped and thought, I find myself giving a single reply to both of the above objections: Language teachers are simply not "mere." They are neither mere technicians nor mere improvisers. They are professionals who make their own decisions, informed by their own experiences but informed also by the findings of researchers and by the accumulated, distilled, crystallized experience of their peers.

Let me then suggest three questions that we might well ask about "method," together with my proposed answers:

1. *What is a "method"?* A method is more concrete than an approach. An approach is a set of understandings about what is at stake in learning and also about the equipment, mechanical or neurological, that is at work in learning. At the same time, a method is more abstract than a teaching act, which is a one-time event that can be recorded on videotape and on the neurocortexes of learners.

2. *Is it possible to evaluate or to profit from an approach without embodying it in some kind of method?* Possible, perhaps, to some limited degree, but not easy.

3. *Is it possible to improvise teaching acts apart from some more or less con-scious approach?* Possible, perhaps, but rare.

"Method," then, seems to occupy a strategic mid-position between approach and act. For this reason, whoever would either think usefully about teaching or would teach thoughtfully can profit from learning about methods. This leads to three questions about approaches:

4. *Are all approaches equally useful, defensible, or comprehensive?* No.

5. *Should we continue to seek approaches that are more useful, more defensible, and more comprehensive than the ones we now know?* Yes.

6. *Should we expect to find, or should we think we have at last found, the one approach whose supreme usefulness, defensibility and comprehensiveness make all its present and future competitors obsolete?* No.

Returning now to methods and materials:

7. *Is there in turn some one method or some set of materials which best or exclusively embodies a given approach for all learners and under all circumstances?* No.

8. *Can one adopt a method without being controlled by it?* Yes.

9. *Can one profit from a method without necessarily adopting it?* Yes.

10. *How?* I hope that reading this book and working through the tasks I have proposed in it will leave readers better prepared to answer this question for themselves.

---

1 *For thought, comparison, and discussion: Think of—or better, look at—a textbook that you are familiar with at first hand. What assumptions does it seem to make about the nature of language learning? What specific things can you point out in the book that support your answer?*

---

2 *For thought, comparison, and discussion: In your experiences as a teacher or learner of languages, have you ever felt "mere" in the eyes of someone else? In your own eyes? In what respects?*

Most of the remainder of this chapter consists of a paper I read to a group of language teachers many years ago. It is therefore quite dated. I wish I could also think it is out of date. Since the days when I wrote it, numerous materials have come to market which beautifully exemplify its recommendations. Many others however, including some that make use of the latest technologies, still raise the concerns that led me to write this paper. Perhaps that is why when I asked former users of *A Way and Ways* which chapters to omit for this book, several of them emphatically replied, "Not the one on Materials for the Whole Learner!" I have therefore decided to retain it in close to its original form.

MATERIALS FOR THE WHOLE LEARNER

Four basic facts

In some years of asking what the "whole learner" is like, I have come across at least four basic facts. Since I have not yet been able to integrate them fully in my own mind, I shall have to be content here with listing and juxtaposing them.

First for me chronologically has been the fact that learning is something that the learner does, and that he does it best when the teacher doesn't stand over him, breathe down his neck, jiggle his elbow, and chatter into his ear. The second fact is that the so-called physical, emotional, and cognitive aspects of the learner cannot in practice be isolated from one another: what is going on in one of these areas inexorably affects what is possible in the other areas. In the same way, and this is the third point, the people in the classroom are not separable from one another: they inevitably make up a more or less successful community. Fourth, the needs of the whole learner go beyond the need for achievement and approval, which are central in the minds of most writers of textbooks. They also include needs for security, predictability, group membership, and the feeling that what one is doing makes sense in terms of some overall and deeply satisfying life pattern. Human beings fulfill these needs principally by the ways in which they interact with one another. People are conscious of some of the ways in which they affect other people and in which other people affect them, but many of the most powerful ways in which we affect each other lie outside the focus of our conscious awareness.

---

3 *For thought, comparison, and discussion:*

- Are there any of these four "basic facts" that you would not consider to be facts, or to be not really so "basic"?

- Are there other facts that your experience would suggest should be added to this list?

- Which of this list of "facts" is most conspicuous in your comparison materials, or in the best method or approach you have used?

- Do you know of any method or approach that ignores or virtually ignores any or all of these "basic facts"? How, if at all, would you estimate that it loses—or gains—by ignoring them?

"Investment," "yield," and power

But what has this has to do with the design of relatively permanent, publishable materials for foreign language courses? Let's take a look at the traditional—and almost universal—relationships among textbook writer, teacher, and student. In describing these relationships, I would like to use a pair of terms that may need some explaining. The first of these terms is "investment." "Investment," as I shall be using the word, means making a choice that leaves one committed irrevocably; it therefore includes the taking of a certain amount of risk (Chapter 3). Clearly there are all kinds and all degrees of risk. Accordingly, the quality and quantity of "investment" may vary from negligible to complete. Clearly also, "investment" with its associated risks can involve any and many of the levels at which we experience need (Chapters 1, 2), and at which we are therefore vulnerable to loss and anxiety.

The second term is "yield." This refers to one person's response to another person's "investment." The quality of the "yield" that one gets in return for a particular act of "investment" has a powerful effect on one's readiness to "invest" further. "Investment" and "yield" thus are two parts of a single pattern of rhythmic alternation whenever and wherever two people interact. Teacher and language students, or the writer and the users of a textbook are no exceptions.

In the traditional relationship, dominated by textbook and teacher, the writer "invests" by making choices of what and how to write, with the risk that the teacher may not adopt the book, or that students may not learn from it, or both. The teacher in this relationship invests by making choices of what she tells the student to try to do; the teacher's risk is that the student will not perform in a way that will bring to the teacher a sense of achievement, or of prestige among her colleagues. The student invests by choosing among alternative ways of trying to do what the teacher has told him to try to do. The usual risk for the student is a low grade, possibly accompanied by the displeasure of the teacher and the disdain of his classmates. In this model, the teacher holds power over the students, and to a large extent over the textbook writer a well. As long as teachers can influence the selection of the book materials they work with, they will continue to have this power over the writer. They will force the writer to collaborate with them to maintain their chosen power relationship with the student. What the writer can do for the teacher depends on what the teacher intends to do with the students.

But the student is not entirely without power over the teacher in this relationship. If the teacher feels a personal need to have successful students, then each student can reward or punish the teacher by doing well or poorly. In schools where enrollment is voluntary, the student favors one course by signing up for it and dooms another by avoiding it.

Blocking the whole learner

The title of this section of the chapter is "Materials for the Whole Learner," (p. 49) yet in the traditional model of foreign language instruction, we never see the whole learner at work. Or to say the same thing in another way, the whole learner is present in every one of his or her acts, but in the traditional model, parts of the learner's mind and personality are not working in harmony with one another. Some parts may be relatively inert, and some may even be working at cross purposes with each other. (Among the three "ways" discussed in Chapters 5–10, it is suggestopedia that is most explicit and most emphatic about the almost qualitative difference between outcomes when just some parts are working in harmony, and when all are. This appears to a smaller extent in Counseling-Learning's concern for the two "selves." It is certainly implied in the Silent Way's pursuit of ever deeper and broader "awareness of awareness.")

The assertion on my part that parts of the learner's mind and personality may not be working in harmony with one another requires illustration. Let me begin with an example taken from something I published almost 40 years ago. As a part of one lesson, I gave the populations of the five medium-sized cities in the United States:

Nashville	173,000
Denver	412,000
Memphis	394,000
St. Louis	852,000
Cleveland	905,000

Pattern practice

with the purpose that the student should substitute this information in the original sentence "Columbus has a population of over 374,000." Obviously I must have wanted students to practice the pattern "X has a population of Y." The learning theory on which that drill was based has of course been seriously questioned since then, but that is beside the point I want to make here. The question I am concerned with is: What are the various parts of the learner likely to be doing during a drill of this kind?

Assuming that the content of the drill is not information that the student has already mastered, her intellect will be fairly busy. She must remember to say "has a population of Y" and not "has the population Y". She must remember how to pronounce the names of some unfamiliar cities, and she must get her tongue around some relatively long numbers. If she does well, she receives the usual approval—from the teacher, from herself, and possibly from a few classmates—that accompanies a right answer in a classroom. If in addition she happens to believe in the efficacy of the method, she also gets the feeling that she has taken one more step toward whatever long-term goal brought her into the course in the first place.

Looking first at this drill in a framework borrowed from Transactional Analysis, the teacher and the textbook together are in the classic stance of Teacher-as-Parent, saying to the student, "Now you try to do this, so that I may tell you how you did." The student, in turn, plays the Adapted Child, trying to do what the Parent demands of him so that the parent can get what she wants from him. Other than that, there is nothing in the drill for the Child part of the student's personality: no physical activity, no fun, no aesthetic pleasure. Nor is there very much for the Adult part of the student's personality, which is the part that is concerned with forming and maintaining an accurate picture of the world as it is. The population figures given in this drill were correct according to the most recent census at the time, but I doubt that these particular facts fitted into any very urgent gaps in many students' personal maps of reality.

Shifting away from the Transactional terminology, we may say that in this drill the student's soma remains almost completely inactive, while at the same time there is nothing much for his or her self to make an investment in. The only choice is which answer to give, and the only risk is that the answer may be wrong.

To look at the same drill from still another point of view, the student's need for security is met to the extent that the format of the materials and the actions of the teacher lead him to feel that he is in firm and competent hands. There is, on the other hand, nothing in this sort of activity to foster the growth of group feeling among students, and thus to contribute toward meeting each individual's need to belong. The need for esteem is met only with regard to the correctness of the answers: the student has no opportunity to explore and enjoy his own powers of originating and of judging for himself. Finally, the need to feel that this drill fits into a total and satisfying life pattern is met only to the extent that this is one more small step toward a linguistic competence that for some reason the student wants.

All in all then, this drill is hardly an activity in which the whole learner is involved in any coordinated, internally harmonious way. In the terms that I used in my 1971 book on materials, it is "light" (non-tiring) enough. It is also "transparent" enough, in that students can readily see what is happening in it. But it is almost completely lacking in "strength"—in rewards offered for effort expended. I have taken this example from my own work in order to avoid the unnecessary embarrassment of pillorying somebody else. But I would not have used page space in this way if I did not believe that essentially the same personal dynamics are present in more recent and more highly regarded materials by other authors. Where those materials go beyond what I've outlined, they don't always go very far beyond it. Sometimes they do provide humor, or attractive pictures, or subject matter especially chosen to fit the student's professional interests, or a carefully limited amount of freedom for the student to devise her own responses. But the overall message to the student often remains the same: "Try to perform this linguistic task so that we may tell you how well or how poorly you performed it." This message is at the heart of the generally "confrontational" or "judgmental" Evaluation Paradigm I mentioned earlier—a pattern that too many teachers and too many students seem to take for inevitable.

---

4 *We have just critiqued the little drill on page 52.*

- Choose an activity out of your comparison materials, or from some other book you use, or one that you have put together yourself.

- Critique it in the same terms as the above drill.

- Exchange activities, but not critiques, with a colleague and apply the same criteria to the second activity.

- Compare your critiques of the two activities with those of your colleague.

Activating the whole learner

The materials I have been describing, then, are definitely not what I would call "materials for the whole learner." Let's turn now to the positive side, and see what such materials might be like. First, a list of five desiderata:

1. There should be something for the emotions as well as for the intellect. That something may be beauty or humor, but it may also be controversy or apprehension. Or beauty and controversy may occur together.

2. The materials should provide occasions for the students to interact with one another as people, or with the teacher as a person.

3. The materials should allow students to draw on present realities as well as on their distant future goals.

4. The materials should provide for the students to make self-committing choices in the areas covered by 1 to 3 above.

To summarize 1 to 4, "whole-learner" materials allow and encourage students to make a much fuller self-investment than other materials do. But will students actually welcome these opportunities for self investment? Some will, but others won't. The student's ability to participate in and enjoy this kind of risking commitment will depend on how safe he feels on each of the levels I mentioned earlier. If he expects that linguistic errors will bring unpleasant consequences, he will be cautious with the form of his sentences: instead of experimenting with them, and instead of using them for the purpose of saying something, he will pick his way through them as if they were a minefield. If he feels uncertain about his place in the group, he will be careful to reveal nothing about his activities and his preferences that might lead to rejection by teacher or classmates. If he finds insufficient structure or clarity in the materials, he may either rebel or withdraw. In any or all of these ways, he avoids the kind of investment that I have been talking about.

There is therefore at least one additional desideratum:

5. Design of the materials should contribute to the student's sense of security.

We have already seen that the quality of the "yield" that a student gets back after making an "investment" is one important source of security. The materials themselves are the other source. *The extent of security limits the depth and intensity of investment, and the depth and intensity of investment are the principal determinants of the quality and the quantity of learning.* Here again is the central role of affect in the constant shaping and reshaping, organizing and reorganizing of memories.

Up to this point, I have been talking in abstractions. It is time to look at some concrete ways in which my five desiderata may be—and occasionally have been—realized in nonephemeral, publishable materials.

The security need represented in the last of my five desiderata is fundamental. It is also complex. The student needs to feel that whatever she is learning from is strong, and that it is strong in a number of different ways. She needs to be able to say at least three things about the textbook.

1. "This book contains something I want to know." Insofar as what the student wants to "know" is "a foreign-language," published materials need to give some evidence that what is in them is authentic. This is why publishers mention the native competence of the authors, the academic and literary attainments of those who have contributed, and the careful checking of the manuscript by numerous experts.

2. "This book can give me access to something I want." This is why we write phrase books for tourists, and particular language courses for engineers or for students of literature or for air traffic controllers. The specially selected vocabularies are undeniably of some practical advantage to the various users.

But I suspect that a large part of the value in studying from a textbook aimed at one's own special field of interest lies in the reassurance it gives to the learner—what in Chapter 10 Lozanov will call its "placebo effect."

3. "This book gives me clear directions what to do." This is surely a large part of the reason why materials ought to be fairly "transparent."

There are additional ways of helping the student to feel secure in working with a set of materials: claiming that the materials are in harmony with the latest linguistic and/or pedagogical thinking; associating the name of the author with fascinating, widely publicized experiments in which pigeons have been taught to seem to play Ping-Pong or with some other spectacular achievement; use of carefully selected typography and paper, and so on. None of these is new; publishers have used them for centuries, and I list them only for the sake of completeness. The trouble is that in all of the centuries publishers have been using them, they have seldom gone beyond them.

One way in which most textbooks could contribute more to the student's sense of security would be to change the Suggestions to the Teacher, printed before Lesson 1. Any set of materials can be used in a variety of ways. Some ways of using materials are more "confrontational" or "judgmental" than others (the Evaluation Paradigm once more), and the uses that authors recommend are commonly near the more confrontational end of the spectrum.

The Suggestions to the Teacher can also contribute more than they usually do to meeting the student's need for belonging, which is one ubiquitous source for the student's affect as I used that term in Chapter 1. They can do so by placing suitable emphasis on work in small groups. Sometimes authors do not mention small groups at all. When they do include them, they often treat the group merely as an expedient for giving each student more air time at the cost of having his or her mistakes less dependably corrected. They almost always ignore at least five important features of groups:

(1) A group of even three or four people is likely to be more reliable than any one of its members when it comes to recognizing which of a set of alternatives is the correct one.

(2) A correction from a peer is more telling because it comes from someone who has had the same amount of exposure to the language, and not from someone with professional qualifications.

(3) At the same time, a correction from a peer is generally less threatening, both because the one doing the correcting is not the person who gives out the grades, and because the correction is less likely to come in a reproachful or other judgmental tone of voice.

(4) Competition between groups is less threatening to individuals than competition between individuals is. At the same time, it can be just as exhilarating.

(5) Working, risking, and suffering together for even a short time can produce noticeable feelings of mutual loyalty.

These, then, are two ways in which an author can improve the whole-person effectiveness of his or her textbook before the reader even gets to Lesson 1.

In writing the lessons themselves, the author will be less preoccupied than we usually have been with the sequencing and presentation of discrete units such as grammatical structures and lexical terms. There is a place for these concerns, of course. But the first and central aim of the writer of whole-learner materials will be to say something—or better, to help the student say something—that is worthwhile and interesting. Within that framework, but only within that framework, the writer will take care to see that the linguistic elements do not get out of hand.

THREE PARADIGMS

There are at least three well-known paradigms—well-known but underused—that lend themselves very readily to "whole-learner" materials.

The Lady or the Tiger.

The first of these paradigms we may call "The Lady or the Tiger," after Frank Stockton's story with that title. As I remember it from junior high English, a princess loved a young man who for some reason was sentenced to go into an arena and open one or the other of two identical doors. Behind one door was a ravenous tiger, while behind the other door waited a beautiful woman who would become his wife. The princess finds out which was which, and so gives a hand signal to the young man as he stands in the arena. But is her signal motivated by love—or by jealousy? The man follows her signal, and there the story ends.

Let's take a look at this story in terms of our desiderata:

The story contains plenty of color and emotion to interest the Child part of the student's personality.

The story ends abruptly at a point where two dramatically different endings are equally plausible. The question contained in the title thus leads naturally to discussion and debate among students.

The story is interesting in itself: it does not depend for its interest on the fact that questions about it will appear on the final exam.

Expressing and defending one's own answer is a self-committing choice.

The story contains plenty of linguistic ammunition for use by both sides.

It is of course true that this particular story requires the student to have an advanced level of reading comprehension, and anyway, not many such stories exist. Let me comment on these two points in reverse order. First, although few stories end with the outcome so uncertain as this one, there are many stories that lend themselves to discussion in terms of "What if. . .?" and "What should. . .?" ("What if Tom had not stayed home with a cold that day?") ("What should Helen have done when she noticed that the porch light had been turned off?") Much fiction, and some nonfiction as well, is suitable for this kind of use, but not all of it is. "Whole-learner" materials will contain more of this sort of text than do materials that ignore this point of view. Once again, the criteria are that the text should carry intrinsic interest for the emotional as well as for the intellectual side of the students, that it should lead to self-committing interaction among the people in the classroom, and that it should supply plenty of raw material for that interaction. From the point of view of Chapter 1, this sort of thing activates nonverbal mental imagery from each learner's unique long-term memory resources, and these images then come to be associated with the words and structures used in talking about them.

The same model may be applied not only at the advanced level, but also in very elementary lessons. Take for example the set piece in which a city or a town is described. This kind of pabulum is commonly concocted in a style that is linguistically antiseptic and emotionally sterile. I used to write things like this for my students:

> Mr. Smith lives in Pleasanttown. Pleasanttown is located in the northeastern part of the state. It is not very large, but it is not very small, either. A river flows through the center of Pleasanttown. On the banks of the river there are a park and the campus of Pleasanttown College. Mr. Smith teaches English at Pleasanttown College. The college is near the center of Pleasanttown, but Mr. Smith lives on the southern edge of the city. He usually goes to work by bicycle. He has to ride through the business district and across a bridge.

This description is followed by a series of "comprehension questions":

> Where does Mr. Smith live?
> Where is Pleasanttown?
> Is Pleasanttown large, or small?

and so forth. These are followed by questions like:

> What does Mr. Smith do every aday?
> Describe Pleasanttown.

and the like. Finally we reach the culmination of the lesson, optimistically referred to as "real communication practice":

> Where do you live?
> Is your town large, or small?
> How do you come to class?
> What do you pass by on your way?
> Do you cross a bridge on your way?

All of us, I'm sure, recognize the author's goals in writing this lesson: Stick to the simple present tense, introduce vocabulary for points of the compass and for assorted landmarks, and provide further practice with "there are" and "has to," which were introduced in earlier lessons. All of this will be useful in the "communication phase" that ends the lesson.

I need not point out to anyone reading this book the generally musty odor of this reading passage, which could hardly have originated anywhere but in a language textbook. The content itself is cloistered, probably originating in a security fantasy of the author's. Now, I believe that this passage is not much worse than much of what we find in many published materials that we sometimes see even today. Yet it fails all five of the criteria that I have set on pages 53 and 54: There is a minimum of color or emotion; the material has no intrinsic interest; it does not lead to discussion, debate, or self-investment; it does not even contain the raw materials for any of these. At best, it can lead to what Eric Berne calls a "pastime," and a rather perfunctory pastime at that: "I come by subway; you come by bus; she usually walks but sometimes she takes a taxi; they come by car." Pleasanttown soon becomes Dullsville!

Whole-learner materials on this same topic would be different in at least four ways:

1. They would be written in a style that had some currency outside of language textbooks.

2. They would convey some emotion, whether enthusiasm or despair or amazement or anger or whatever.

3. They would be less bland in their content. Some neighborhoods in Pleasanttown might turn out to be run-down, and certain parts of town might actually be dangerous.

4. They would provide alternatives. There might be two or more descriptions of the same place from different points of view, or there might be descriptions of different towns. Either would enrich the student's vocabulary, but more important, materials of this kind provide what Keith Sauer once called a "basis for disagreement," and therefore for nonperfunctory interaction.

Twenty Questions.

A second paradigm is one we may call "Twenty Questions." The reference is to the game of the same name, which is an old standby for language teachers. For our purposes here, however, I would like to let it represent a much wider range of activities, in which factual information is unevenly distributed, and in which there is at least one objectively correct solution waiting to be arrived at. One team of students trying to duplicate another team's configuration of cuisenaire rods through the use of language would be an example. Asking one another about weekend activities is another example, and the accumulated techniques of language teachers down through the centuries could supply many more.

From the "whole-learner" point of view, some of these "Twenty Questions" activities are much better than others. All of them, of course, provide occasions for students to interact with one another. But they differ widely in their aesthetic and emotional impact, in the immediacy of the interest that they arouse, and in the scope that they provide for student investment beyond a relatively shallow intellectual level. Obviously they differ also in the amount of linguistic raw material they provide.

In illustrating some of the possibilities in the paradigm of "The Lady or the Tiger," we looked at alternative treatments of our city topic. To explore some of the potential in the "Twenty Questions" paradigm, let's turn to an equally ubiquitous theme: "My House/Apartment."

One kind of lesson on this theme is sometimes drawn from real estate or apartment rental advertisements. The task given to the students might be to read a series of five or ten advertisements with the prices deleted and try to rank-order the advertised properties according to cost. This can be done by teams of three or four students, with the winning team determined by reference to answers printed in the back of the book. With students for whom accurate knowledge of the housing market is a valued survival skill, this exercise meets the five desiderata for the "whole-learner" materials. So far, so good.

But remember that we are talking about publishable, nonephemeral materials. A column of ads taken from the New York Times may be highly suitable for students living in the New York City area, but they will have less appeal in Miami or Cairo. Even in New York, ads that are a year or two old are of less interest than ads that came out this week. The very process of publication places a limit on freshness.

This brings me to an observation about authors of textbooks, and about what they expect of themselves. They seem to think it's up to them to provide everything that the users are going to need. This is a big part of the freshness dilemma I have just mentioned. What they might better do, it seems to me, is to provide a full-sized sample of lessons based on apartment ads or supermarket ads or weather forecasts or sports stories or what-not, but not to think that they have to go on and fill up a whole book in the same format. Instead, they might supply a few examples, with sufficient vocabulary and technique to meet the security needs of the users, and then invite the users (teachers together with students) to make up similar lessons, as many or as few as they need, from local and current sources.

Incidentally, and outside of the "Twenty Questions" paradigm, a column of apartment ads can provide quite a range of activities, which involve many different parts of the student's personality.

In appealing to the students' curiosity, for example, or to their desire for achievement, we might ask them to make a list of all the words that occur only once in the column, or all of the words that occur five or more times. The former would be a basis for vocabulary expansion, while the latter would provide information about the core vocabulary for this particular subject matter. Or we might invite the student to rewrite the ads in complete sentences, with all of the necessary function words, and with all of the abbreviated words written out in full. In this way, students could verify their comprehension and at the same time get practice in guided composition. This activity is suitable for small-group work, with the teacher or a paraprofessional native speaker serving as referee only when needed. A further activity, also suitable for small groups, might be to compare the prices given in the sample with local prices for similar accommodations. Students could draw upon both the local newspapers and their own experiences. This would work equally well whether the students are in the same currency area as the sample advertisements or in a different area. Finally, students might look at the ads with the eye of a detective or of an anthropologist, to see what inferences they can draw about life among the people by whom and for whom the ads were written.

Moving now from the practical to the realm of daydreams, which of these apartments would you want for yourself, or for yourself and your family, and why? Or suppose that you were advertising your own house or apartment for rent. What might the ad say?

Some students might want to move from the verbal to the graphic, drawing pictures or floor plans to correspond to the printed ads. Other students might then interpret these productions back into words.

The Tower of Babel.

Now let's take a quick look at a third paradigm, which is probably the most powerful one of all. Remembering the story about an occasion when people were still using a single language to coordinate their efforts and almost solved their real estate problems permanently, we can call it the "Tower of Babel" paradigm. In a "Tower of Babel" activity, the goal is not to express and defend a point of view, or to solve some problem for which a right answer exists. Instead, the participants are using language in order to do something that they want to do for reasons that are independent of (unrelated to) their study of language. Some examples that I have actually run across in other people's programs around the world, are:

- Teaching the teacher and fellow students how to make linoleum block prints.

- Teaching others how to lay bricks.

- Planning a religious service for the end of the language training period.

- Sharing memories of early experiences related to rain, bread, etc.

- Learning to convert mentally between the English and metric systems of measurement.

Published material can contribute to many of these activities of teaching, learning, planning, sharing, and doing together. Instructions for knitting, or paper folding, or writing Chancery Cursive script, can be cast into language that is suitable for the ESL classroom so that a person who already has one of these skills can teach it without unnecessary linguistic impediments.

In summary, then, materials for the whole learner will aim first of all at helping the learner to make self-committing choices in the new language. These choices will involve as much of the learner's personality as possible, and not just the verbal part of his or her intellect. To this end, whole-learner materials contribute to the security of learner and teacher, both by providing adequate linguistic models and by suggesting techniques that make for wholesome interaction among the people in the classroom.

---

5 *For thought, comparison, and discussion: From your experience as a learner or as a teacher and from your comparison materials, provide examples of the three paradigms. Then pool your contributions with those of one or more colleagues and consider the following questions:*

- Do any of these examples show characteristics of more than one of the three paradigms?

- Which example of each paradigm is smallest in scale?

- Can you devise a workable example of each paradigm that could be executed in less than two minutes? Less than one minute?

PUBLISHED EXAMPLES OF THE ABOVE PRINCIPLES

Shortly after I wrote the above paper, I began to find more and more books breaking the bonds of what was safe and emotionally sterilized.

The first such book I came across was *No Hot Water Tonight*, by Jean Bodman and Michael Lanzano. My own first real teaching experience was in Manhattan, and I remember the difference between life as we described it in our lessons and life as we and our students lived it in the slums and the subway. In *No Hot Water Tonight* we find a central character who is an elderly, sometimes lonely widow; a mother who as a single parent faces uncertainty about whether her teenage son is on drugs; and young single adults who do or do not pick up dates (or get picked up) in a bar. The book's pedagogical format was not unusual, though some of its vocabulary had an authenticity that ours had lacked thirty years earlier. The important contribution of the book is the way in which by its own example it invites students to talk in class about the realities of their own lives. Many other books, not explicitly but again by their example, have warned students that the painful and the seamy sides of their lives have no welcome place in the language classroom.

Another book that grew out of Manhattan Island was *Getting Into It: An Unfinished Book,* by Dave Blot and Phyllis Berman Sher (Language Innovations, Inc., 1978). It contained 13 brief "stories," written mostly in the first person. Each story tells how one student or teacher sees the study of English, and some of the things that have happened to that student or teacher in using the new language. Following the story are a few discussion topics and writing assignments designed to get the students talking with one another as well as with the teacher.

---

6 *For thought, comparison, and discussion:*

- Make a list of topics that are clichés in language textbooks:
  - ordering a meal in a restaurant
  - planning weekend recreation
  - and so forth
- Next, make a second list, this time of topics traditionally avoided in language textbooks:
  - drug use
  - insolent fellow passengers on public transportation
  - and so forth
- Exchange or compare lists.
  - Discuss which of these topics should be covered with the specific classes, or the categories of students, with which you work.
  - How would you describe your comparison materials with respect to their choice of topics?

A little later, Francis Riccardone brought to my attention L. G. Alexander's *For and Against,* which he had used with great success overseas. Each lesson is on one topic about which people are likely to disagree. It provides a full statement of one point of view on the question and then outlines, in fragments of sentences, two sides of a possible argument. The grammatical incompleteness of these two outlines forces the student to contribute at least some connecting words, and from there it is only one step to developing the ideas further, changing them and adding new ones.

A larger-scale example was *Challenges,* written by Brian Abbs and others in 1977. These materials called themselves a "multimedia project for students of English." They consisted of:

A 100-page paperback book, with many black and white pictures.

A series of 35-mm slides.

A number of short films.

Tapes containing:
    Short programs.
    Exercises or drills.
    Stories or other comprehension material.

(I myself have seen only the book.)

The "project" is divided into six parts. Each part has its own theme. The themes are:

Somewhere to Live
Someone to Love
Somewhere to Work
Somewhere to Go
Something to Say
Something to Do

Each of the six parts is divided into half a dozen "chains." A "chain" is made up of three to seven "steps." Each chain generally begins with a step that presents interesting, culturally authentic information. It ends with one or more "tasks," in which the students do something that is like what they might need to do one day in an English-speaking country.

Some features of Challenges.

Each of the six themes is a need that everyone has, and that underlies everything that we do. These themes are therefore able to catch and hold the student's interest. At the same time they are broad enough so that a wide variety of material can be included under each theme.

The students often have to use more than one medium at a time. For example, they may find a series of questions in the book. The information they will need in order to answer the questions is not on the tapes, and the book does not contain a copy of the conversation.

Some of the steps take a single goal of communication and pull together a number of ways—grammatically quite different from one another—by which people commonly reach that goal. Thus for the goal of "Making a tactful suggestion," the book offers:

> Let's. . .
> What would you think of. . . ?
> What about. . . ?
> Perhaps the best thing would be to. . .
> Why don't you/we. . . ?
> Can't we. . . ?
> etc. . .

Free discussion is frequently helped by charts that give it a "notional" or a grammatical outline, but that still allow the students to say things that they really want to say.

The book, tapes, and visual materials contain some English that is more complex or idiomatic than the students are ready to produce: "Here we lived and fed in a family fug. . ." Or it may be in a style for which the student is not likely to find much use: "What's the magic ingredient for the party of the year? An army of waiters? An expert chef? No, it's you alone with the Kitchen-made Electric Blender." There are examples of newspaper headlines, obituaries, and application forms. Here the writers are taking advantage of the fact that people can understand far more than they would be able to say by themselves. Students are allowed and expected to get the meanings from context, from asking other students or the teacher, from guessing, or from using the dictionary. They are even allowed to miss some of the details. But what they are expected to say and write is carefully planned so that they can work successfully within their limits.

This gap between what people are supposed to understand and what they are supposed to produce has several good effects.

- It allows the writers to include authentic and lively materials; genuine, unrehearsed conversations; brochures; literature; advice columns.

- The liveliness and authenticity of the materials help to remove some of the students' feeling of having severe limitations on their language and on their ability to learn.

- The liveliness and authenticity also awaken parts of the students' personalities that are ordinarily asleep in a language class. Language practice therefore comes closer to language use.

- Students may actually pick up some of what they have found there—things too complicated for explanation or formal presentation.

At the end of each "chain" the students find one or more realistic "tasks" to be performed: deciding which of a set of housing advertisements they would follow up first, which never, and so forth. These tasks pull together the activities of the earlier steps in the chain, and they also show the student why the earlier activities were worthwhile.

In some of the steps, students work individually; in others they work in pairs; in still others they work in small groups. The materials therefore do *not* depend on the personal energy that is set free in only *one* of these patterns.

Because these materials draw energy from so many sources within the student, my guess is that more energy will be available for use in learning. It seems to me also that the cross-cultural content of this course gives life to its grammatical and notional machinery, while at the same time the machinery helps the student to work his or her way through the cross-cultural content without getting lost.

Incidentally, I have talked with one person who reports having used ideas out of *Challenges* successfully in developing materials in a non-Western language for English-speaking students. The book by itself, even without the accompanying tapes and visual aids, is a concentrated package of stimulating ideas.

The books that I have described up to this point are books to be placed in the hands of students. But we're finding also an increasing number of what we may call "idea books" for teachers. Though these books may contain a certain amount of general discussion about teaching, their most important feature is a list of techniques from which teachers may choose and adapt to suit their own needs.

One such book is *Drama Techniques in Language Learning* by Alan Maley and Alan Duff (Cambridge: 1978; second edition 1982). In spite of its title, this is not a book about putting on foreign language plays. As the authors explain in their opening paragraph:

> Let us be clear from the start what we mean by "dramatic activities." They are activities that give the student an opportunity to use his own personality in creating the material on which part of the language class is to be based. These activities draw on the natural ability of every person to imitate, to mimic and to express himself through gesture. They draw, too, on his imagination and memory, and on his natural capacity to bring to life parts of his past experience that might never otherwise emerge. They are dramatic because they arouse our interest, which they do by drawing on the unpredictable power generated when one person is brought together with others. Each student brings a different life, a different background into the class. We would like him to be able to use this when working with his fellow students.

The authors also assure us that their "drama techniques" are not a substitute for the psychoanalyst's couch.

Maley and Duff divide their manual into two parts. In the first, which covers fewer than 30 pages, the authors set out their thinking about what they have done, and why they have done it as they have. At the same time, they give us a highly readable overview of what language teachers will find useful in much of the research of that day: research on language-in-society and on language-beyond-the-sentence. This section of the book could in fact easily stand by itself as a short, nontechnical introduction to that research.

The second part of the book lists and describes five dozen techniques, most of them with variations. The first 10 are built around the student's powers of *observation;* the next 24 enlist the student's powers of *interpretation;* in the remaining techniques, students *interact* with one another and talk about their interactions. Within each of these three groupings, the authors present first those activities that make the smallest demands on the student, and move gradually to activities that require more and more from the student, either of language or of imagination or both. Under each technique, they first tell us "What to Do"; they then offer a few "Remarks" in which they share with us their own experiences, or give us hints about the purpose and the principles behind the technique. The language is straightforward, mercifully clear, and appropriately colleague-to-colleague in its tone. This latter part of the book, like the first, could stand by itself.

All of the techniques follow a single dependable formula:

1. The teacher sets the activity up. In setting up any activity, the teacher must be sure to do two things:

   (a) Establish some area of tension or uncertainty—something for the students to work out in their own way.

   (b) Make clear what the students are to use in resolving the tension or the uncertainty, and the rules they are to follow. The "tension or uncertainty" is not limited to the cognitive plane, and does not depend on uneven distribution of information among the students. Most of the activities include a strong aesthetic or emotional component.

2. The students use the resources that the teacher has given them and work within the rules in order to reach the goal. At this time, the teacher largely withdraws from the center of the stage and gives only as much help as is absolutely necessary.

3. Students discuss what they have done, among themselves and sometimes with the teacher. (This third step is not stated explicitly with every technique, though is stated with most and is possible with the rest.)

Two examples will illustrate how this formula works itself out in Maley and Duff's techniques. In one of the activities in the section on "Interpretation," the entire class is given a fragment of a conversation, such as:

A. A man came to see you.

B. Oh? When?

A. While you were out.

B. What did he want?

A. He didn't say.

The students are to work in twos. Each pair is to imagine who the speakers are, and where and what they are doing. Then they go through the dialog, adding to the beginning and the ending but leaving the original lines as they were. Finally, they try out their versions on other pairs of students. The five-line fragment quoted above shows how *very common words, in short and structurally simple utterances,* can set up uncertainty—even uneasiness or dread—while at the same time they give students a nucleus of language around which they may gather their own ideas and put them into words. This is one of several techniques that show students, without telling them so, that the meaning of what is said comes mostly from the context, and only partially from what they can look up in dictionaries and grammar books.

In one of the "Interaction" techniques, the students work in groups of three. Each group decides on a situation that involves some tension: the wives of trapped miners waiting for news, lovers having a quarrel, etc. They work out a *silent* scene to show what the tension is about. Then each group pairs off with another group and tries to guess the meaning of the other group's scene. The guessing, discussing, and commenting of course produce a great deal of language. Finally each group takes the silent scene *of the other group*, puts words to it, and acts it out before a *different* group.

As I described it in the preceding paragraph, this technique seems to need a class with a certain amount of imagination and fairly good control of the language. Or perhaps we would be surprised at how much a class could do with this technique after only a few weeks or months of study! In any event, if students need more to work with, it can be given in the form of "briefing papers," one for each of a set of situations that the teacher has thought out ahead of time. The "briefing paper" need not be in dialog form.

In ordinary "free conversation," and in some language games, the students are expected to give birth to ideas ("what to say") and to clothe those ideas in words ("how to say it") at the same time. In most of the techniques that Maley and Duff offer us, this is not the case. In the miming activities the ideas may be brought forth in silence, so that the inventing of thoughts and of words are completely separated from one another. But even in other activities, emphasis falls first on "talking about what to say," and then on "saying it." It seems to me that there is value in protecting the student from having to fight a two-front war, or from having to juggle two quite different sets of objects simultaneously, at the beginning of an activity.

Maley and Duff emphasize that their "drama" activities are only one side of a complete course. The other side may contain quite a bit of fairly conventional presentation and controlled practice. Even in the "drama" activities themselves, the authors provide a clear structure with its own "electrical charge," its own life. These activities will become productive, however, only when the students add their own "charge," something from and for themselves. After all, an electric current flows between positive and negative terminals; both sperm and egg must be alive if anything is to come of their union. So the authors avoid the trap of throwing out drilling altogether in favor of "doing," or of assuming that the classroom deserves to be called "humanistic" only to the extent that the students have been given responsibility for their own learning, or of seeming to say that telling a student what to do—on some level, at least—may not be a necessary part of helping that student to grow.

This chapter has been concerned with methods and materials in general. In Chapters 5–10 we will see some of these same principles at work in three unconventional approaches.

7 *For thought, comparison and discussion:*

- With one or more colleagues, try out the portion of the first Maley and Duff activity described on p. 65. Write out your results.

- Do the same activity again, this time limiting your vocabulary to words that might be available to a relatively new speaker of the language you are teaching.

- Now go back and edit your written conversation with an eye to simple vocabulary. (Be sure to keep the language authentic, however!)

- Together with one or more colleagues, write a new starter exchange comparable to the five line fragment that begins the Maley and Duff activity. Try to maintain interest, even suspense, along with simplicity of vocabulary and authenticity of language.

5

COUNSELING-LEARNING: BASIC IDEAS

In the mid-1970s Irene Dutra and I were among a number of language teachers who received training in Community Language Learning (CLL), a method created by Charles A. Curran. A year or two later Irene took part in a 12 hour demonstration of CLL in which the target language was Swahili. I was the teacher. Irene's narration of the two days provides a real context for some of the basic theory behind Curran's approach. She titled her account A Roller Coaster Ride to Swahililand or: Nobody Loves a Skeleton. *Here's how it began.*

A RIDE ON A ROLLER COASTER

Irene (1): Recently a group of New York teachers of English as a Second Language participated in a Community Language Learning (CLL) experience learning a foreign language in a new way. We discovered that indeed "learning is persons" and that the skeleton (bare bones grammar) of a new language is lovable only when encased in a warm human body: first, in that of the teacher-counselor and then, as the learners grow in linguistic independence and peer interdependence, in the body of the learning community. The following is not meant to illustrate a *typical* CLL experience, for each experience is unique: rather, it is a personal account of what happened when a teacher and a few learners came together for two days of Swahili and "let a community come into being."

FOUR ESSENTIALS

Looking back over the years, I suspect that my early contacts with Curran's work were what planted in my mind the seed that later became the question "What's at stake?" Curran's overall approach to education is called Counseling-Learning, and what is called Community Language Learning is only the application of that approach in the field of language study. In her opening paragraph, Irene touches on four essentials of Counseling-Learning:

■ **CL-1** *"Learning is persons."* This is a sentence that I heard often from Curran's lips. As a psychotherapist, his view of the inner dynamics of persons lay at the base of his contribution to the learning and teaching of languages.

■ **CL-2** *People may or may not grow in independence and in interdependence, and there is no necessary contradiction between the two.* This kind of growth takes place best in a community.

- **CL-3** *A group of people may also become a community, or it may not become one.* Communities can come into being, but they cannot be constructed just by following rules or procedures.

- **CL-4** *A community is more likely to come into being when the person who is teacher functions also as "counselor."* This is the most controversial of the four points, partly because it makes heavy demands on the teacher's maturity and self-discipline.

We will look at these points in more detail as we continue with Irene's narration.

THE SARD ACRONYM

Irene (2): The first morning the teacher-counselor and five students boarded the roller coaster bound for Swahililand. We didn't know we were climbing into a roller coaster; we thought we were boarding a relatively smooth-riding train—anticipating, of course, occasional jerky stops and starts.

Two days and 12 hours of Swahili later, with wobbly legs and emotions, students and teacher stumbled off onto level ground, murmuring "Wow!" What had happened on that ride? Well, we had learned (in passing) quite a bit of Swahili, but more importantly, we had learned something about ourselves, about our fellow passengers, and about the complexity and subtlety of the group learning process.

Words like "Wow!" and "wobbly" go directly to the heart of Curran's approach. He liked to summarize the learning process under the acronym SARD:

- **CL-5** Any person at any given moment feels more or less **S**ecure. (This is an example of "affect" as I used that term in Chapter 1.)

- **CL-6** To the extent, and on the levels that one feels secure, one is able and willing to **A**ssert oneself—one's existing purposes, motivations and needs as well as one's existing cognitive resources—into what is going on, and to give it **A**ttention. This is clearly related to what was said in Chapter 1 about the centrality of "affect" in learning. This is the box turtle of Chapter 2 again, or the country rooster who can't or won't crow in the city (p. 29).

- **CL-7** One is best able to **R**eflect on, and so to **R**etain, material that has been the object of attention. (In the terminology of Chapter 1, cognitive networks that include strong elements of affect are more likely to bring appropriate verbal and nonverbal imagery onto the "worktable" of working memory.)

- **CL-8** As one retains material and reflects on it, one is able to respond to new **D**ifferences. (What one has noticed on the worktable becomes available for incorporation into one's inner resources.)

To put the same ideas into reverse order, one can't learn to tell the difference between things unless one can remember them; one can remember them best if one has somehow been involved with them; and one hesitates to get involved where one feels unsafe.

I must confess that I too had expected the Swahili experience to be more like a train ride than like a roller coaster, and that the students' levels of security bounced around more than I had intended. This was one of my early experiences as a "language counselor," and I was still very much a teacher trainer who was hoping to do something brilliant and memorable. I therefore placed great emphasis on giving the group as much responsibility as I could, as soon as I could, in the hope that a beautiful community would spring to blossom in those two brief days and bear spectacular fruit in the form of language mastery. The language results were in fact gratifying, but I was also using the group for my own purposes. On the other hand, I doubt that a sedate train ride through expertly presented language lessons would have led to many new differentiations in self-awareness or in awareness of the complexities and subtleties of the learning process.

> **Irene (3):** We started out that first morning, five slightly apprehensive learners sitting in a circle with a tape recorder and a microphone. Our teacher stood outside the circle. Dave, a student, asked the group (in English) who was going to start. The teacher moved behind him, lightly touched his shoulders, and in a low voice gave him the Swahili translation. Dave turned to the group, snapped on the mike, and asked "Nani ataanza?" Lee responded, "You're going to start." The teacher quickly moved behind her and said, "Wewe utaanza." Lee took the mike, turned it on, and playfully informed Dave, "Wewe utaanza." And so it went for about a dozen utterances, everyone taking a tentative whirl at the language.

I have found it useful to distinguish between Community Language Learning (CLL) in general, and what I call the "Classical Community Language Learning" (CCLL) method in particular. CCLL was the first CLL method, and was developed by Curran and his associates in their research seminars in Chicago. The above excerpt from Irene's account exemplifies certain features of CCLL, but these features themselves are less important than the principles they illustrate:

- Learners record their own voices, but not the voice of the knower. *Principle:* An authority figure's voice would be alien, carrying with it implied demands and threats; one's own voice will not have these effects. Compare the Security element in SARD.

- The knower stands outside the group of learners. *Principles:* This arrangement enhances Security by removing a literal confrontation between teacher and students. The resulting power vacuum also dramatizes the need for Assertion on the part of the learners.

- In supplying utterances in the target language, the knower stands behind the learner who wishes to speak. *Principle:* Security again. The knower touches the learner lightly on the shoulders. *Principle:* This reassures the learner that the supportive knower is indeed there. (Learners not infrequently report that they were not *consciously* aware of the actual contact.) The knower speaks from a point 3 or 4 inches from the learner's ear. *Principle:* This is close enough to get inside the usual boundaries of the learner's personal space, so that the knower's voice may seem to the learner to be coming from inside his or her own head. At the same time, the distance is great enough to avoid threat of contact.

> **Irene (4):** I was feeling very good about myself, my peers, the teacher, and the Swahili language. This was going to be fun!

We then listened to the entire conversation on tape (only our Swahili, not the teacher's, was recorded). It sounded pretty good, rather "African." We smiled at each other in delight.

We listened a second time, sentence by sentence, with each student supplying the English translation of his or her own sentence. We had no trouble recalling the meanings of our utterances.

We listened a third time while one student attempted to write a transcription of the Swahili in the board, looking frequently to the rest of us for help. The teacher verified the transcription. A student copied it on a sheet of paper, and carbon copies were given to each of us as page 1 of our "text."

[Readers need to know that Swahili is a very regularly spelled language in which vowels have about the same values they have in Spanish and most consonants have about the same values as in English. With some other languages, letting a student try transcribing in the first session would not have been feasible.]

The learners' ability to supply the overall meanings of their own utterances is a simple example of the power of Assertion, or of affect. This expedited the replay steps, which introduced the Reflection and Retention components of SARD.

Several features of the activity were contributing toward community-building among the learners:

- As I have already noted, the knower was outside the circle, and was not controlling who was to speak or what was to be said.

- The taped conversation was a product of the learners working together.

- The written transcript was done by one learner with the help of the rest, and the handwritten copies for distribution were the work of another.

No wonder these learners "smiled at each other in delight"!

> **Irene (5):** Now with our first Swahili conversation transcribed, some students felt moved to analyze its grammar: "That must be a pronominal prefix." "Nime- and mimi both seem to mean 1st person singular, but when do you use one and when the other?"
>
> My stomach muscles started tightening. I didn't want to look at the bony skeleton of Swahili. I was getting annoyed at my peers for performing this ghastly dissection, and at the teacher for permitting it. Only 45 minutes had gone by, and my emotions had run the gamut from delight to discomfort to annoyance!

Here in the fifth excerpt we come to the reason for an approach called *Counseling*-Learning. Irene's "purposes, needs and motivations" are suddenly not being matched by what is going on outside her, and she has the emotions to prove it! In the terminology of Chapter 1, her working memory is being flooded with all sorts of cognitive by-products of the mismatch ("clutter"), and the delightful learning she reported in the fourth excerpt has ground to a halt.

Just what was running through Irene's mind at this time? We have no way of knowing, of course. Here is a sampling of the possibilities:

- "The learning that I thought a few moments ago was progressing so smoothly seems to have left unanswered questions. Was that progress all an illusion?"

- "Let me see. What meaning am I supposed to attach to Susan's phrase 'pronominal prefix'? And how can a 'prefix' be a 'pronoun', anyway?"

- "Analysis is something I've never been good at and don't enjoy."

- "Instead of keeping up with the rest, I'm going to fall behind them!"

- "If I start to fall behind, they'll look down on me!"

- "In fact, they may not even accept me as a member of their precious community!"

- "In doing this analysis at this time, they're engaging in a power play at my expense."

- "I'm angry, and holding anger in has always been difficult for me. Will I further disgrace myself by a display of temper?"

- "I want to cry/crawl under the table/leave the room and not come back."

- "What would they say if they knew what's going through my mind?"

Other methodologies have no systematic way of dealing with this kind of "clutter" on the learner's "worktable."

THE ROLE OF THE KNOWER-TEACHER

Irene (6): The language learning round was over. The teacher, now in the role of counselor, joined us in the circle for a group feedback session in English. It became clear that I was not the only one irritated by the grammatical dissection that had ended our first round of Swahili. One or two others admitted getting knots in their stomachs. Listening to them share their feelings lessened my own discomfort: I wasn't alone in my feelings. As we opened up bit by bit and the teacher reflected back our comments and tried to "catch" our underlying emotions in his counseling responses, it emerged that to varying extents four of the five of us wanted to approach the language more intuitively. The fifth, however, expressed a strong need to approach it analytically. A definite conflict in learning styles had emerged in our little group.

The "counselor" with his "counseling responses" (or understanding responses) seems to have had three good effects here:

- Irene's discomfort and feeling of aloneness were reduced, and along with them some of those internal sources of "worktable clutter" that I listed above.

- The individuals in the group got better acquainted with one another in this context, thus moving a bit in the direction of community.

- Some potentially usable information about learning styles emerged.

What, then, *is* this special kind of response? In my understanding of Curran, it has seven characteristics:

- It has a verbal but also a nonverbal side: words, but also body language and tone of voice.

- It is supportive and nonjudgmental.

- In its form, it is an attempt to verify that the counselor is understanding what the other person is communicating, particularly in the realm of feelings.

- In its purpose, it aims not only at verifying the counselor's understanding, but also at leaving the other person with the assurance of having been understood and accepted (though not necessarily agreed with).

- It reflects the literal message of what the speaker has just said, but also takes into account the speaker's feelings.

- It is nondirective: the counselor doesn't try to tell the other person what to do or how to react.

- It is nondefensive: the counselor doesn't resort to self-defense if criticized or attacked.

Very briefly, then, this kind of "understanding" needs a listener who can:

- **CL-9** *See and hear* the other person as that person is, without turning away, without fighting back, and without trying to control the other person.

- **CL-10** *Believe* that the other person has the desire, and much of the wisdom, to straighten out what is within her or him and to make it more harmonious.

- **CL-11** *Speak and act* in ways that flow out of what one has seen and heard and believes, and out of what is appropriate to the situation in which one finds oneself.

This special kind of response will be treated more fully in the last half of Chapter 8.

> **Irene (7):** A change in procedure was therefore proposed: the next time, instead of "attacking" the grammar as soon as the Swahili conversation was transcribed on the board, we would spend a few minutes silently "communing" with it, mentally noting any points that interested us, making any hypotheses we chose to make. After this period of silent reflection, we might or might not choose to share a few of the hypotheses we had formed. Finally, we would test our hypotheses—even the unarticulated ones—by generating new sentences, using the data we had before us.
>
> Everyone agreed to give this new way of working a try; so we went on to a second round of Swahili, similar to the first but with the changed procedure at the end. As we generated new sentences, the teacher gave us nonjudgmental feedback on the correctness of our hypotheses: "Yes, we could say that in Swahili" or "I would say ____ instead."
>
> In the feedback session that followed we all voiced our pleasure with the new procedure. Susan, however, who had initially expressed her need for a more analytical approach, said she still felt the need for more explicit grammatical analysis. The four others outvoted her, and we broke for lunch.

One reason why this negotiated procedural change seems to have reduced tensions is perhaps that people with contrasting learning styles differ less in what they can do than in how nimbly they can do it. The period of silence allowed all five learners to make comparisons and construct guesses at their own rate, rather than being left in the dust by Susan's rapid acceleration.

However, the essential purpose of the feedback session was not negotiation. What negotiation there was came as a by-product of the learners being understood and overhearing others as they were being understood. If the feedback session had been only a matter of "I want this and you want that and she wants the other, so let's ____," the proposals would have been on the surface, and underneath there would have remained unspoken anxieties, frustrations, and resentments. The outcome might have been a bit of temporary accommodation, but with no prospect of fundamental personal growth or change.

> **Irene (8):** I came back from lunch feeling too lethargic to jump into Swahili again. I was annoyed that my peers seemed peppier and more interested than I; everyone should feel logy after lunch. I sat there rather sullenly, barely participating in the Swahili conversation. In the feedback session I hesitantly expressed some of my negative emotions. Strangely, as I did so and as the teacher "caught" my feelings in his counseling responses, I began to get a surge of energy, and by the time we began another round of the language, I was animated and interested again.

> The value of having negative emotions understood and accepted by the teacher was becoming clearer.

This excerpt illustrates four points of interest:

- A vote is not a community transaction, just a power transaction.

- **CL-12** One can have feelings about feelings: annoyance that one's lethargy is not shared by others, for example, or shame at feeling annoyance.

- **CL-13** The sources of feelings (in this case lethargy and loginess) can be ambiguous. Attribution to the time of day was certainly plausible, but the disappearance of the feelings as Irene was understood suggests otherwise.

- **CL-14** Being understood can be liberating.

FIVE DEVELOPMENTAL STAGES

> **Irene (9):** And so it went for two days—a Swahili conversation followed by a feedback session, the group making slight changes in procedure as we felt and voiced the need to. In the Swahili conversations we were taking more risks, venturing more into Stage II (the "kicking stage") and Stage III (the "birth stage") by trying to use words and structures from previous sessions. We were also looking more to our peers and less to the teacher to supply a word or finish a phrase for us. At a certain point we invited the teacher to sit in the circle instead of standing behind us. At the time it seemed spontaneous, but in retrospect the invitation may have been an unconscious acknowledgment of his changing relationship to us. Yet even as we were trying to become more independent of the teacher, we were aware that he was always there, warm and supportive, for the times we needed him, for the times we wanted to return to the womblike security of Stage I.

Curran talked about the students being in one of five "stages," which he compared to the stages of individual birth and maturation. Stage I is like the womb, where the learner has as much security as the knower/teacher can provide for her. As the learner gains a bit of knowledge and some confidence, she begins to take small risks by trying things out on her own. This is what Irene called Stage II—the fetus working its way into the outside world. The knower is close by, however, to provide security whenever the learner seems to want it. To switch figures of speech for a moment, in a swimming lesson the Stage I learner keeps her feet on the bottom of the pool. The Stage II learner tries floating, always with the teacher's hands an inch or two beneath her. The Stage III swimmer has great fun jumping into the water and paddling around with her friends. All she needs is a lifeguard to warn her when she is getting into a dangerous area, and to rescue her in case of real trouble. The Stage III swimmer, however, has little patience with the expert who wants to show her the fine points of swimming faster or more gracefully. Returning to the developmental metaphor, Stage III is a combination of carefree childhood and complex adolescence. The would-be teacher may therefore feel considerable frustration and pain, both because he feels rejected by the student and because he sees all that the student is missing by refusing to learn more.

By the end of our 12-hour Swahili workshop, the learners began to get into Stage III. For the sake of completeness, however, let me summarize the two remaining stages. In Stage IV, the roles of the knower and the learner are reversed. In Stages I–III it was the knower who provided security; the learner was free to stick her neck out or not, according to the amount of security she felt. The knower had to be very cautious not to destroy that security, whether by the wrong kind of correcting of mistakes, or by loading learners down with more than they could handle. In Stage IV, on the other hand, the learners are secure enough so that they are able to take care of their own anxieties. They are also able to see some of the anxieties of the knower: his fear that what he has to offer will not be valued by the learners, his pain at the way they are mangling his language (or whatever subject matter he is teaching), and so on. They are also able to help the knower with his anxieties—and at the same time to help themselves learn better—by welcoming his corrections and suggestions. In an ideal Stage IV, the knower continues to have an "understanding" attitude toward the learners, so that the relationship is one of mutual support. Each side puts into the learning enterprise what he or she is able to supply, whether knowledge of subject matter, or knowledge of what she or he is ready to take in next, or appreciation of the contribution of the other, or awareness of their own reactions of perplexity, elation, anger, or fatigue. Each side also accepts the contributions of the other freely and nondefensively.

Stage V is like Stage IV except that now most errors are behind the learners, so that both the learners and the knower can turn their energy to polishing and perfecting the new skill of the learners.

These five stages are not an inflexible series, and a learner may shift from one of them to another from moment to moment. But they do show how the relationship may grow and become more mature. In the first three stages, the learner is locked into herself, her own purposes, and her own anxieties, and sees the knower either as a source for getting what she wants, or as a threat, or as both at the same time.

■ **CL-15** Moving from Stage III to Stage IV may prove to be a very turbulent experience, bringing with it pain, anger, and confusion. Curran compared it to the crisis of moving through adolescence into adult-adult relationships.

In Counseling-Learning, as in most approaches, not all learners get beyond Stage III. This is therefore the part of the approach that requires of the teacher the greatest strength and deepest inner stillness, the surest maturity.

> **Irene (10):** In the feedback sessions too, we were taking more risks. Susan shared with the other students how rejected she had felt when they twice seemed to spurn her analytical way of learning. On the first day, she said, her emotions had gone up and down and up again, initial delight turning to feelings of rejection, near tears turning to contentment as she started feeling understood and accepted by her peers. I tried to express the awful tug-of-war I felt between my own needs and the needs of the group, having always to make the choice of subordinating one to the other or reaching some harmonious balance. Jean confessed she felt subtle group pressure to speak and participate more, which infringed on her learning space and made her feel crowded in. At times she wanted and needed simply to sit there in silence, letting the language "wash over" her.

■ **CL-16** This excerpt shows how Curran's sequence of stages appear not only in the use of the new language, but in the development of community as well.

Going through the stages together is itself a community-building experience. Incidentally, it is interesting how Susan and Irene, with their conflicting learning styles, had apparently gone through the same up-down-up swing of emotions.

> **Irene (11):** By the second day we also felt freer to criticize the teacher in feedback sessions. He gave us understanding counseling responses as we did so: he had been rather authoritarian in abruptly starting off the class that morning; he had been brusque with Susan when she got off on a tangent. I said he broke off eye contact with me too soon when giving me new Swahili phrases, causing my mind to block completely; and that in his effort to be nonjudgmental, he was sometimes "inauthentic." I even criticized him for innocently greeting me in Swahili outside of class; as an insecure beginner I panicked at this intrusion of Swahili into the real world. (Surprisingly, a few days later when I met him in the real world, it was I who initiated the Swahili exchange; my fears had totally vanished.)
>
> Yes, we were all in this together: students and teacher. Our emotions were surfacing, our sensitivity to the dynamics of the group was developing, our trust in and care for each other was growing. We were allowing ourselves to become more vulnerable, more transparent. A "fragile community" was forming.

For some readers, the conspicuous part of this excerpt may be the criticism of the teacher. For me its overriding theme is the progress toward, and the fragility of, a nascent community. Any criticisms of the teacher, and any of his responses to criticism, are only means toward and evidences of that community.

But is this much time and attention to the learners' reactions and feelings feasible? In a two-day class with five learners, maybe. But with 20 or 30 learners, wouldn't it swamp all other activities? When would they find time for exposure to the language they're supposed to be learning? These are natural questions.

Let me guess what Curran might have said:

■ The teacher's nondefensive and understanding responses to criticism serve three purposes:

(1) They encourage learners to offer further criticisms, which are useful in informing the teacher about what is going on and in suggesting possible modifications of technique. But the number of different criticisms will not grow in proportion to the size of the class.

(2) As we have seen in earlier excerpts from Irene's story, such responses have a beneficial effect on individual learners. But hearing one's own criticism understood and accepted when it has been put forth by another learner can also lead to feelings of acceptance and community.

(3) "Understanding responses" establish and maintain an atmosphere in the class as a whole. This third purpose can be served with a class of any size.

■ The criticisms offered by learners are products of the moment. As we see in this excerpt, a learner may later have second thoughts about a criticism, and may recognize it as simply a sign of where she needed to grow cognitively or emotionally rather than as evidence of some error on the part of the teacher. (Not all criticisms, though! Since I was the teacher in this episode, let me make clear that I believe most of the ones reported here were in fact valid. Many of my errors stemmed from a desire to perform a *tour de force* and impress my colleagues.)

Irene (12): The strain of participating in this intellectual and emotional adventure began to show by the middle of the second day. At lunch, exhilarated after a good morning session, Dave, Lee and I concocted a hilarious fantasy involving a pompous linguist and his microphone. (Did this reveal veiled hostility to the mike we used—and somewhat feared—in class?) There was much camaraderie and hysterical laughter, tears rolling down our cheeks. During the Swahili session after lunch, I started giggling every time I looked at the mike. Unable to suppress my giggles, I—a usually serious sedate adult—fled the room, feeling like a silly first-grader.

When I returned for the feedback session, I apologized for my childish (or was it childlike?) behavior and confessed I didn't understand what had happened to me. It emerged that most of the group had been feeling giddy since lunch, and that the giddiness was perhaps a release of tensions. No one in the group had been aware of great tension during the two days; for the most part it had been a pleasurable learning experience. Yet there were necessary tensions involved in learning a foreign language, in gradually opening up to each other, in coalescing as a group—even in realizing that our fledgling community would soon be disbanding.

Community Language Learning was much more complex than I had imagined.

Just as I was playing the multiple roles of teacher, counselor and teacher-trainer, so Irene, Dave, Susan, Lee, and Jean were in the double role of language learners and teachers examining a new approach. Under these circumstances, there may have been some sources of tension and anxiety in their group that would not have been present in a class consisting of people who merely wanted to learn Swahili.

This should however not blind us to the fact that there is more of this kind of thing than we like to think about under the surface of an ordinary class, where it is typically suppressed by social convention and by teacher-applied sanctions. The position of Counseling-Learning is that suppression does not do away with such tensions and conflicts; it only diffuses their effects and makes them harder to deal with.

> **Irene (13):** Our last Swahili conversation was a breakthrough. For the first time, instead of safe, somewhat superficial topics, we chose to speak in the foreign language about our deeper concerns and feelings. We tried to make the same connections with each other in Swahili as we had made in English.

There seems to have been further progress in Curran's five stages, both with regard to community building and with regard to the use of Swahili. There is complex and subtle interplay between the purposive and emotional sides of "affect" as that term was used in Chapter 1.

> **Irene (14):** Time was running out, but we still had a little left. We didn't feel like learning any more Swahili; we were drained. The roller coaster was slowing down. Someone suggested the teacher teach us an African song, so he sang us a soft Bantu lullaby, and our roller coaster ride came gently to an end.

"Bantu lullaby"? I do not now know nor have I ever known anything that could be described in that way. Maybe it was *Mwari komborerai Afrika* in Shona. The only thing I've ever sung successfully is children to sleep, so even that grand song may have come out a bit soporific.

SUMMARY

For convenience, here is a list of the numbered points about Counseling-Learning/Community Language Learning appearing in this chapter:

The first four points are very general:

- **CL-1** *"Learning is persons"* (page 68). That is, learning involves more than just one brain at a time and a batch of new information.

- **CL-2** *People may or may not grow in independence and in interdependence, and there is no necessary contradiction between the two* (page 68). Put negatively, building interdependence doesn't necessarily establish dependence.

- **CL-3** *A group of people may also become a community, or it may not become one.* (page 69)

- **CL-4** *A community is more likely to come into being when the person who is teacher functions also as "counselor."* (page 69) This assertion is distinctive for Curran's approach to education.

Points 5–8 are an outline of Curran's SARD acronym summarizing how and why security is so important for learning:

- **CL-5** *Any person at any given moment feels more or less Secure* (page 69). Various degrees of security are felt on a number of levels: physical, social, and so forth.

- **CL-6** *To the extent that, and on the levels where one feels secure, one is able* *and willing to Assert oneself into whatever is going on* (page 69). This applies to one's existing purposes, motivations, and needs as well as one's existing cognitive resources.

■ **CL-7** *One is best able to Reflect on, and so to Retain, material that has been the object of attention* (page 69). This is hardly surprising, but it is an essential link in Curran's reasoning.

■ **CL-8** *As one retains material and reflects on it, one is able to respond to new Differences* (page 69). This is obviously true for abstract concepts, but probably applies also to sides of experience that cannot be put into words.

Points 9-11 have to do with what is needed in the teacher:

■ **CL-9** *See and hear the other person as he or she is, without turning away, without fighting back, and without trying to control the other person* (page 73). Among its other effects, this allows the teacher's personal security to help reduce a learner's insecurity.

■ **CL-10** *Believe that the other person has the desire, and much of the wisdom, to to sort out confusions and conflicts within him or her and achieve more inner balance* (page 73). Without this assumption, CL-9 is inappropriate.

■ **CL-11** *Speak and act in ways that flow out of what you have seen and heard and what you believe, and out of what is appropriate to the situation in which you find yourself* (page 73). Trying to do otherwise contributes to insecurity in the teacher, and from there ultimately to the undermining of the security of the learners.

Points 5–8 were concerned with one kind of feeling: security. Points 12-14 are about feelings in general:

■ **CL-12** *One can have feelings about feelings* (page 74). This simple observation often makes it easier to give "understanding" responses to other people.

■ **CL-13** *The sources of feelings* (in this case lethargy and loginess) *can be ambiguous* (page 74). Not realizing this can lead us to premature and overly simple conclusions.

■ **CL-14** *Being understood can be liberating* (page 74). Liberated from, among other things, the need to keep up pretenses.

Two additional points are:

■ **CL-15** *Moving from the stages where one is receiving emotional and other support full-time, to a stage where one is expected to give as well as receive, is an essential part of the goal of the CL/CLL system as a whole* (page 76). This can involve stress and turbulence, and not all learners make this transition.

■ **CL-16** *Curran's sequence of stages appear not only in the use of the new language, but in the development of community as well* (page 76). Curran's personal discovery of this parallel took place in a situation where he himself was being tutored in French, and led eventually to his creating CL/CLL.

A REMINDER

Needless to say, a teacher who wishes to use Community Language Learning or Counseling Learning should have some live, face-to-face training in it. As I indicated in the Prologue and in Chapter 1, the descriptions in this book are intended to illustrate certain general principles, rather than to teach readers how to use the approaches for themselves. Meanwhile, the reader may wish to consult what other writers on methodology such as Larsen-Freeman (1986), Richards and Rodgers (1986), Blair (1982), and Oller and Richard-Amato (1983), have said about Counseling-Learning. My own treatment of the approach in Stevick (1990) was concerned primarily with explaining the thinking behind it, rather than with how to put it into practice.

1 *The interview quoted in Chapter 1 included the following exchange:*

"Aggie": Yes! And furthermore, the presentation seems to leap around from topic to topic. Every hour the teacher starts something new, and it's not always related to what came before. I get so confused.

Interviewer: There seems to be no continuity for you to hold on to.

The interviewer's reply is a good example of a "counseling response." Here are eight other things the interviewer might have said:

- "Are the other students having as much trouble as you are?"

- "Yeah, I remember a similar experience when I was studying Russian."

- "Do you also have trouble in following other kinds of communication?"

- "Whenever you begin to get this feeling of confusion, I'd suggest you pause and take a few deep breaths."

- "I'm sure this will all work out all right as you get further into the course. If it doesn't please feel free to contact me again."

- "Actually, most students have found that teacher to be highly effective, and no one else has complained about confusion."

- "Have you any ideas how you might deal with your problem?"

- "You get confused because the teacher is always starting something new."

In what respects do these replies fail the criteria for a "an understanding response"?
What effects might each one have had on "Aggie"?

2 *Here is an excerpt from another interview. Carla had picked up a fair amount of German just by living in Germany, and has recently been placed in an audiolingual class with students who had studied the language academically from the beginning. She tells the interviewer:*

"Carla:" I feel restrained in the class. And on the other hand I feel dumb. I feel restrained because the vocabulary is there in my head, and the thought patterns are there, a little more complex than where the other students are right now. But I also feel very dumb because I don't know any of the endings! I don't know what I'm doing!" (Taken from Stevick 1989.)

Working if possible with a group of colleagues, suggest at least five responses that an interviewer might make to Carla at this point.

Then compare your responses in the light of the criteria for a "counseling response" listed on pages 72-73.

---

3 *Carefully listen to or read someone else's account of a language learning experience. Prepare, compare, and evaluate five or more responses a listener might give to this account. (Don't forget to be alert for the feeling side.)*

---

4 *In the Classical Community Language Learning procedures Irene describes, in what ways do you find the teacher exercising "control" as that term was used in Chapter 3? What kinds of learner "initiative" do you observe?*

---

5 *Again with reference to the techniques examined in TASK 4:*

- We know that students differ greatly with regard to temperament and learning style. Suggest possible negative comments that a student might make concerning one of these techniques.

- What would be an appropriate "understanding response" to each of these criticisms?

---

6 *Irene (page 71) says that the five learners started out the first day "apprehensive."*

- What did they have to be apprehensive about?

- How are they like and unlike your own students in this respect?

---

7 *Pick out from Irene's narration as many evidences as you can of Irene's emotional state.*

---

8 *For each of these quotations from the "Voices" in Chapter 2, suggest one or more ordinary conversational replies that would not qualify as "understanding responses":*

- "When someone approaches me in French, whether she is a native or a non-native speaker, I am unwilling (not incapable) to respond for the fear of making a mistake."

- "I hid in the intellectual study of the language and kept postponing a deliberate effort to use Japanese because I couldn't hold my own in conversation with a native speaker. But why did I feel it was necessary to hold my own in a conversation? And what, in fact, did I mean by "holding my own"? I think self-image was an important part."

- "Though the students seemed to appreciate my 'warmth, acceptance, and understanding,' their needs were not being met."

- "I was soon put into what was called 'the slow group'."

Now suggest and evaluate possible "understanding responses" to these same statements.

6

OTHER APPLICATIONS OF COUNSELING-LEARNING IN LANGUAGE TEACHING

If one has seen only a single example of a principle in operation, one may find it hard to distinguish between the principle itself and the particular details of the example. In this chapter, therefore, we will look at additional incidents that illustrate the ideas set forth in Chapter 5.

FROM A ONE-DAY WORKSHOP

The first excerpts are from a one-day demonstration in a Master of Arts in Teaching program, again using Swahili. Excerpt 1 summarizes preliminary contacts that took place before the beginning of the overt instruction.

Teachers' Voices

EWS 1: The members of the program had already been introduced to basic concepts of Counseling-Learning by a resident staff member. On the evening before the Swahili course, I talked with all 56 members of the program for about two hours. One incidental effect of this session was, I hope, to reduce any general anxiety that the 12 prospective Swahili students may have felt with respect to me as a stranger.

On Friday morning, I began by reminding the learners of the first step in the procedure, which they had read about before my arrival, and with which they had already experimented on a small scale. My purpose in doing so was threefold. First, I wanted to be sure that they had the information fresh in their minds so that the first step would go smoothly. On a deeper level, I wanted them to feel secure with respect to the way their time was going to be structured for the next few minutes. Deeper still, the content of what I said at this point was only a vehicle for a tone of voice and overall manner that I hope conveyed calm and self-assurance on my part. The first two of these goals could have been reached without the third. The third could have been reached without the first two by talking about some external topic such as the weather. By using the CCLL (Classical Community Language Learning) procedure itself as the content, I hoped that the three aspects of what I said would enhance one another.

From previous experience, I knew that people often become very anxious while making the tape-recorded conversation because they are aware that they can't remember what they have said. For that reason, I casually remarked that the learners were not expected to remember anything at this time, but that later steps would provide for retention.

I chose my clothing with the learner's security in mind. They were young adults in their twenties, living on a campus where life is quite informal. They therefore wore clothing such as blue jeans and sweatshirts. I could have tried to dress the same way. If I had, however, I would have felt that I was saying to them, "See, I'm one of you!" which would have been false. To have said that would have implied, further, "When I'm around you, I'm not comfortable with being a member of your parents' generation." If my way of dressing had in fact come across to the learners in this way, it would have had an unnoticed but not negligible effect on their security with me. And I was sure that, in any event, I would myself feel like a hypocrite in clothes like theirs. My own insecurity at this point would have been transmitted to them in subtle ways. I therefore wore wool slacks, a warm brown dress shirt, and a tweed jacket. As a token of informality, I did not wear a tie.

Investigations

1 *In the above paragraphs, how many specific references can you find to concern for learner security (page 69 of Chapter 5)?*

- On which different levels do you find these references?

- On which levels, if any, was security apparently ignored?

- At what points in the account did the teacher take risks with regard to the security of the prospective learners?

2 *Take a few minutes to recall a trainer or teacher you have recently observed.*

- List some ways in which he or she showed concern for learner security. If possible, compare your list with someone else's.

- In which respects, if any, did he or she appear to ignore certain aspects of security?

3 *Take a few minutes to recall a class or group you have recently led.*

- List some ways in which you showed concern for learner security. If possible, compare your list with someone else's.

- On which levels, if any, did you ignore certain aspects of security?

- What risks did you take, either deliberately or not?

4 *In the sense developed in Chapter 3, how does Excerpt EWS 1 illustrate more or less subtle forms of "control"?*

The first session the following morning followed the same conversation circle technique described at the beginning of Chapter 5. Interested teachers and others sometimes raise certain concerns about this technique. One such concern has to do with the quality or accuracy of the knower's translations of the learners' sentences in the conversations. My response would be that even a native speaker of the target language is likely to introduce at least subtle distortions under these circumstances, and a nonnative like me is likely to encounter gaps in his own vocabulary. Both of these things do happen. Neither causes serious trouble, however. The purpose of the translation is not to produce an exact equivalent, but only to provide for the learner a sentence in whose content she can feel some sense of investment. If the knower-counselor cannot come up with a word that is essential for even an approximate translation of the learner's sentence, he simply says "Blank" and goes on. This happens to me on an average of once in a ten-minute conversation, and the learners say that it doesn't bother them. The important thing seems to be that the counselor-knower himself, through his nonverbal communication, convey a sense that he himself is comfortable with the gap.

Another frequently expressed concern has to do with the learners' tendency to fumble the mechanics and the timing of the tape recorder as they originate new conversations. It is indeed true in my experience that that during the first few conversations, the learners generally have trouble with the stop-start switch on the microphone. As a result, the first parts of some sentences don't get recorded; or the counselor's voice, or even the learner's native-language sentence may get recorded. In the succeeding steps of the procedures, these sentences will be treated exactly as though they had been perfectly recorded. In the meantime, it is important that the counselor avoid anything that could be interpreted as even joking disapproval or derision. This includes grimaces.

This demonstration included certain techniques not described in Irene Dutra's account (Chapter 5). One of them was used after the third group conversation had been taped and then transcribed onto a flip chart:

> **EWS 2:** I drew two vertical lines on the blackboard, thus forming three columns. For one of the verbs on the recorded conversation. I put the subject prefix at the top of the first column, the tense prefix at the top of the middle column, and the verb stem at the top of the last column. Then I relinquished the chalk to one of the learners, who agreed to serve as secretary for the group. The task was to fit the verbs from their sentences into these columns. I sat at the back of the room and made occasional interventions or answered questions, but at least 95 percent of the talking was done by the learners.
>
> The overall effect of this step was the learners' discrimination of prefixes and stems. My staying physically out of their way contributed to their security with me and their confidence in themselves. My drawing the lines on the board and dissecting the first verb contributed to their security by giving them a clear framework within which to proceed. On the other hand, leaving the initiative to them allowed them to invest themselves by contributing data to be fitted into the diagram. My asking for someone to serve as "secretary," rather than calling on someone to "recite," protected the security of that person and of anyone who might take his or her place.

Following the tabulation exercise, the learners got to try a new type of production. I divided the learners into groups of three and gave blank 3 by 5 cards to each group. The group was to write an original Swahili sentence on each card, without English translation. I circulated while this was going on, looking over people's shoulders to see the sentences as they were written. Most of them were correct, but I suggested changes where necessary. When each group had at least three sentences, they passed their cards to the next group, which figured out what the sentences meant.

Here is a further technique that some teachers might not have thought of using after only four or five hours of instruction. After a break, I told the learners that I was going to talk to them for a few minutes in Swahili just so they could get some idea what connected speech sounds like. I told them that I would not question them or otherwise put them on the spot with respect to what I was going to say. I said that while they might recognize some things that I said, I would make no attempt to stay within the vocabulary that they had been exposed to.

My monolog lasted for something over five minutes, with great animation and continuous eye contact. I sat where I could see the sentences that we had written from all three cycles, and drew on them, but said whatever else I felt like saying. I repeated myself frequently, but in ways that would be appropriate to a similar monolog where no foreign language is involved.

Following the monolog there was a long silence, at the end of which people began telling me what they had thought I had said. They were usually right, and among them they retrieved most of what I had said. I confirmed or disconfirmed their guesses with brief, matter-of-fact replies.

In the above I knowingly took certain risks. This step seemed to leave the group with some feeling of elation. Since much of what I said was based on what had been in their recorded conversations, the monolog was in some sense a diffuse "reflection" of all that the learners had done up to that point. I have done this same kind of thing with several other groups under similar circumstances. Both the learners and I are always amazed at how much they have understood. I suspect that this result could not have been obtained if I had not maintained their security by (1) assuring them that I would not quiz them; (2) refraining from quizzing them; and (3) acting casual about the successes and occasional failures of their guesses. These guesses were, after all, a further form of self-investment, which could have dried up immediately in an atmosphere of evaluation.

Now here is the final technique in the one-day demonstration: As the last activity of the day, I engaged in two or three minutes of vigorous conversation with each of the learners. Before I began, I told them that whoever I was talking with was free to ask help from the others, either in figuring out what I had said, or in deciding how to reply; and if they didn't feel ready to reply in Swahili, they could always reply in English.

During the conversations, I spoke rapidly and with great animation at all times. If a learner didn't understand something, I was willing to repeat it, but not to slow it down. My part of the conversations consisted almost entirely of (1) questions based on sentences they had met earlier in the day; (2) my "understanding" responses to their replies to my questions; and (3) my "understanding" recapitulations of what the learner had said during the entire interview.

In this technique, the conversations, like the monolog, were a diffuse reflection of what the learners had created earlier. My questions required the learners to make appropriate discriminations in order to understand and reply. Their replies, in turn, became new investments that I had to meet with nonthreatening responses in the form of Swahili-language reflection. These responses, together with the privilege of replying in English if they needed to, seemed to keep the learners' security at a fairly high level.

THE "ISLAMABAD PROCEDURE"

The principles of Counseling-Learning and Community Language Learning can also be applied outside the framework of the classical technique based on a group-originated conversation. One that has been widely cited and adapted is the so-called "Islamabad Procedure," named after the subject matter chosen by the first learner who used it. There are four basic steps.

1. A learner serves as originator. The originator describes a city (or other place) [a] *that no one else in the room has ever seen.* With each sentence of the description, she [b] *puts one or more cuisenaire rods—colored wooden (or plastic) objects a square centimeter in cross section, ranging in length from 1 to 10 centimeters—into place to represent what she has said.* The rods, with their ten lengths and ten corresponding colors, soon form a striking pattern on the tabletop. (This is particularly true if the tabletop has been completely cleared beforehand.)

   The originator speaks [c] *either in the target language or in her native language or in a combination of the two.* Whatever the originator's language or combination of languages, *the teacher gives for each sentence an "understanding response" in the target language.* With beginning students, the form of the teacher's response [d] *follows the form of the originator's sentence as closely as possible.* With more advanced students, [e] *the response should usually be more flexible.*

   During this first step, [f] *the other students simply watch and listen.*

2. The teacher [g] *retells the description in the target language.* It is generally helpful to [h] *point at each rod as it is talked about.* Some teachers like to retell the description in [i] *a more or less hesitant way.*

3. The other students take [j] *turns pointing to the rods and telling things that they remember from the account.* It seems to be important that each student [k] *tell only one fact per turn.* As in Step 1, the teacher gives [l] *"understanding responses,"* not approval, correction, or praise.

4. In the last step of the Islamabad Technique, the other students [m] *ask the originator questions about the city (or other place) that she has described.* [n] *Rods are added or moved to reflect new information.* The teacher [o] *moves to the edge of the conversation, but is still available as a*

"counselor" to paraphrase questions and answers. [p] Again it is essential that his nonverbal communications be such as to say, "I'm an interested participant in this conversation."

---

1 *Read through the entire description looking for ways in which the Islamabad Procedure exemplifies or fails to exemplify what was said in Chapter 1 about affect and memory; what was said in Chapter 3 about control and initiative; and what has been said about the SARD components (page 69) and the growth of community.*

---

2 *A number of points in the description have been italicized and marked with a letter enclosed in [ ]. For each, suggest a common alternative (e.g., instead of [a], describing a place that all the learners are familiar with).*

---

3 *What may have been the thinking behind each of the lettered points in the Islamabad description (above)? (There are no "correct answers" to this question!) First make your own guess, then compare it with the correspondingly lettered items in the following list, which represent my thinking at the time. (Again, these are not the "correct answers," but are given only for comparison!)*

a. This guarantees that what is said will be genuine communication. It also means that the listeners will not be tempted to superimpose their own memories on what the originator says, thereby distorting it.

b. The visual clarity and simplicity of the resulting configuration is first of all an aid to concentration, particularly if the tabletop has been completely cleared beforehand. In addition, it provides reference points for visual images that the participants form as the narration unfolds. These will be useful as subject matter for language in the later steps.

c. To limit the originator to the target language would severely restrict the spontaneity, genuineness and interest of what she would say, and turn the activity into a proof of her already-existing control of the language.

d. Otherwise it might create confusion.

e. Otherwise it may become monotonous.

f. This simplifies the role of the listeners as well as of the originator. To do otherwise at this point would both break concentration and contribute to insecurity.

g. Linguistically, this both repeats the language that the teacher had supplied in the earlier step, and pulls it together. Psychologically it is reassuring: "Something usable and interesting has been produced."

h. This gives an occasion for connecting the spoken language with whatever mental images the participants may have attached to the rods.

i. With their sentence intonation and their facial expression, they ask the originator to verify the facts in what they are saying. This contributes to the originator's feeling of status, and therefore to her overall confidence.

j. This keeps the originator and her narration at the center of attention while providing the others with opportunities for assisted production.

k. Otherwise, this step can become a contest to see who has the best memory for this sort of thing. This may invigorate the best students, but it very quickly discourages the others. People seem to differ from one another less in their ability to remember *single* facts that they themselves have *chosen,* and to differ more in their ability to reproduce a *paragraph-sized* description that *someone else* (in this technique, the originator) has provided.

l. By listening to the "understanding response," the learners correct most of their own mistakes. At the same time, they are spared the deadening impact of the nonverbal messages that come along with conventional corrections.

m. Now the rest of the students can begin linguistically freer production in which, guided by their own purposes, they are working from and on their own mental images. Two-way traffic between "Files" and "Worktable" (p. 13)!

n. The moving of the rods allows long-muscle and visual activity that fits what is being said. It also serves as physical recognition that information has actually been conveyed through the new language.

o. This conveys nonverbally that the knower/teacher is after all a temporary, though necessary, foreign object within the learning community.

p. Under these circumstances, students still notice and correct most of their mistakes, but the conversation continues. If the teacher's non-verbal communication says, "You've just made an error that you can correct by listening to me!" then the footmen turn into mice, the coach into a pumpkin, and the conversationalists into students who are trying to please their teacher.

WORKING WITH VERSE

Advice

If you try to pull a stamp off an envelope
You're likely to tear it,
But if you hold the stamp and pull the envelope away from it
The stamp will not tear.
This really works. Try it sometime!

People are like that.
You can take a lot away from me
If you will leave me as I am,

But if you try to pull me away from something I've stuck myself to
It will be hard for you, and very hard on me.
I hope you won't forget this next time.

A final example is based just as deliberately, though less obviously, on Counseling-Learning. It is designed for non-beginners and makes use of small bits of verse such as the one above. The procedure is:

UNDERSTANDING THE WRITER

Language: Silent reading. Reading aloud by the teacher. Members of small groups try to clarify meanings for one another, referring to the teacher whatever questions stump them.

Ideas: What was the writer trying to say? On how many levels? Write a paraphrase.

Feelings: How did the author feel as he or she was writing? What makes you think so?

UNDERSTANDING ONE ANOTHER

Feelings: How do you feel after reading this text? What in the text makes you feel that way?

Ideas: Do you agree with the ideas you find in the text? Why, or why not?

Related experiences: What does this text remind you of? Can you provide illustrations that confirm or that contradict what the author is saying?

NOTE: *In both halves of the above plan, whatever a student says constitutes an "investment" of him or herself, which may receive a supportive, understanding response from teacher, fellow students, or both.*

---

4 *Concerning the above lesson format:*

- How does it exemplify principles of Counseling-Learning?

- In what other ways may short texts of this kind be used in language instruction? How do those other ways exemplify or not exemplify the principles of Counseling-Learning?

---

5 *How do the ideas expressed in "Advice" themselves relate to basic concepts of Counseling-Learning?*

7

COUNSELING-LEARNING AND WHAT'S AT STAKE

One perceptive and largely accurate comment on A Way and Ways *was that my vision of human beings seemed to include the idea that people in general, and learners and teachers in particular, are commonly in some kind of psychological difficulty (Allard and Young 1990). I of course do not think everyone needs psychotherapy, and I happily recognize that many people lead emotionally healthy lives in general. On the other hand, I have seen up-close too many examples of the effects of psychological factors on language learners to deny that the potential for some degree of psychological difficulty is present in whatever we do, and that such factors may work either toward success or toward failure in pursuit of language competence or of any other overtly chosen goal.*

In this book I have been suggesting that much of what is called "psychological difficulty" consists of attempts to deal with conflicts among what the learner has "at stake" on various levels. This is of course related to the central place I gave to Becker's "denial of death" concept in Chapter 2. Some readers have objected to both these themes. It seems to me, however, that writers on these matters differ less concerning the existence of widespread psychological difficulties than they do concerning their convictions about the sources of those difficulties and their recommendations as to what can or should be done about them in an educational context. All of this is, I believe, consistent with my emphasis on the powerful and complex role of "affect."

The present chapter will take a fuller look at "what's at stake" from a Counseling-Learning point of view, and then go on to describe more fully the "understanding response" mentioned in Chapter 5, showing how it can be useful with the kinds of psychological difficulties that often interfere with learning.

EXPECTATIONS: HARMONY AND CONFLICT

People since the 1960s have often talked about "getting it all together." With these words, they have come near to one of the insights at the heart of Counseling-Learning: the insight that doing and feeling and knowing (what scholars sometimes call the "somatic, affective, and cognitive aspects of living") cannot be fully untangled from one another. We may choose to look at only one or two of them, but then we will not see the whole; in some kinds of research we may cut them apart artificially, but in so doing we cut ourselves off from life.

This is true for one learner at a time, but it is also true for all of the people in a classroom as they work with, on, and through one another.

But as we well know, there is more to "getting it all together" than "unity of body, mind, and spirit," whatever that may mean. We also have a need—even a strong drive—to get our *expectations* together. I know that "getting expectations together" is a clumsy way to put it, and that it sounds as if I am making up my own private jargon. So let me try to spell out what I mean by it.

In simple English, my "expectations" are whatever I think is likely to happen. What I think will happen—the way I think things are going to be one year, one hour, one second from now—is built up out of all the things that I have learned to tell apart from one another, and from the ways in which these things have fitted themselves together in my mind—in those "networks of my long-term memory" mentioned in Chapter 1. Rain is not snow, but when spring comes both will run downstream as water. Red is not green, and a motorist faced with a red light almost always stops. Girls are not boys, and margarine is not butter, and irony is not quite sarcasm. These things, and more subtle things, and more complex things—these things and the ways in which I have seen them fit together in the past—make up my picture of the world—my expectations. One might even say that they *are* my world—the only world I know. This in one sense is that "world of meaningful action" that Adler, and after him Becker, talked about: the very world in which at the end my life will have been worthy or will have been lost. What I am—the world in which I have meaning—is made up of what I have learned to expect.

A well-known example of what I am trying to say is the fact that where English has a word "snow," the Eskimo languages have fifty or more words for different varieties of white frozen water. They need them because those who have lived for generations in the Arctic have learned to *tell that many "kinds of snow" apart*. They also know what to expect from each in terms of heaviness, ability to bear the weight of a snowshoe, and so on.

A striking example came up one day when I was talking with a group of people from Northern Europe. During the conversation, they said that many of their American colleagues did not greet them or even acknowledge their greetings when they met them in the hallways or the elevators. This did not meet their expectations of how people show courtesy to one another. I then raised my eyebrows, and asked them whether *that* would be enough to make them feel that another person had acknowledged that they were there. At first they were not even aware of what I was talking about. Then they saw the raising of my eyebrows but appeared unable, without a little practice, to distinguish it from a wink. I suspect that most of the time the Americans who they thought had ignored them had actually greeted them silently by a friendly raising of eyebrows. These Northern Europeans and I were different from one another in what facial movements we could *tell apart,* and in what *we expected* other people to do.

A language is also a complex network of telling things apart and knowing what to expect of them. The most obvious examples are the "phonemic" distinctions: speakers of one language hear and use the difference between *r* and *l*, or between nasalized and nonnasalized vowels, while speakers of other languages do not use them, cannot hear them dependably, and so ignore them. Another example first described a number of years ago that still receives attention these days is "cloze" testing, in which a person's strength in a language is measured by his or her ability to fill in blanks where words have been left out of paragraphs. To say that a person has "communicative competence" in a language/culture is to say that he or she has the same expectations as the lifelong members of the culture about what a person may try to do when, and about what means are appropriate for what ends, and so on.

But useful as expectations are, there are several ways in which my "expectations" can get me into trouble. First of all, my expectations may not always agree with one another. To take a simple and very trite example, someone may set an extra piece of pie in front of me. I can safely expect that if I eat it my taste buds will send me happy messages, but I may also expect that eating the pie will make me weigh more than I want to weigh. So my expectations pull against each other; whatever I do, whether I eat the pie or not, will contain those expectations within it and will be shaped by the conflict between them.

Conflicts are found in all parts of life, of course, and not just at the dinner table. If I write what I really think, I can look forward to a good feeling that comes from knowing that I have been straight with myself and with my readers. But I may also have reason to expect that saying what I mean will make some people turn away from me—people whom I do not want to lose.

There is no end to the examples we find in the foreign language classroom. I set some of them out in the second edition of *Memory, Meaning, and Method:* pronouncing the language well may please the teacher but lead my friends to feel I am disloyal to our native land and language; succeeding through methods that are different from and easier than what my first teachers used may leave me both feeling good and feeling that I have cheated someone and will soon have to pay for it; saying, in the foreign language, something that is important to me may be at the same time satisfying and risky. Even when the student does outwardly only what the teacher or the textbook or the tape tells her or him to do, these inner conflicts twist, in great ways or in small, her or his doing of it. We sometimes see this twisting literally in the microphone cords of language laboratories: I know of at least one university that went so far as to install worry beads in its booths, just to drain off the nervous energy that was causing nonmalicious damage to its equipment. Side remarks inadvertently recorded on the student tracks of lab tapes sometimes give us amusing, yet also sobering, glimpses into what is going on inside the student. But even when we cannot see the twisting, it is there: feelings, attitudes, and the conflicts among them are parts of the whole act of learning. *They are therefore stored in the networks of the student's long-term memory (Chapter 1), intertwined forever with the word or sentence or rule or paradigm that she or he has learned along with them.*

As I write, I see that the preceding paragraph is itself an example of conflicting purposes. Because it is about learning languages, I can hope that it will help to keep the attention of other people who may read this, most of whom I expect will be language teachers. At the same time, however, it may take a reader's mind away from the general groundwork that I am trying to lay for explaining what I think is at stake from the point of view of Counseling-Learning.

With this in mind, let's go back and look more carefully at two limitations of the S- and R-arrows in the Bloomfieldian diagram on page 5. For one thing, this diagram obscured the fact that what was coming through Jill's eyes and other sense organs was not just one simple "stimulus" to be represented by a single wire. What comes in from outside and impacts the inner resources is less like a single wire than it is like a cable with many strands representing the various senses.

The second point is more serious. Bloomfield considered himself a strict behaviorist and so he avoided terms like "mind." Whatever was in there, inside the head of a learner, was to him a "black box" into which we could not look with any hope of making valid, dependable observations. He therefore omitted any reference to the internal resources that receive and are shaped by the incoming S-arrows, and that enable, influence and limit the nature of the R-arrows. These resources appear in the diagram on page 13 as the big box with all the networks in it—as "long-term memory. He was even unwilling to recognize any such concept as "consciousness" in the self that interacts with its environment. For that reason, his diagram could make no provision for anything like what in Figure 3 on page 13 shows up as a "worktable," or for the vital two-way traffic between working memory and long-term memory. Some of this traffic carries messages that we're not even aware of. Furthermore, these non-conscious or peripheral messages may disagree among themselves. To say that someone "has got it all together" would be to say that all these messages are in harmony with one another. I don't suppose any human being ever "gets it together" 100 percent, or not for long anyway. Some people are closer to it than others, and each of us is closer to it at some times than at other times.

In any event, lack of harmony among the many parts of a living, acting self can keep that self from doing what it wants to do as well as it would like to; too much conflict within a self can bring real trouble, or may even tear the self apart. So the Self (if I may capitalize the word) instinctively abhors the chaos within and has a deep drive toward healing itself—toward making itself whole and harmonious. As I have said, it never completely succeeds at this, partly because it is a prisoner of those very same expectations that are in conflict with one another. Or it is like a woman trying to apply makeup without being able to see her face in a mirror.

But Becker showed us that the Self's drive to put itself into the best order it can has another and deeper source. It does not come *only* from the desire to do well whatever it wants to do. It is also more than just a wish to have fewer internal stresses and strains. We also have a strong need to feel that we are somehow consistent with the way things finally are (whether that "final reality" be what some traditional religion or other system of thought teaches, or whether it be the "reality" of materialism, or of humanism, or of nihilism).

"Spill and Spell": A Special Stake

Some years ago, I came across a game that caught, in a way that is easy to see, something of this inner drive to bring harmony into one's self, or to get the pieces of one's self to fit together. I think the game was called "Spill and Spell." It consisted of nothing but a plastic cup and a set of 15 dice. Instead of spots, each face of each die carried a letter of the alphabet. The first player puts the dice into the cup, shakes them, and spills them out onto a tabletop. The player than tries, within a limited period of time, to fit the dice together so as to spell words with as many as possible of whatever 15 letters came up. The words may cross each other as in a crossword puzzle or in Scrabble. Each letter scores a certain number of points when it is used, with the rarer letters scoring most and the very common letters counting least. Normally it will be impossible to use all 15 letters at once, so the player must decide which letters to leave aside.

It seems to me that this game is true to life in at least four ways. First, things seldom or never come out entirely even. Second, the choices that the player makes depend on what she thinks the rules are. If one religion, or one culture, or one philosophy, or one outlook on life says that the letter j is worth more than the letter z, and another says that z is worth more than j, then two players who follow different philosophies will make different decisions, and starting out with the same 15 letters they may end up with quite different configurations of words. Third, once a player has begun to build up one particular pattern of intersecting words, she would rather look for more words to fit into that pattern than start all over and try to use her limited stock of letters in an entirely new way, even though the new arrangement might turn out to be the first step toward an even higher score. Fourth, if a player does not know a particular word she cannot use it, but if she learns a new word, she then becomes able to use it. Fitting the new word into her configuration of words may take work, but it may also change her score upward or downward. The player must decide whether within the time she has left she is willing to do the work, and run the risk, that the new word would cost her. The worst outcome—the lowest score— would be if time ran out after a player had torn up one arrangement and before she was able to put a new one together. Life in this respect is harder than the game, because we never know how much time we have left.

What I have said so far, then, is this: that what each of us does (an R-arrow in Bloomfield's diagram) begins in the Self; that what looks like a simple act has many parts; some parts are physical movements of the body, other parts have to do with purposes, emotions, attitudes, expectations, and so forth; that each of these parts of an act has its roots in some part of the Self; that the various parts of the Self are more or less in harmony with one another; that the Self wants to organize its parts so that they work smoothly with one another, but that it never succeeds completely at this task and sometimes has real trouble with it. The Self is aware of some parts of many of these arrows, but some parts run beneath or outside conscious awareness.

As incoming information reaches the inner resources of a Self, much of it fits readily into the network of expectations that that Self has already put together. Some of the information, however, does not fit. Perhaps two things that the Self has always seen as alike now need to be treated as two different things: for example, a belief that all members of a given ethnic group act alike may not hold up if one is willing to look at what two or more members of that group actually do. Or, to take an example from language study, English speakers as long as they are speaking English do not need to hear the difference between the vowels in French *pur* and *pour.* But in using French, we need to reshape our expectations so that they will be able to handle that difference.

Other information, perhaps, does not fit because it says that the Self needs to give more weight to something than it has given to it in the past. In an everyday example, the Self may have been aware that regular visits to the dentist are important, but a visit after a lapse of three years may bring results that cause the Self to come back sooner to the dentist's office and more frequently in the years that follow. Here the Self is not asked to make a new distinction, but only to change the weight it gives to something it already knows about. A language example may be the speaker of a western European language who has distinguished all his life between masculine and feminine in *third* person pronouns, but who starts to learn Arabic or Hebrew and suddenly finds that those languages have separate masculine and feminine forms also in the *second* person. On another level, someone who has succeeded in a language by a certain approach may resist a program that asks her to abandon familiar formats and practices, and to follow a quite different approach.

Going back to the player of "Spill and Spell," when new information comes in it is as though someone had suddenly changed the game, either by adding new letters or by taking some letters away or by changing the number of points that each letter is worth. It is easy to understand why the player might become annoyed, might tell the other person to go away, or might try to pretend that the other person was not there at all.

A player of "Spill and Spell" needs to feel that he knows the rules and that at least some of the other players will give him credit for the words that he puts together by following those rules. If one part of his life tells him the rules are like this while another part tells him they are like that, and if he cannot in some way decide when to follow one set of rules and when the other, then he may with one sweep of his hand knock all of the dice onto the floor. Or if he knows the rules but sees that with his letters (e.g., G, Q, Q, V, V, V, X, Z) he can put together nothing that is acceptable by the rules, he may do the same thing. Even a player who has usable letters may fling the dice away if he cannot make a score that gives him the status he seeks with the other players. Here is a paragraph from a story by Michael Dobbs in the *Washington Post,* May 21, 1978:

> N____ was one of the most successful women in Hungary.
> She had a large circle of friends, ran a smart fashion salon in
> Budapest, and made frequent trips abroad. Last year she killed
> herself at age 70 by jumping from a high-rise apartment building.
> According to her family, the reason was that a pair of false teeth
> implanted in her gums had started to rot. For most people, that
> would not have been the end of the world. But for a woman who
> had made a highly successful career in the beauty business, it was
> impossible to bear.

By contrast, some players find that their arrangements of letters are valued even more highly than they had dared to hope, and are judged by exactly the rules they had been working by. Vice President Mondale said of Hubert Humphrey:

> In looking back over Hubert's life, it seems as though all the disappointments that were visited on him were suddenly settled in his favor in that last year, when everyone wanted him to know they appreciated what he had done for them and for their country.

I have already said that expectations are built into all levels of memory and of personhood. In those of our expectations that lie next to the rock on which our safety rests, we may find even the slightest changes to be unbearable. Here is the small child, whose bed is her best replacement for the womb, listening to a familiar bedtime story read by a parent, who is her all-powerful protector. She will object to, and correct, any syllable that strays from the original.

Because we are constantly interacting with what's outside us, we find that even if we do manage to "get it all together," we can't stop there. We have to *hold* "it" together against a steady stream of new inputs. We can do this by hiding from those inputs, or we can try to fight them off, or we can use them in a constant process of rebuilding our inner resources, our Self. This rebuilding takes work of course, but fighting the new arrows off takes work too, and so does hiding from them. Sometimes hiding may be the best way of reacting, and sometimes fighting back may be. Most often, perhaps, the best reaction would be to rebuild, but this may require more energy than hiding or fighting, in the short run at least. Furthermore, to change one's habitual reactions away from hiding or fighting and toward rebuilding is itself, on a deeper level, an act of rebuilding. What is it that determines which way we react in any given situation? I don't know, but this brings us to the next point.

From "Inside" to "Between"

Of course each person has her or his own unique inner resources and is subjected to a unique set of new inputs. When two people come together, therefore, we have two Selves. That is to say, we have two long-term memory boxes, two sets of expectations, two systems of values. Not least, we have two bodies, each with its own eyes, ears, and tongue, its own heart and lungs and arms and legs, its own will to go on living and to cheat various kinds of death.

So what comes out of one person's inner resources and is consistent with that person's expectations becomes a part of the new input to another Self into whose existing resources and expectations it may or may not fit. If it does not fit, then the second person will have to work either to fight it off, or to pretend that it is not there, or to rebuild his or her own system of expectations so as to make a place for the new input. This of course applies in both directions.

We all learn about this at a very early age. We learn that certain kinds of outputs from us will cause somebody to punish us, whether physically, or by turning her or his back on us or even by leaving us altogether. We also learn that other kinds of actions from us will force the other person to produce actions that fit in with our system as it already stands—or that some actions from us will at least keep the other person from actions that are troublesome for us. The other person has of course learned comparable things. Therefore when two people come together, each must decide how much of his or her self he or she had best hold back out of the sight of the other, and in general how to act so that the other will behave to fit his or her expectations. There may be a power struggle, and such a struggle may last for just a few seconds or may go on for years.

The English word *expectation* has two separate meanings, which in their effects on other people are quite different from each other. One kind of expectation is something that one thinks is likely to happen: "I expect it will rain tonight." The other kind places someone else under pressure to fulfill it: "I expect you to answer this question correctly (and you'd better not let me down!)" "I expect you to do the dishes before you watch television!" These expectations can be conveyed either with or without words. In a language class, the unspoken message, "I expect you to do well/get this right" may carry either the first kind of expectation or the second. The first lifts the student's spirits, while the second is a warning to the learner to defend herself. *To recognize and control this difference within his or her own behavior is one of the most delicate tricks a teacher can master, but it is also one of the most useful!*

What, then, can happen when I meet you? I may find many things that I know, and see, and perhaps would like to say, about which I've learned I must not talk to you. You likewise know that there are certain things about which it would be unwise to talk to me. So we are partly cut off from each other. There may be some things that I feel I must not talk about with anyone. I may feel this way because of something that happened many years ago between me and other people. So it is not only that I am cut off from you. Even worse than that, I feel that those parts of myself which I think others are not willing to look at or hear about are "bad," and I feel shame for them; I myself may not be able to look at them steadily; not being able to look at them, I am unable to deal with them, to set them right. In these parts of my life, I am lost; I am alone; I am cut off not only from other people, but even from myself. This is the first of three things that happen when people meet one another: We may hide from each other.

The second thing that may happen is the opposite. Instead of hiding from you, I may use whatever strength I have and whatever cunning to get you to act in ways that will tell the world, and will tell me, that my system of expectations is right and good and worthy of being held by all people. Perhaps you will yield to me altogether and set about rebuilding your own acts, your own habits, your own system of expectations, so that they will fit what I seem to want. Or perhaps you will fight back, using your own strength and your own cunning to reshape me just as I have been trying to reshape you. Or finally, you may be careful to put out R-arrows that you think will not displease me, yet without really changing your inner self. To do this, somewhere inside you you must build for yourself a little model of what you think I want from you. Moreover, you must give to this little model a place within your own inner resources. But the shape of this foreign model will not agree with your basic self, and so the two will rub and pull against each other. After some time, the two may become more like each other so that one of them or both of them have changed. Or perhaps they go on forever chafing and pulling at each other. Then the actions that they put out may show the effects of that conflict.

There are many ways in which we lay our expectations onto one another.

Direct orders and open criticism are only the most obvious. If a student says he is discouraged at the end of the first week, and if I tell him, "There, there! You shouldn't feel that way!" I am laying my own expectation onto him. If in explaining the formation of the past tense I use a tone of voice that says, "Now, always remember. . . !" I'm doing the same thing. If I give someone a suggestion about how to get rid of her headache, and then an hour later ask if her headache is better, I'm probably more interested in vindicating my own suggestion than I am in her physical state. A driver who follows too close behind the car ahead of him along a road where there is no possibility of passing is using a nonverbal way of laying his expectations on the other person. Compare also the knowing, reproachful fluttering of eyelids by the actress in a television commercial, as she informs us that she takes a patent diet supplement "*every day*—and so should you!"

But interactions don't always bring disagreement and conflict. Sometimes one person's acts become exactly the kind of thing another person needs in order to fill out what is missing within his or her own inner configuration. In the physical realm, sexual attraction may provide examples of this. In the realm of food and eating, Jack Sprat and his wife are an instance from folklore. If a person who very much needs to see his or her own solution of the "Spill and Spell" puzzle confirmed by how faithfully other people copy it meets someone whose inner self has been a howling wasteland crying out for order, then each may find in the other exactly what he or she had been looking for. In all of the examples I've mentioned in this paragraph—sexual attraction, dietary complementation, the relationship of guru and disciple, (and in other similar relationships)—the people who are involved may describe their relationship by saying that they "love" each other. If a third person comes along and tries to break the partners away from each other, they will fight that third person, and in this fighting they will do things beyond what they or anyone else would have thought them able or willing to do. Likewise if one of the partners turns away from the other, terrible things may happen. By the very fact that this other person had shared so fully and so deeply my cherished configuration, I find it all the more frightening to watch that person go off and leave me, and see her or him succeed in getting along without what the two of us had once agreed was both good and necessary. All of us, being human, need and use and appreciate from other human beings the kind of support that I've been talking about. But insofar as we depend on that kind of support, what we call "loving" and "being loved" can become clutching and holding and controlling.

In life seen in this way, then, the acts of one person may become for another person an input that is welcome and helpful, or unwelcome and unhelpful, or welcome but unhelpful, or unwelcome but helpful. When should one act, and when hold oneself back? In a religious or ecclesiastical context, this is the question of the ethics of evangelism:

> *The impatient gate, that swings both in and out,*
> *Whose work is lost when no one passes through;*
> *The faithful fence, that marks off false from true—*
> *No time for hanging back, no room for doubt—*

Exist, not in the world, but in the mind.
Yet God forgive if what is there for me
I either hide, or try to press on thee,
To shout thee deaf, or leave thee lost and blind.

This dreadful choice sets brother against brother,
Either to injure, or to fail each other.

This same dilemma is equally present in contexts which are not religio-ecclesiastical. So we organize our existence and institutionalize it against the dread of these choices, and against the dread of chaos and oblivion. Society then consists of:

chain-link lives
twisted tight,
even, stout,
to keep Us
In,
Them and It
Out.

("It," I suppose, is the chaos, oblivion, and knowledge of death about which I have been writing.)

In life, of course, we "play Spill and Spell" on many different levels at once. We may challenge, and even break up, one another's configurations, and we may do so on one or more of these levels. Thus you may call into question the *words* I have spoken, or the *deeds* I have done. Or you may attack the *purpose* that I had in my speaking or acting. Deeper still, you may say (or show without saying it) that in your eyes the *kind of person* who would give himself or herself to these purposes of mine has no worth—that the world would be better off without such people. Any of these attacks may frighten me into hiding or fighting, or it may not. What I do will depend on where I feel secure and where I do not. When I have that stillness at the center, then I see that all these games of "Spill and Spell" are only games, and that I, the player, stand outside them. Then you may do your worst: you may prove my words wrong, you may show that my purposes work against each other, you may even cast scorn upon the kind of person I have tried to be, and I can still "understand" you. When I do not have that stillness, then if you attack my purposes I need to have you tell me that you still see worth in the kind of person I am. Otherwise I may panic. When I am not sure within myself about the kind of person I have chosen to be, then if you attack my words or criticize my deeds, I need to believe that you at least agree with my purpose. And if I am not at one with myself even in my purposes, all I have to hold onto is your approval of my words and deeds. Then if you do not take and use my words, if you do not praise my deeds, I feel great threat. I may run away, or fly at you, or fly apart.

1 *Think about the following questions and, if possible, discuss them with colleagues.*

- When in your own experiences with other cultures (or with other parts of your own culture—a new campus or new in-laws, for example) have you run into trouble or embarrassment by failing to make a distinction that was taken for granted there?

- When did the same groups disappoint you or appall you by their failure to make a distinction that you had been taking for granted they would make?

2 *Write a note or short letter (50-100 words) to the author about this book. Include the words "For me, at least. . ." or some equivalent.*

- Where are your expectations of this sort of book reflected in what you wrote?

- Where are your expectations of the author's possible reactions reflected in what you wrote *or in what you left unwritten, or in how you wrote it?*

b. Exchange papers with another reader and answer the same two questions about what the other person has written.

c. Draft a reply from the author to the other person.

- How does this reply reflect (your expectations of) the author's expectations of what the writer of the note might be willing to accept?

- To what extent are your expectations of the other reader's readiness or unreadiness to accept certain replies parallel to your own readiness or unreadiness?

3 *Assign numerical weightings from 1 to 6 to these six letters on the faces of a die used in the "Spill and Spell" of language teaching:*

a. The students work in an orderly manner.

b. The class shows up well on standardized tests.

c. My students like me.

d. They and I feel a healthy exhaustion at the end of a session.

e. They and I feel relaxed and rested at the end of a session.

f. The students show frequent spontaneity in what they do.

THE "UNDERSTANDING RESPONSE": A POWERFUL TOOL

The last paragraph of the preceding section depicts a state of affairs that I have observed all too often in dealing with learners and teachers of foreign languages, including me, over the years. It is a state that is a constant source of "clutter for the worktable," of lost time, of misdirected effort, and of emotional stress. As a remedy for this state, Curran proposed a special relationship characterized by an unusual degree of "understanding," and as a means for building and maintaining that relationship, he trained teachers in a form of disciplined attention that he usually called the "counseling response." In this chapter, however, I will use a more descriptive term that Curran also used: the "understanding response". The remainder of this chapter will be devoted to that topic.

Knowledge about this attention and this relationship, often under some such name as "active" or "reflective listening," is more widespread now than it was in 1980. I have included it here because many readers of *A Way and Ways* seemed to profit from it, and because it has been of immense value in many parts of my own life other than language teaching. What follows (pp. 102–110) is a first-hand account written not by a professional counselor, but by a language teacher (EWS) who had recently learned some of the skill.

How this kind of response is unlike ordinary conversation

In "understanding" as in normal conversation, there is a constant stream of what in the Jill and Jack story of Chapter 1 I called "R-arrows" (i.e., responses) from the person who is being understood becoming "S-arrows" (i.e., stimuli) for the person who is doing the understanding (the "understander"), and back again from the understander to the person being understood. In the process, each person's inner resources are being constantly changed. But "understanding" is unlike normal conversation in at least five ways.

First, the understander sees himself and the person being understood in a special way. Someone once gave me a quotation from Rainer Maria Rilke that puts into words the difference between two kinds of "love." He said that, "Once the realization is accepted that even among the closest human beings infinite distances continue to exist, a wonderful living side by side can grow up, if they succeed in loving the distance between them which makes it possible for each to see the other whole against the sky."

The heart of this sentence lies in the way Rilke sets next to each other the words "closest" and "infinite distances." In our everyday use of these words, both of them cannot be true at the same time concerning the same two people. In saying that they cannot be, and yet are, true at the same time, Rilke is trying to lift us out of our everyday reality, for our everyday reality is full of the same hiding and fighting and controlling and holding on that I have already described. In everyday reality, we have no way of knowing others, or of being known, except through those same the S- and R-arrows of the Jill and Jack diagram. These lines are the tubes through which we have been nourished, the cables through which we have received the messages that have shown us how to grow into whatever we are, and the messages also which reassure us day by day that we are who we think we are. But what we do not always see is that these lines are not merely threads that are all that keeps us from a fall into nothingness. To put the same thought into other words, if Jill is lucky, she may someday see, for an hour or for a minute, that she is more than just a place where R———►S lines and S———►R lines converge. She has her own being, and if she has her own being, then Jack may likewise have a being of his own. Looking at Jill now as an "understander" rather than as a language learner, when she sees Jack (as the person being understood) and herself in this light, then she becomes able to treat him in a new way. The S- and R-arrows have not disappeared. They are still there but now they are no longer as they were before, because Jill's inner resources are no longer as they were before. Now the word "love" (in a nonromantic sense) can take on a new and deeper meaning. In this new relationship, a person being understood may in his turn see what the understander has seen—see himself as partaking in, yet at the same time free of, the web of S- and R-arrows; he may know he has been loved, and so he may know that love is possible. With this vision comes a stillness to which great philosophers and spiritual teachers have through all ages borne their witness. Only, I think, from within the stillness can the vision turn itself to flesh and blood—to R-arrows that carry the vision to another human being. It can be bedrock upon which is built great teaching regardless of method.

I think Rilke is telling us here, if we can understand it (and I would not claim I understand it completely), that something is possible that a series of mechanically-generated S- and R-arrows cannot account for. Although the understander and the other person are in close, perhaps intimate communication with each other, still each one has her or his own wholeness, her or his own worth, which is unlike the wholeness and worth of any other person and is independent of any other person. It is this view of the person being understood, *and also of her- or himself,* that enables the understander to listen, without turning a deaf ear, to anything that the person being understood says, and without judging it as good or bad, and without trying to reshape what comes from the person being understood into a pattern that comes out of the understander's own private set of expectations, needs, and desires.

A second difference from ordinary conversation is that as she listens, the understander tries to form in her own mind a picture of the Self of the person being understood, or at least a picture of that part that that person has shown to her. As I said earlier, a picture or a model within the understander's Self is not in a watertight bag. There is a real chance that some part of it will leak out and make changes within the understander. But in the stillness that I talked about earlier, and in the knowledge that she is who she is and belongs to herself, the understander can take that risk without hiding or fighting back. (Since no human being is in perfect stillness all of the time, it would be more accurate to say that *insofar* as we have that stillness and self-steadiness, to that degree we will be able to be open and nondefensive in our listening.)

We are all familiar with how hard it is to listen to—or to talk about—certain drastically painful topics. One of a group of teen-aged cancer patients reported that "When they told me I had Hodgkin's disease, . . . they never said the word cancer. Then one day I looked the disease up in the encyclopedia and saw the word cancer, and I nearly fell over. It was six months before anyone else said the word." But as a language teacher I can remember brushing aside much less serious things that my students were trying to tell me simply because what they were telling me would have caused me pain or inconvenience. Perhaps I was not always wrong to do so: each of us has a limit on what he can carry. But I *did* turn away.

In this kind of "understanding" also (and this is the third difference), much of what the understander says has as its purpose to be certain that the understander's *picture* of what the other person is saying really does fit what that person *is* saying. That is at the heart of this kind of "understanding" for at least two reasons. First, as in ordinary conversation, there is no use in two people talking about two different things when they think they are talking about the same thing; that only leads to wasting time and to frustration. So the understander needs to check out her own understanding by telling the person being understood what she thinks she is hearing.

Some people, however, have gotten the idea that in this so-called reflective listening the understander simply repeats or paraphrases the other person's words. If that were true, then this sort of "understanding" would be nothing but a technique, and a rather superficial one at that. (Curran himself was quite emphatic on this point.) When I am trying to give this sort of understanding, however, I find that most of my words are descriptions of whatever has been taking shape in my mind. The words of the other person serve me first as a source for (much of) that picture. The paraphrasing of words into other words plays only a secondary role.

But there is another reason for "reflective listening" that is even more important than verifying what the other person is saying. When the other person feels that the understander has truly understood him and yet has not turned away in boredom or disgust or tried to change him, then he feels less cut off. He is not alone. He sees that he is not, or does not appear, unworthy, foolish, ugly, horrible as he had feared.

This holding back, this self-discipline on the part of the understander, is the fourth way in which this kind of "understanding" is unlike the conversation of a sympathetic, solicitous friend. The "understander" avoids criticizing what the other person says, of course. But she is equally careful to keep from agreeing with it or praising it or trying to solve the other person's problems. To do either would be to put herself into the position of a judge. The other person, perhaps without knowing it, would then try to please that judge, or try to overthrow her, or both. In any case, the other person could no longer work and speak out of his own wholeness, which is unlike the wholeness of any other person. Instead, he would become entangled in the web of the *understander's* expectations.

The fifth and last point has to do with the understander's own contributions to the conversation. A person who is trying to give this kind of understanding holds back from asking questions, and from telling about her own experiences, and from making suggestions. Again, the reason is that she has faith in the other person's ability, working freely within his own wholeness, to come up with what he needs. Questions, suggestions, or the understander's own experiences would only lay onto the other person the understander's own expectations; which is to say that it would be like pulling the other person into the understander's world and asking him to conform to it.

What the understander is trying to do is in fact exactly the opposite. She is trying to see the other person's world through that other person's eyes, without reaching into it and changing it. If she can do that, she can then reflect that world back to the other person. In doing so, she uses a very special kind of R-arrow. She tells the other person what facts and what feelings she sees in that world, but the understander's own *feelings* as they come through on this kind of communication do not copy, and do not react against, the *feelings* that she sees in the world of the person being understood. For example, she does not weep with one who is weeping. If the person being understood is angry with her, she does not become angry or defensive or conciliatory in return. She talks *about* the other person's feelings, but the feelings that she herself sends out are *whatever kind of support is appropriate to the situation.*

But to say that in this kind of "understanding" the understander holds herself back, or to say that she does not react directly in the usual way to the feelings of the person being understood, is not to say that she is just an uninvolved observer. On the contrary, the understander is involved with the other person *more* deeply than is usual in normal conversation. This brings us back to the paradox in the Rilke quotation: infinite distance in greatest intimacy.

---

4 *For thought, comparison, and discussion: Look again at the introduction to Chapter 4. On page 49, Investigations task 2 asked: "In your experiences as a teacher or learner of languages, have you ever felt 'mere' in the eyes of someone else? In your own eyes? In what respects?" The task there was to focus on the experiences themselves. This time, using the same or other recollections, narrate your experience to one other member of your group, limiting yourself to no more than three minutes. The role of the other person will to be to give understanding responses. At the end of the narration, focus your discussion on the responses themselves in the light of pages in the earlier part of this chapter.*

Investigations

Effects of This Kind of Response

Teachers' Voices

When the communication of the understander follows these rules, then the new S-arrow that the other person receives is also unlike most. Because the emotional tone of the understander's communication is neutral and supportive, the person being understood does not have to defend himself from it. He is therefore free to hear more clearly what the understander is saying, and to see how it fits together. It is as though he is trying to straighten out a bureau drawer that is completely full, with no way of leaving some of the contents outside the drawer for a short time so he can sort them out and rearrange the other things in the drawer. In this metaphor, the understander is providing the person being understood with a table top on which he can lay out some of the things that have been all tangled in together, and untangle them, and sort them out, and see them in a new and clearer way, and decide what he wants to do with them. He recognizes the same *facts* that he had been describing to the understander; but he also finds that his own *feelings* are coming back to him from what the understander has seen and heard of his feelings. And all of these facts, as they are carried in the understander's communication, are accompanied by the understander's own feelings of nonjudgmental, unquestioning, supportive interest. In another figure of speech, the understander is providing a rack on which the person being understood can hang some of his mildewed clothing in the sunshine and fresh air for a while.

After being listened to in this way, a person being understood often finds that he is "hearing himself better" than he had before. He may feel less cut off, not only from the understander and not only from the rest of the outside world, but even from himself. He may still have the same basic feelings that he started out with, but his *feelings about those feelings* may be less bad. The fresh air may take away some of the mildew. And it is often those feelings-about-feelings that had led into the vicious circle that left the person being understood feeling cut off, a prisoner of his own uniqueness. Another of the teenage cancer patients tells us, "People with cancer don't want you to talk. They want you to know what they have to say. They want someone who lets them talk about what it's like." Again, the examples in language classes are less dramatic. But I remember clearly how much better I felt, *and* how much more easily I learned, in a demonstration class in Chinese after someone successfully "understood" how I felt about the study of tones.

As a representative of the outside world, then, the understander has power over the person being understood, either to tighten the circle around him, or to make a little break in it. Through using this power, she can reward the person being understood or punish him, and so shape what the person being understood does, and even what he thinks. It is therefore important the understander not use her power in order to sell the other person life insurance, or change his religion, or otherwise exploit him. But even in a nonexploitative relationship, the understander's choice of words and images can lead the other person subtly, therefore compellingly. The good understander needs to watch out lest in this way she distort what the other person is saying.

If I may oversimplify the picture of the arrows, the understander communicates to the person being understood through two channels: most obviously through words, but also through body posture, facial expression, tone of voice, and so forth. It would be misleading to say that the word channel carries what the understander has understood and nothing else; or that the other—the nonverbal—channel carries the understander's attitudes and nothing else. Certainly the main use of the word channel is to carry, and to verify, what the understander has heard. At the same time, however, subtle choices of words or of phrasing—the kind of thing that would show up even in a typewritten transcript of the conversation—can also carry hints about how the understander feels toward the person being understood and what the person being understood has said.

In much the same way it is true that the main use of the nonverbal channel is to carry the feelings of the understander. At the same time, however, it can be used in very specific ways, which can let the person being understood know that the understander is following in detail what he is staying. On two occasions when the situation was one in which I was not permitted to speak, I have—with apparent success—conveyed understanding through the nonverbal channel for periods of over 15 minutes. This is quite different from just sitting silent with a benign look on one's face. (Someone did that to me last week, for just 5 minutes, and I found it unsettling.) Normally, of course, the understander uses both channels at once.

Nevertheless, if I had a choice between bungling the verbal or the nonverbal side of communication with someone to whom I was trying to give this kind of "understanding," I would without hesitation choose to get the nonverbal part right and let the words go. The words are the precise lines of a fine pen, but the nonverbal communication is the surface on which they are drawn.

---

5 *Here's an exercise that works especially well with groups of three to five people, though it can be done with just two.*

- Take a moment to imagine yourself into the situation described by "Aggie" or "Carl" or one of the other voices we heard in Chapters 1, 2, and 3. Or you can think of a student with whom you have worked in the past or are currently working.

- Play the role of that person as she or he tells a study adviser (played by a colleague) about it. Talk for at least a minute, filling in details that may be absent from the printed account. The "study adviser" will offer understanding responses, but at this time will withhold any actual advice. (Any other members of the group just listen and make notes.)

- At the end of no more than 3 minutes, break off the interview and discuss your reaction to the "adviser's" responses, and their effects on you. (Did you in fact feel understood, or not? What was there in the "understander's" words or manner that contributed to this feeling?) In this step, it's generally better to let the role-player speak first, followed by the "understander," and finally to invite comments from any observers.

- Then switch roles and repeat the exercise.

When to avoid and when to use this kind of response

I have said that the supportive nonverbal communication from the understander should be of "whatever kind is appropriate" to the situation in which the two people find themselves. Some of us first learned this kind of listening by watching psychological understanders plying their trade, and then trying to imitate them in our practice sessions with each other. This worked very well while we were in training. It also worked very well outside of the training institutes, with colleagues, students, friends, and family *as long as* there was a clear agreement, spoken or unspoken, that this was what the other person wanted: that she welcomed, for the time being at least, a series of responses from an understanding person that consisted of little or nothing except reflections of what she had said, and that carried with them feelings of warmth, acceptance, and support. We found that by responding in this manner to people who wanted us to respond in this manner, we could often be helpful in ways that had been closed to us before.

This new skill was not only helpful to our friends and students, however. It at the same time opened to us new and deep sources of satisfaction. I can remember three such sources especially. Most obvious was the feeling of having been helpful. Alongside that was seeing that the people to whom we had given this simple help often had good feelings toward us: warmth, gratitude, admiration, and the like. Not least was the pure joy of craftsmanship: like an artist who has caught a likeness truly, or a bowler who has just made a difficult spare. For all of these reasons, I'm afraid we sometimes acted like the child who received a new carpenter set for Christmas, and who went around pounding nails into the piano and sawing the leg off the dining table. We looked for every opportunity to do this kind of "understanding," whenever anyone expressed anything but the simplest fact. We did so even though we had been clearly told that this sort of understanding relationship would probably take up no more than 10 to 20 percent of our daily activities. I'm quite sure that we never did anyone any damage in this way—one of the things that I like about this kind of "understanding" is that it does not push, or probe, or tell people what to do, or look for emotional blisters that it can lance. But we did every now and then make our chosen "person-being-understood" pretty annoyed with us.

I can remember two kinds of annoyance that came up more than once. The first was that we were trying to work some kind of psychological trick—to play psychiatrist with them. This made them feel manipulated, and nobody likes to feel that way. The other annoyance arose from the fact that in this kind of "understanding" the understander gives himself entirely to hearing what the other person is saying, and reflecting it back faithfully. A person who is "understood" in this way for a long time without wanting it may begin to feel that the understander is holding himself out of sight, or that he is even running away from her. (And I suppose it is true that this kind of "understanding" can be used for that purpose.) At any rate, the people who trained us had warned us that "understanding without a contract" could get us into trouble, and they were right.

At the same time, we also saw people react in exactly the opposite way. A person who had been "understood" for three or four sentences, even without a contract, might flash a "hurt" look if the person who had been "understanding" her suddenly began to talk about his own related ideas, or to offer advice, according to the conventions of ordinary conversation.

So while I accepted the rule against "understanding without a contract," I could not get away from the idea that skill in this kind of disciplined understanding had a place outside of the "understanding contract," and that my reasons for feeling this way went beyond my personal needs to receive gratitude and to have a sense of craftsmanship.

I have gone off on this detour about how some of us used and overused our "understanding" skills because I think that what happened to us sheds light on the kind of feelings that the understander should send to the person being understood. We were taught that the "understander" should show "warmth, acceptance, and support," and we also picked up, without anybody telling us to, a sort of professional, consulting-room air that sometimes came across fairly plainly. For people who had asked for this kind of understanding, the faintly professional "warmth, acceptance, and support" proved to be reassuring and clearly welcome. It was appropriate to the setting. To others, it could be objectionable. In their situations it was inappropriate. In some situations, an appropriate feeling is intense personal interest in the factual side of what the person being understood is saying. In some situations, it is appropriate to agree, to commiserate, even to raise objections. All of these were discouraged (and with good reason) by those who trained us in the formal "understanding" relationship. They also discouraged us from taking the center of the stage and telling stories about our own experiences or our sufferings. Yet I have found that telling the person I was "understanding" such things about myself can be highly appropriate and effective, *provided* that the story is not too long, and *provided also* that the end of my story *ties back in* to where the other person had left off.

In his last, posthumous book, Curran made it especially clear that "understanding" is not just a form of "spiritual soothing syrup." The "understander" does not spend all of her time in understanding the other person. She sometimes takes a stand of her own. When she is "understanding," she may occasionally sandwich in a bit of "standing," i.e., taking a stand of her own. When she is "standing," by the same token, she may sandwich in a bit of "understanding." But one of the skills that a good understander offers to a client is the ability to serve these two roles as the bread and meat of a sandwich. By contrast, the well-meaning friend who is listening sympathetically but without this skill is likely to flit back and forth haphazardly between "standing" and "understanding." The result is less like a sandwich and more like hash. It destroys the clearness and cleanness that can be so welcome to an anxious person who is being "understood."

When the understander does take a stand of her own, she may simply express her own views. Or she may force the other person to come face to face with how what he does and what he has said contradict each other. She may even engage in "creative destruction," just as a dentist may drill a hole in the patient's tooth to take out what is rotten in order to fill the tooth and save it. The dentist does not passively accept the patient's teeth as they are, or merely reflect an x-ray picture of them back to the patient. On the other hand, he is careful to be certain, before he begins work, that he has seen the patient's teeth *as they actually are*. As he works, he watches the patient carefully to see where the areas of pain are, and to be sure that the pain does not become too great. So the skilled "understander" moves back and forth between "understanding" and taking stands of her own. "Destruction" can be "creative" only when the person being understood is in the fourth or fifth stage of relationship with the understander (Chapter 5). Otherwise it will be truly destructive, and therefore irresponsible on the part of the understander.

All of this is true when the understander is in the role of therapist. But I am finding that it is equally true in any ordinary conversation except the most trivial: people want a certain amount of opinion, or narration, or whatever, from me (or from you or from anyone else), but if they get too much, they soon begin to feel crowded, annoyed, resentful. So the understander needs her skill on two levels: first, to hear what the other person is saying; second, to see when the other person needs that first kind of understanding, and when he needs something else. But there is yet a third level: the understander needs to be aware of her own needs, her own interests, and her own resources. Being aware of them, she does not entirely keep them out of the picture; rather, she draws on them and controls them, both while she is "understanding" and while she is "standing for herself." I concur with Kathleen Graves' suggestion [private communication] that "understanding (via understanding responses) is the way Curran sees a teacher (and learners) in Counseling-Learning responding to the conflicting expectations that we have of ourselves and the conflicting expectations others have of us."

So the second kind of "love"— the kind that Rilke was talking about—is as simple as the paradox of closeness and infinite distance. At the same time it is complex, because putting that kind of love into action must be done with sensitivity on several levels at once. There may be a few people who do this instinctively, but many who think they do so are (in my experience) not fully aware of how they are coming across to the people they are "understanding." Most of us can profit from systematic practice followed by frank feedback from the persons we are trying to "understand."

What I have said about this kind of "understanding" is then just an elaboration of three points I made in Chapter 5: That *we* should try to *see and hear* the other person as he or she is, without turning away, without fighting back, and without trying to control him or her; that we need to *believe* that the other person has the desire and wisdom to pursue clarity and harmony; and that we ourselves should then try to *speak and act* in ways consistent with what we see and believe.

Looking back now, I find myself asking whether one can become very adept at giving understanding unless one deeply understands the need for understanding; and whether one can understand this need unless one accepts its existence within oneself; and whether, as one understands more deeply the need for understanding, one feels more pain when it is withheld, whether from others or from oneself.

6 *After what I have said in the previous section about the kind of "understanding" that is so integral a part of Counseling-Learning, it is probably evident that to try to teach anyone this skill in a few simple exercises would inevitably be misleading. In my experience, such brief, disconnected-from-principles exposures only reinforce the all-too-prevalent notion that a teacher's effectiveness is largely determined by the size of his or her "bag of tricks." Therefore in hope of being more helpful and preserving the authenticity of my representations of this powerful way of relating with students, I've decided just to focus on a few of the objections that have reappeared over time. Each in its own way helps to shed light on some of the misunderstandings of the "understanding response" that are in circulation.*

Here then are four objections (labeled A, B, C, and D) that one sometimes hears in reference to the kind of "understanding" that is so integral a part of Counseling-Learning. Work in pairs or in groups of three or four. One member of the group begins by voicing one of these objections, and another member tries to answer it in terms of his or her own understanding of Curran's position. After three to five minutes of exchange, get out of the attacker-defender roles and discuss the issue from a neutral point of view. At the end of this exercise [and not before!] you may wish to peek at my comments (below) for a brief indication of some of the points I would probably keep in mind as I answered.

A. "Why all this concern for 'security' anyway? It's quite possible to get along with people even when they're making you feel a little insecure—or when you're making them feel insecure, for that matter. In everyday life, in fact, this is the norm, not the exception. Why is a language classroom any different?"

B. "You can be more helpful to a person—even a person in trouble—by interacting with him or her normally than by backing off and subjecting the person to some kind of methodical, self-conscious, artificial 'understanding'!"

C. "As a result of all this 'understanding' the 'understander-teacher' receives a mass (and a mess!) of information about the students' feelings and other reactions. This information may be digestible and usable for a demonstration like the one we read about in Chapter 5. But over the days and weeks of a real course, it is inevitably going to accumulate and lead to progressive complications upon complications, and this is going to leave everybody confused and bewildered. Students may actually wind up even more insecure and demoralized than the students in a conventional course!"

D. "Since this kind of listening originated in the field of psychology, if we do it as teachers aren't we just practicing amateur therapy without a license and aren't we in danger of violating a person's private world?"

My Comments

A. Some of the ideas out of which I might put together my reply to Objection A are:

- The most obvious reason for being considerate of the feelings of those entrusted to one's care is that that's what we're supposed to do. As scrawny little Pansy Yokum used to explain to Li'l Abner after she had subdued the latest villains with her bare fists, "You see, son, Good is stronger than Evil because it's *nicer*!" I think this is part of what the speaker in (A) is questioning.

- There's a large difference in productivity between groups that are working under duress and inner conflict, and what is accomplished by groups working in harmony and with high morale. You can slice bananas with a dull knife, but to slice oranges you need to keep the blade sharp.

- Yes, I do think there's something special about the learning of a language as contrasted with renting an apartment or applying for a job. (a) Language learning is by definition the pairing of forms and meanings in new ways. (b) This takes place within the learner's brain. (c) As we saw in Chapters 1 and 5, learning goes best and lasts longest when the meanings are rich, deep, and subtle. (d) What will be actually present in the learner's working memory depends largely on affective factors.

B. My basis for responding to Objection B includes:

- To a large extent I agree with the statement. But the "understanding" attitude needs to be a genuine part of the teacher or other person who is doing the understanding, and so does the inner discipline that will enable the understander to maintain this special style of interaction. Then it's no longer "methodical, self-conscious, or artificial."

- And remember that if "normally" means "in the usual manner," normal interaction is frequently self-centered, often unpleasant, even destructive.

C. For Objection C, I would keep in mind:

This objection points out a real danger in an overly-simple copying of the format of a brief demonstration of CLL, trying in effect to repeat that demonstration indefinitely. There is however a difference between on the one hand (a) giving learners the impression that they're responsible for planning the learning experience, and that the knower is supposed to bend to their every expressed need or complaint; or on the other hand (b) making clear by deeds that while the knower is still a teacher, in charge of decisions as to what to do next and how to organize activities, he or she hears and in one way or another takes into account what is going on with the learners.

D. Concerning Objection D:

Objection D raises two very important issues. The first is "practicing therapy without a license," and the second with violations of privacy. Let me consider them one at a time.

During the influenza epidemic of 1918, my mother was one of many young women who took a course in home nursing. There she was trained to recognize common symptoms such as fever or swelling, to deal with those symptoms in simple ways, and to know when to call for the intervention of nurses or doctors more skilled than she was. She also picked up simple skills like bandaging and keeping wounds clean, and how to maintain a home environment that would minimize the risk of common hazards such as food poisoning or upper respiratory infection or transmission of communicable diseases. These skills stayed with my mother ever after, and contributed to a healthy home life for our family long after the influenza epidemic itself was past.

I can't imagine anyone accusing my mother of "practicing medicine without a license," even though the principles she followed and the techniques she used were derived from medical science and taught to her by medical professionals. If on the other hand she had taken it upon herself to decide whether someone had pneumonia or just a bad case of the flu, or if she had distributed prescription drugs freely to anyone displaying this or that symptom for which doctors *sometimes* prescribed it, she would have been out of line. I do think that some teachers may be disposed to get carried away with their heady, close-up exposure to working psychotherapists. For such teachers, the first half of Objection D is indeed a useful reminder to keep their new skills in perspective.

As for the "personal space" concern, I can accept it too as a valuable warning. The importance of personal investment—of personal involvement—in what is being said is a major theme of this book. Anyone who witnesses even a moderately successful demonstration of Counseling-Learning will see this principle dramatically vindicated. What more easily escapes notice, however, is the sensitivity with which the knower-teacher *enables* personal data to emerge rather than pressuring learners to "share" them. In the birth analogy that Curran used so often, it's like assisting at a normal delivery, and not at all like performing a C-section.

It is also impressive to a newcomer to be present as strong emotions accompanying personal data express themselves openly and are dealt with in a wholesome way by the knower-teacher. This again can be pretty heady stuff, and might tempt some teachers to tease out emotions, tears, and the like just for the excitement and the feeling of power that they the teachers hope to derive from dealing with them. I once was a member of a Saturday-morning training session on something or other in which the trainer seemed bent on "finding emotional boils to lance," and the results were of the kind that the writer of Objection D is warning against. I'm happy to say that that person had never been trained by Curran or any of his associates. Certainly the same warning applies to Counseling-Learning, however.

8

THE SILENT WAY: BASIC IDEAS

What in you is educable?

The weather outside the open windows was sunny, fresh and full of possibilities, and the tone of our meeting matched the day—almost. If it just hadn't been for that one fellow sitting over by the wall who kept making discordant noises! Finally someone said, "All right, Dr. Gattegno, after lunch we'll all get together in the library and you tell us about the Silent Way."

And so we did, seating ourselves in a large circle with our doctoral degrees on our sleeves. The twelve of us were together for two days of nothing but creative thinking. Our task was to design a brand new kind of program for a Master of Arts in Teaching Languages, one whose graduates would not only control a variety of methods and approaches but would know firsthand what was behind them—who would be able not only to apply what they had learned in the past, but also to see what they needed to learn from the future and to learn it without further help from us. So the morning had been exhilarating, all except for the unsettling reactions of the man who faced us now. The leader said, "Well, Dr. Gattegno, what is the 'Silent Way'?"

There were several long seconds of silence, broken by a five-word question from Gattegno. His question was: "What in you is educable?"

For perhaps a minute nobody said anything. Finally someone ventured some kind of answer, which was immediately shot down in flames by a few words from Gattegno. And so the session continued, the pauses getting longer and the answers more thoughtful, but always with the same result. As the hour came to an end someone asked, "We give up, Dr. Gattegno. You tell us. What in us is educable?"

Gattegno waited a few seconds for the question to reestablish itself in our consciousness. Then he said, "The only thing in you that is educable is your awareness." We thanked him out of politeness, but as we resumed our exciting work back in the main house, I suspect we'd all pretty much put him out of our minds.

Caleb Gattegno liked to compare himself with Kipling's Cat Who Walked By Himself—a maverick, as we would say. His great achievement was a "Science of Education" that was in reality a comprehensive approach to all of living. What is called "the Silent Way" is only the application of that science to the learning and teaching of foreign languages. As we will see, the light Gattegno casts on the question "What's at stake?" comes from an angle almost 90° from Curran's.

Gattegno's name is not one of the most widely cited in our field. (When asked why his work wasn't better known, he sometimes responded, "My mother used to say, 'Truth has short legs!'") Nevertheless, his work has enabled some people to attain amazing results. One teacher who used his approach to teaching native-language reading reported:

> **Alice Mick:** "Larry" was most noticeable at the beginning of the year because he stuttered so badly it was difficult to understand what he was saying and because he reacted to any request with a firm, "No, that's impossible. I can't do it." Four months later he reads comfortably, and "I can't do it" has become a joke which he throws out only as a matter of form.

Similarly a district administrator who visited a first grade class learning arithmetic according to Gattegno's approach commented:

> **Alan White:** While the most advanced group of [first-grade] children in my school was still working on 7+8= ? there were four youngsters in [this] class who were reading and solving problems like: "If a tractor tracks at a speed of 18 mph and goes for 3 hours, how far will it go?"

I've observed comparable results with foreign languages, and even obtained a few of them myself. A teacher who had participated in a rather routine demonstration of the Silent Way in Southern Europe once exclaimed to me, "You are a magician!" The compliment to me was richly undeserved, but it does indicate something of the extraordinary power of the method. And a group of East African teachers of Swahili to whom I had passed along a few simple Silent Way techniques used those techniques to reach not only vastly superior results for their trainees, but also an enhanced degree of job satisfaction for themselves. What, then, are the ideas behind this approach of Gattegno's, and how does it look in action? We will consider the first of these questions in the present chapter, and the second in Chapter 9.

IDEAS BEHIND THE SILENT WAY

Caleb Gattegno was an original thinker who worked long and hard to learn about learning and to make what he learned available to others. He was intensely concerned about the accuracy of his ideas and about being careful that his own actions should remain consistent with those same ideas. He once told me he was actually not very concerned either about the acceptance of his ideas or about being consistent in the details of how he expressed this intricate set of concepts from time to time. Moreover, in stating his conclusions he employed a highly specialized set of words, some of them with meanings unlike the meanings they have in everyday speech. It also happened that most of his writings were published quite informally and are not widely available today. I will not be able within the scope of this book to give a full account of Gattegno's ideas. I can only sketch some broad outlines. For details, I must refer interested readers to a sum-

Alice Mick, in Educational Solutions, Inc. Newsletter, 3(4), April 1974, p. 8.

Alan White in Educational Solutions, Inc. Newsletter, 3(4), April 1974, p. 1.

This summary appears as Chapter 6 of *Humanism in Language Teaching* (1990).

Ted Swartz in Educational Solutions, Inc. Newsletter, 6(2-3), Dec 1976-Feb 1977, pp. 14-16

mary he saw shortly before he died, which he told me was essentially accurate. Let me introduce some of Gattegno's basic ideas with an example not from reading or from arithmetic or from languages or from any academic subject, but from parenting. A young teacher who had studied with Gattegno shares these reflections on a recent experience as a new father:

Ted Swartz (1): Consider with me the apparently innocuous event where a father is feeding cereal to a two-and-a-half month old child for perhaps the second or third time, and is placing the food in the baby's mouth at a rate inconsistent with the infant's capacity (or desire) to swallow what is being deposited. The father's beliefs are that the more the baby eats, the better, and that the more quickly the cereal is put into the baby's mouth, the more the baby will eat. In addition, the father is in a hurry to have the food consumed, since he thinks it would be more fun to be doing something else (probably with the baby, such as holding the baby and dancing around the living room).

1 *Most of this chapter will be built on a young father's narration of his experience in feeding his first baby. I have broken his story up into seven segments. Take time now to read through all seven (pages 116–122), for the moment skipping the Frameworks comments you will find in between them. Then consider the following questions:*

- Have you ever tried to feed an infant? If you have, or if you've ever watched someone else do it, in what ways does Swartz's account seem to fit your observation? In what ways if any is Swartz's experience atypical?

- What suggestions would you make to anyone who is undertaking this activity for the first time?

- Can you remember any specific experiences of your own that lie behind your suggestions?

- What analogies can you find between Swartz's experience with transmission of oatmeal, and other kinds of activities including language teaching?

SW-1. This first excerpt from Swartz's account illustrates a common assumption that Gattegno considered inappropriate in education, namely that what is to be learned is to be transmitted one morsel at a time to the learner from and by the teacher. In fact, the spoon metaphor comes up frequently in this regard. I remember once hearing an army officer who had no patience with "easified" methodologies warn that "If you feed it to them on a silver spoon, it'll just go in one ear and out the other!" Gattegno saw learning as something done by the learner, and repeatedly asserted the subordination of teaching to learning.

SW-2. A second point is that the father's (or a teacher's, or a student's, or anyone's) actions are (as I would have stated it in the terminology of Chapter 1) *enabled, influenced, and limited by complex interactions among a range of internal resources.* Swartz here mentions beliefs and desires, but as we saw in Chapter 1 and will see further in this chapter, there are other kinds of inner resources as well. Swartz continues:

Ted Swartz (2): The outcome of the father's beliefs and actions may be familiar to other people who have fed infants, but for those who have not:

1. the baby spends a lot of time sputtering, spitting, bubbling, and otherwise ejecting the cereal back out of its mouth;

2. the baby at some point begins to choke, becomes startled, and cries;

3. the father, immediately certain he may have done irreparable damage to his child's digestive system, grabs up the baby.

4. This abrupt movement results in:
   a. a baby covered with sticky, warm cereal,
   b. a carpet with sticky, warm cereal on it, and
   c. a father with sticky, warm cereal on him.

At the close of this vignette, we find a baby who is unwilling to eat any more at this sitting (and perhaps is not fully satisfied), a father who is cleaning up a mess and feeling a bit shaken (and certainly is not at all satisfied), and a good opportunity to study a particular kind of mistake.

This excerpt illustrates two further principles of Gattegno's science of education:

SW-3. *The occasion for learning* is not merely the existence of some further spoonfuls of the multiplication table or of the past subjunctive or countries-and-capitals waiting to be placed into a passively opened brain. It is rather *a mismatch between the expected or hoped-for outcome of one's action, and the observed outcome of that action.* In life in general, the world outside one's skin is constantly providing a random series of such challenging mismatches. In Gattegno's Science of Education, the role of the teacher is to constantly study the learner and to provide a controlled series of such challenges, each shaped so as to lead the learner toward something the teacher knows the learner will someday need.

SW-4. In the incident I recounted at the beginning of this chapter, Gattegno highlighted the place of "awareness." The young father's recognition of a mismatch between his expectation and the actual outcome is certainly one example of awareness in that sense. Gattegno emphasized, however, that *awarenesses are not merely numerous, they are also layered.* (This is one more example of what in Chapter 1 I called "degrees of abstraction.") Due at least partly to his study under Gattegno, the father is aware not only of the dispersed sticky, warm cereal and not only of the mismatch, but even of the fact that he is facing "a good opportunity to study a particular kind of mistake."

---

2 *For thought, comparison and discussion: Recall recent experiences in which your "expectations were not matched by outcomes." In particular:*

■ Think of one with a duration of less than 30 seconds: Trying to loosen the screw cap on a jar, for example, or not getting from someone the response you were expecting or hoping for.

■ Think of one with a duration of a week, several weeks, or a semester.

Ted Swartz (3): The sources of the mistake [EWS: what I have been calling a "mismatch"] are in the father: in his prejudices about how much a baby should eat; in his lack of sensitivity to the needs of his child; in his less than adequate respect for the dignity of his child; in his selfishness; in his misconception of what is important. This list could perhaps be extended, but it is sufficient to indicate the depth and variety of the inner movements which had come together to produce the impetus and support for the actions.

Investigations

3 *For thought, comparison and discussion:*

- What within yourself contributed to the mismatch you reported in Task 2 (above)?

- How might the mismatch modify your expectations for the future?

- What changes might you deliberately make in your inner awarenesses that would affect your actions in similar situations in the future?

Gattegno liked to say, "In teaching, patience is not a virtue. It's a necessity!" Most obviously, excerpt 3 is a detailed statement of the antithesis of "subordination of teaching to learning" (SW-1). The words "inner movements," "impetus" and "support," however, point to a further and very important element in Gattegno's thinking.

SW-5. Gattegno saw himself first of all as a scientist, and in that role he wished to be as parsimonious as possible in his basic assumptions. He therefore postulated *only two realities: energy and time,* and saw all of life, all of learning, and all of existence as made up of interactions between them. By this Gattegno does not seem to mean primarily that what we know as matter is made up of energy by the law of e = mc². Apparently what he has in mind is more like the energy that's required in order to make neurobiological changes in the networks of the brain (Chapter 1). In any case, we will see how this materialistic premise permeates Gattegno's thinking and the terminology that flows from it.

Ted Swartz (4): As the mistake occurs, the feeling is that it is unavoidable, so deep are its roots. In spite of a gnawing suspicion that trying to get so much food in so fast is wrong, the doubt is kept at the fringes of consciousness. It seems that an enormous amount of energy is behind the mistake and supporting it. And so what comes to maintain and carry the mistake is a rather morbid curiosity as to whether the child will indeed manage to keep up with the rate of introduction of food. The mechanisms for carrying out the mistake appear automatic, as well as powerful, and therefore imply firmly rooted ways of being. Such well integrated inclinations can only be met with a movement for changing them which is at least equal to them in energy content. And this is the most important and interesting point.

The central word in this excerpt is one that doesn't appear in it at all. It is the implied actor in the passive verb phrase "can. . . be met."

SW-6. For Gattegno, *that subject is "the Self." The Self consists of energy* of a very special kind: energy that is capable of *awareness,* capable of *comparing,* capable of *choosing,* and capable of *controlling other forms of energy within a person.* Its chief limitation is that *it can only deal with one very restricted task at a time.* I believe this is the same limited capacity that we found for **working memory** in Chapter 1.

As Gattegno saw the theater of life, the Actor is the Self, the Stage is the whole world outside the Self, and the Play is limited in Time. (This is my metaphor, not his.) The Self, the other actors, and the Stage are Energy. Energy, as every schoolchild learns, is the "capacity to work." So the Self is energy that works on all that comes into its body through its eyes, its ears and all its other senses. It works to organize these inputs, forgetting them or holding them as new parts of itself. The Self as Energy is not Work; it is "Capacity to Work." What it does or does not do within the time it has may lead or may not lead to freedom: freedom to "stop being lived, and live," as Gattegno put it, freedom to enter the future fully human. This is a one-paragraph summary of what I hear Gattegno saying. In the pages that follow let me expand it just a little.

The Self begins its work at the very moment of conception, to build a body for itself. Here, as it will through its life, it draws on what it has within itself. The earliest inner resource is DNA—hereditary matter provided by the parents. Working with what it has, the Self receives from outside itself things over which it has no control (the mother's nutrients) and builds them into itself. As it does so, it adds to what it has, and so increases the range of what it will be able to use in dealing with future inputs. *This is the basic wonder that Gattegno sees recurring in one form or another throughout life: that what is not-Self becomes, through the Self's work, part of the Self.*

The Self exists and work is done in four realms at once. The first three are the electromagnetic realm of atoms and molecules, the cellular realm, and the animal realm of the body and the instincts. The fourth realm, unique to *homo sapiens,* is one that "makes [us] know [our] knowings" or, in the terminology we met back at the library, a realm in which we become "aware of our aware-nesses ." No one of these realms replaces or denies the existence of any of the others. So along with the body the Self creates a Mind. The Mind may act on and make use of the brain but is not the brain, for the brain is only one more organ in the body-realm. Because both Mind and brain [capitalization sic] are aspects of a single Self, we need not wonder how both can exist at once.

Much of Gattegno's writing is concerned in one way or another with how the Self responds when it runs into a new limit or meets some new challenge from outside itself—what a few paragraphs ago I was calling a "mismatch." Its best way of meeting this "aggression," as Gattegno termed it, is through Learning. Learning, as we saw in SW-5&6, means a reshaping of whatever lies within the power of the Self to shape. This same continual and appropriate reshaping in answer to whatever demands the here and now may place upon us also defines full living (or full humanity), if living is more than animal existence. Practitioners of the Silent Way sometimes use the phrase "living in the present." There is of course the choice of shutting out or ignoring these "aggressions," but to do so cuts off learning. The seeing Self, if it is to do the work of truly seeing, must see itself as seeing—"awareness" and "awareness of awareness" again. When it does not see and learn, the Self may lose self-knowledge and sink back into that universe that it will never reach, and never learn to deal with, within the time it has.

Just as the Self must "see itself as seeing," so must it also use itself in its working with other things and reshape itself in its reshaping in other things. For Gattegno, learning was not so much an accumulation and recognition of facts as it was the learner's coming to use himself better. This is true for what we ordinarily think of as the learning of new material. But it is also true for what we call "the correction of errors." Errors are to be corrected by the learner, who uses for this purpose a system he or she has already built inside him or herself. They are not and cannot be "corrected by" outsiders. All that an outsider—a teacher or a parent—can do is bring to the learner's attention the fact that a difference exists between what he or she says (if the error is in language) and what is said by those around him or her. This information then becomes for the learner a new "limit," "challenge," or "aggression" from outside. As with any other new "aggression," or "mismatch," the learner must decide whether and how to work with it. Under these circumstances, students often quoted him as saying, "The answer to that is within you!"

His corresponding advice to teachers was, "Grant your students everything, but take nothing for granted."

One of the purposes for which the Self uses energy is to shape the body (the "soma"), including the brain, according to the results of past experiences. In so doing, it modifies the way the body functions. Once the body has been shaped in this way, it can operate outside the direct control of the Self. Here is the source of what Swartz in excerpt 4 on p. 117 calls "mechanisms," and the source of the apparent automaticity of the mechanisms, as well as the source of difficulty in changing them. Gattegno, however, gives us a message of hope: Not only is change possible, it can even be done efficiently if we know what we're doing.

SW-7. The essential first piece of information that Gattegno strove to transmit to the Selves of his readers, and even eventually into their Somas, is this: That *just as the Self has created those mechanisms through the use of energy, so it can modify them or even do away with them through further application of energy.*

> **Ted Swartz (5):** In reliving the event and letting the implications of it permeate one's being, it is possible to learn from the mistake, in the sense that one is changed so that the inclinations which produced it are divested of their capacity to do so again. Even more profound is the recognition that other mistakes with a similar source are less likely to occur.

As I read Gattegno, the one who does the "learning" in this excerpt is again first of all "the Self," though the Self may of course use what it has learned in order to reshape the mechanisms. This high concept of the Self is what allows Gattegno to avoid reaching a mechanistic conclusion even though he started from a materialistic assumption.

SW-8. We may be only energy configurations passing through time, but that doesn't keep us from being free.

> **Ted Swartz (6):** But what is it in the virtual reenactment of the occurrence that is able to generate the sufficient amount of energy to accomplish the change? In [this] case, reliving its occurrence produces the very disturbing association

with scenes of force-feeding that had once been viewed on a television program. The association is effective because it is an exaggeration on the one hand, and yet on the other, finds its bridge in the truth that both the actual situation lived and the one acted out in the program yielded at least one similar result—a person made to suffer discomfort in the act of eating, which ought to be a satisfying, relaxed and nourishing activity. (Here also, a direct analogy is easily drawn to situations where teachers try to force students— through drills, testing, rewards, grades, approbations, etc.—to "digest" a certain predetermined amount of knowledge.) The energy that swells inside at the experience of the association—felt as revulsion, anger, empathy, etc.— immediately seems to envelop the sources of the mistake, and the automatisms responsible for its emergence are dissolved. There is no effort in this: rather, the simultaneous awarenesses of the sources of the mistake and the nature of its results, once fully experienced and realized, bring about the dissolution just as naturally, easily, and necessarily as the appropriate muscles cause air to be breathed in and out of one's lungs. As is true for any learning to be gained from any mistake, it is clear that the awarenesses are reached by the learner [in this case the father] in his or her own terms and only through the intervention of his or her will. Without the need for any discipline (since the will has been fully and effectively mobilized), the mistake does not occur again. At the same time, the impetus for perhaps many other mistakes is greatly diminished. [emphasis in original]

Let's consider two long-standing commonplaces of teacher education. (1) When students have done something right they should be rewarded. (2) The atmosphere in the classroom should be basically pleasant, but disapproval and correction contribute toward unpleasantness. Therefore approval and affirmation, perhaps in the form of a nod of the head or a quiet "Mhm!" should be frequent in a well-run classroom. Usual conclusion: Let's see more nods of the teacher's head and hear more quiet "Mhms."

Swartz's reference to "rewards, grades, and approbations" indicates that Gattegno did not concur in this conclusion.

SW-9. For Gattegno, learning consists in building into one's mechanisms a set of *"inner criteria"*: connections that truly reflect what goes with what, and what is likely to lead to what, in the world. At the end of a learning moment, the student should be able to say to him or herself, "Ah! Now I have a reliable new link between that letter shape and what I need to do with my throat and mouth!" or "Now I control the connection between this word and that color." This happens best when the learner's attention is focused on the throat and mouth muscles, or the letter shape, or whatever is to be connected with what, and this in turn is best done through meeting challenges or performing tasks.

SW-10. In the Silent Way, this often takes place in a gamelike atmosphere.

SW-11. I've said (SW-6) that the Self can only deal with one very restricted task at a time. Because of that, a Silent Way teacher carefully selects each next goal for the learners so that it will be very clearly defined for their attention. The learners quickly discover that they are expected to work only on this point, using whatever resources they already have at their disposal (what Gattegno sometimes called "working pinpointedly.") This discovery, once made, contributes noticeably to positive affect and the reduction of "clutter on the work-table" (Chapter 1).

SW-12. The way the learner gets *confirmation* that an action has been right—that it has proceeded from the needed inner criteria—comes through *discovering that no new work is needed at that point.* To throw in a series of "Mhms" or other forms of teacher approbation is at best to dilute the learner's attention, at worst to distract and distort it.

SW-13. Similarly, where something is not yet what it needs to be, *the teacher points out where further work is needed, but does not provide a new model of the desired response.* This is subtly but crucially different from "correction" in the usual sense.

Compare the discussion of "life motivations" and "academic motivations" in *Memory, Meaning & Method,* Second Edition, p. 8.

SW-14. In order to keep from distracting or distorting the learner's attention, *the teacher commonly gives both these kinds of information silently.*

SW-15. One feature of the Silent Way that would not appear in Swartz's account of interaction with just one child is that learners do much of their learning by observing their classmates and the teacher's reactions (SW-11,12,13) to them.

> **Ted Swartz (7):** Perhaps to some people all of this may seem like a tank being used to kill a fly, but in my life as the father who made the particular mistake described it would have been a mistake to believe that less was required. That also could have occurred. But it didn't because the necessary vigilance was at work. A bonus of such an experience comes from the awareness that the vigilance which is at work on one's own mistakes can be used to greatly improve one's teaching if it is made to work on generating its equivalent in students. For it is only when they come to know how they use their energy in similar ways, both to perpetuate and to bring about changes in set patterns that produce their mistakes, that they can be truly independent and responsible in their learning. This way of knowing is not intellectual in nature (though it can at some point take that form): rather it is an intimate and wholly personal contact with one's ways of being which can only come from a face to face confrontation with the real nature of one's functionings. Imagine how much increased the yield per hour of learning anything can be when teachers accept to work on generating the necessary vigilance, [with]in their students, which will result in that con-tact[!] [emphasis in original]

Much of what I have said so far about the Silent Way (SW-1–15) could be regarded as simply a set of observations on how learners' minds work.

SW-16. Where the Silent Way really comes into its own as a system of educa-tion is in its recursive nature: in the fact that *its principles can be applied to the outcomes of what happens when one follows them, and further to those very applications themselves, and so on and on.* This shows up nicely in this final section of Swartz's account. "It would have been a *mistake* to believe that less was required [in dealing with my *mistake*]." And if "vigilance" can be taken as a near-synonym of "awareness," then "the *awareness* that the *awareness* which is at work on one's own mistakes can be used" in generating *awareness* and *awareness of awareness* in students. "For it is only when they come to be *aware* of how they use their energy, that they can be truly independent and responsible in [the education of their own *awareness*]." In further recursion,

SW-17. Being a Silent Way teacher involves much more than just learning subject matter and then passing it on to one's students. It requires continuous learning of one's students and of oneself.

SW-18. The end result of this kind of education is a building up within the learner not only of subject matter knowledge, but also of three qualities: *independence* (the ability to recognize and draw on resources that one already has within oneself), *autonomy* (readiness to make choices about how to deploy those resources of knowledge and awareness), and *responsibility* (willingness to live with the results of one's choices and to correct mistakes when they appear). Swartz mentions the first and third of these qualities, but amply demonstrates in his own example the second as well.

This, then, has been a brief overview of some basic principles of the Silent Way in the very nonacademic setting of one father's kitchen. Before going on in Chapter 9 to samples of how they may be applied to language teaching, let me list them in brief:

1. Education is not just the transmission of information from and by a teacher into a passive learner.

2. Rather, it is the building and shaping of internal resources.

3. The value of these resources lies in helping the learner to interact with the outside world in ways that produce consistent results of kinds satisfactory to him or her.

4. These resources and their successful shaping *consist of* awareness, *require* awareness, and *develop* awareness.

5. The basic realities behind life and awareness are of only two kinds: energy and time.

6. At the heart of Gattegno's system—and of every person—is the Self, a special kind of energy capable of awareness, comparison, and choice, and of controlling other energy. The Self is free, even though it is severely limited in the size of tasks in which it can exercise its freedom at any one time.

7. Through its use of energy, the Self can create mechanisms that can deal with larger or more numerous tasks. Just as it has created them, it can also change them when the need arises.

8. It is in this sense that the Self is free, and this precious freedom is what makes the educational process both possible and worthwhile.

9. An important kind of inner resource consists of criteria: a set of dependable connections that accurately reflect what goes with what, and what is likely to lead to what.

10. There are advantages to developing these criteria in a gamelike atmosphere.

11. Work is directed toward one sharply defined goal at a time.

12. The learner concludes that he or she has a particular point right when he or she notices that the teacher seems to think no new work is needed on that point.

13. Similarly, where something is not yet what it needs to be, the teacher points out where further work is needed.

14. In order to keep from distracting or distorting the learner's attention, the teacher commonly gives both these kinds of information silently.

15. Learners do much of their learning by observing their classmates and the teacher's reactions

16. These principles are recursive. That is, one can be aware of awareness, and of awareness of awareness, and so on. The Self can build mechanisms that control mechanisms. A teacher can learn about him or herself as a learner about learners.

17. Being a Silent Way teacher requires constant learning of oneself as well as of one's students.

18. The goal is to develop within students three qualities: independence, autonomy, and responsibility.

THE SILENT WAY AND THE FRAMEWORK IN CHAPTER 1

I see some striking similarities between the first nine of these points and certain features of the contemporary view of memory sketched in Chapter 1. Both lists are concerned not with shaping behavior directly, but with building and modifying the complex, multilayered inner resources that account for behavior. Both recognize the basic physical or material nature of storage, within which certain processes take place automatically. At the same time, however, both lists imply an essential role for intervention by a conscious and possibly non-material self, which is both the proprietor of the storage facilities and the user of what has been stored in them. For both lists, the scope of the user's direct intervention is quite limited in comparison to the total size of the lasting resources. Beliefs, desires (Swartz 1), and emotions (Swartz 6) play an important role. Learning is therefore not simply intellectual in nature (Swartz 7), but involves the whole person. These similarities become all the more striking because my sketch of memory was derived principally from an experimental tradition on which Gattegno seems not to have drawn, based on work by investigators who had little or no knowledge of his writings.

At the same time, Gattegno did go beyond my memory sketch in a number of respects. In the first place, he drew a number of more subtle distinctions. For example, within what I have called simply "inner resources," Gattegno distinguishes at least "awareness(es)" and "criteria." In the present chapter I have adopted his term "the Self" and his concept of "energy," but I have omitted a whole set of subordinate terms he uses: "psyche," "affectivity," "will," "intelligence," and the like.

The last 7 of the 18 points show that Gattegno did not stop with a mere description of the inner working of the Self and other forms of energy. He added to this description a radical and passionate conviction about what, in education and in living in general, we may best try to do with that inner working, and how most efficiently to go at it. His goals of independence, autonomy, and responsibility are a far cry from our traditional goals of accuracy, fluency, various kinds of competence, and the like. Similarly his means toward those goals—respect, silence, and the subordination of teaching to learning—are in their simplicity more sophisticated than most of the means we usually think about.

What Gattegno has produced, then, is much more than an educational technology. It even goes beyond what we think of as "education" in the usual academic sense. There is good reason for speaking not of the Silent "Method" but of the Silent "Way." It is a "way" not only for the teacher but also for her students. Any Self is "an evolving system endowed with awareness and the capacity for self-education." By developing his awareness the learner becomes more and more free, better able to live "more respectful of the truth in Reality." The evolving Self creates "new forms that integrate [its own] past"—and so it finally "contributes to collective evolution." As he becomes more fully human the learner discovers that those two worlds, the Outer and the Inner, are after all intertwined. Gattegno himself used to say, "With the focus on learning [rather than on content, EWS], one perceives the language to be the vehicle for learning, and its mastery is experienced as the by-product of learning." Compare the common assumption that it is learning that is the vehicle for getting at language. In the same vein, he would tell his hearers, "I don't teach the language per se. I involve my students in specific activities which require them to work on their own functioning *with regard to the reality* of the language. And they end up functioning in the language!"

The long goal of such development, then, is that the Self should add its own unique contribution to its world. A goal within but at the same time beyond that goal is "to recast [one's] world in a manner that makes more sense to more people and leads [them] to accept that [they] were not 'seeing' outside reality as it is." I think this last sentence describes what Gattegno himself was doing for many of us.

Clifford Bax expressed a similar humanistic vision in the English of the early twentieth century:

> *Earth might be fair, and all men glad and wise.*
> *Age after age their tragic empires rise,*
> *Built while they dream, and in that dreaming weep:*
> *Would man but wake from out his haunted sleep,*
> *Earth might be fair, and all men glad and wise.*

A REMINDER

Needless to say, a teacher who wishes to use the Silent Way should have some live, face-to-face training in it. As I indicated in the Prologue and in Chapter 1, the descriptions in this book are intended to illustrate certain general principles rather than to teach readers how to use the approaches for themselves. Meanwhile, the reader may wish to consult what other writers on methodology such as Larsen-Freeman (1986), Richards and Rodgers (1986), Blair (1982), and Oller and Richard-Amato (1983), have said about the Silent Way. My own treatment of the approach in Stevick (1980) was concerned primarily with explaining the thinking behind it, rather than with how to put it into practice.

3 *In 1969 a pair of authors recorded their impressions of certain contemporary trends in education:*

> The *goal*, they said, is something called "covering content": getting into students' heads a series of assertions, definitions, and names as quickly as possible.

- Aside from whatever Gattegno may or may not have said on the subject, would you agree with the predicate of this sentence? If not, what would you replace it with?

- Which of the 18 points on p. 123f are relevant to this statement about "goals"?

4 *The same authors continued:*

> The *method* consists of a series of questions posed by the teacher or the materials intended to lead the student to produce right answers that the teacher or materials already knew.

- Actually the goal and method the authors are describing in this quotation are those of "programmed instruction," a then-current precursor of much that today is known as "computer assisted language learning." In my experiences as a Silent Way learner, by far the greatest portion of our time was spent with the teacher posing one sharply defined, "pinpointed" challenge at a time (SW-11) and silently notifying us when our responses didn't agree with his preset goal for us. He was thus exemplifying SW-12, 13, 14. In spite of this superficial similarity, the assumptions and techniques of programmed instruction were almost 180° at variance with Gattegno's thinking and intent. How can this be true?

5 *A more recent book for teachers lists (but does not necessarily espouse) some commonly held ideas about language learning:*

a. Languages are learned mainly through imitation of models.

b. Parents usually correct young children when they make grammatical errors.

c. The most important factor in second language acquisition success is motivation.

d. Teachers should present grammatical rules one at a time, and learners should practice examples of each one before going on to another.

e. Teachers should teach simple language structures before complex ones.

f. Learners' errors should be corrected as soon as they are made in order to prevent the formation of bad habits.

g. When learners are allowed to interact freely they learn one another's mistakes.

h. Students learn what they are taught.

- How consistent is each of these beliefs with what your own experience has shown you about language learning?

- Among these eight statements are there any that you instinctively dislike even though you think they are largely correct? Any to which you feel drawn even though you believe them to be wrong?

- How consistent is each of these beliefs with what you know about the Silent Way? [Warning: I would find it hard to give a short, simple reaction to most of these statements.]

9

THE SILENT WAY
IN PRACTICE

*The late 1960s were the heyday of language training in the
United States Peace Corps. The number of host countries grew
almost monthly, new volunteers poured in for training, and there
was still adequate money. Whatever language was needed, we
found someone to put together a training program for it, and
whatever method was devised, the Peace Corps was ready to give
it a try. Those were exciting times, and also very instructive ones,
during which I was fortunate to be assigned part time to assist
the Peace Corps Language Training Office in Washington.*

*One day I came back from a trip out of town and asked
the other staff members what had happened while I was away.
"Oh, some man came down from New York and demonstrated
a method using little colored sticks," they replied.*

"How was it?" I asked.

"You didn't miss much," was their assessment.

The matter was dropped.

In fairness I should report that a few years later the Silent Way did receive serious use in the Peace Corps, with apparently excellent results. The above anecdote is however all too typical of how teachers and teacher trainers have often
reacted to this or other unconventional methods, focusing on striking but superficial details and not noticing the heart of what was going on.

The things that any outsider notices first about any language teaching
method are its materials and its techniques. In the rest of this chapter I will enu-
merate some materials and techniques that are commonly used in foreign language courses taught by the Silent Way.

A STANDARD BEGINNING

If there is a language that the whole class can read, the teacher commonly begins
by having the learners read aloud from a "fidel" for that language. A fidel is a
wall chart that shows the spelling or the multiple spellings for syllables of the
language. The symbols on the chart are printed in various colors, in such a way
that symbols that are to be pronounced alike (for example *ee, ea,* and *i* as in
English *feet, feat, elite*) are colored alike. This enables learners to ignore the
shapes at least temporarily and depend on the colors. They are therefore unen-
cumbered by anxieties about the shapes, and left free to concentrate on the new
sounds. The learners first use their knowledge of familiar shapes to learn the
phonetic meaning of the colors. Then, switching to the fidel of the new target

language, and guided by the teacher's gestures, they use their new knowledge of the pronunciation of the colors in order to read the syllables aloud from it. They also use the teacher's silent messages to verify for themselves whether they have a given point right or not. This works even when the writing systems of the two fidels are totally unrelated to each other: Spanish and Chinese, for example.

Let's look at this much of the description in terms of Chapter 1 and also of our list of 18 points (pages 123-124). The very existence of the fidel with its simple but highly professional execution carries certain messages, one of which is that the people who put this course together seem to know what they're doing. Another message is that there's an impressively large but still limited amount of material here. Both of these messages can contribute positively to the security need, though security is not a main focus in the Silent Way.

As it stands, the fidel is neutral with regard to SW-1—the degree to which learners will be passive or active in absorbing the information it contains. It is however a bird's-eye view of where learners will need to create new internal resources (SW-2).

The use of colors as an intermediate stepping stone between the resources from their native language reading ability (SW-9) and the new language provides an occasion for *independence* (drawing on existing resources) and for *autonomy* (deciding when and how to do so) as in SW-18. It is enough for this use of color to get into holding memory; permanence is not necessary.

The teacher's responses are illustrations of SW-12, 13, 14.

Where the new language contains sounds that are absent from the familiar language, the teacher may silently focus the learners' attention and then give them a single clear audible example of the sound. Otherwise the teacher may up to this point have remained completely silent. During this first phase the teacher shapes the learners' pronunciation of the target language (largely) by means of her reaction—or lack of reaction—to their efforts.

Again we find SW-12, 13, 14. Because the teacher is almost always silent, learners hear more sharply what she does say. It probably also reverberates longer in their working memory than if it were preceded and followed by the usual amount of teacher vocalization—a very special variety of "clutter on the worktable" both in itself and for the subtle messages the teacher's tone often brings with it.

After the learners can pronounce the sounds of the new language well enough so that no native would misunderstand them, the teacher moves on to a second phase.

Here is an example of "constant learning of one's students" (SW-17). Of course a certain amount of this goes on in any method, but the Silent Way requires a much finer grained sort of attention.

This second phase centers around a second set of charts, which contain miscellaneous words carefully selected from among the most common words of the language, including the words for numerals. Using these words together with written numerals, the teacher writes numerals on the board and leads the learner to produce long numbers up to a million, a billion, and beyond. In my observation this has been done in a bouncy, fun-filled way that provides the game-like atmosphere of SW-10.

In the third phase the teacher typically puts into use a set of cuisenaire rods, the same devices used in "The Islamabad Procedure" described in Chapter 6 (pages 87f). For their combination of simplicity, flexibility, power and portability, cuisenaire rods are the best educational aid I have ever found. They provide a classic example of input in a number of senses at the same time (Chapter 1). Visually their well-matched colors range from somber to almost but not quite gaudy. Though they are small, I have used them and seen them used with over 50 learners at a time. A rod or a configuration of rods on an otherwise empty table top naturally focuses learners' attention. It is also an excellent locus for forming and stabilizing their mental images of all sorts of things. In terms of touch, rods are simple and pleasant to handle. Kinesthetically they are light in weight and precisely enough shaped to allow for stable three-dimensional combinations. Acoustically, they just sound good on a tabletop. (I should say that in all of these respects the wooden rods are vastly to be preferred over the plastic version!) Overall, rods lend themselves very well to the ingenious devising of sharply focused tasks (SW-11).

Using the charts together with gestures and perhaps a few spoken words, the teacher leads the learner to talk about various configurations and uses of the rods. At first the work is on numbers and colors, but soon it moves into relative locations, and beyond that to virtually any and all grammatical structures that the teacher thinks the learner needs. If this is not to lead to confusion, the teacher must monitor the learners very closely (SW-17). And she is more likely to use a fun-having and slightly mischievous manner rather than a heavy pedagogical manner that says, "All right, class, here's the next thing for you to learn!" SW-10 again.

There are other materials that are used later in the course. I will not describe them here because my purpose is only to show examples of how the basic principles of the Silent Way are realized in practice. The later materials and techniques embody the same principles as the three phases that I have already described. Readers who are interested in an account of the later phases, and in fuller, more authoritative treatment of the first three, should carefully consult Gattegno's book *The Common Sense of Teaching Foreign Languages*.

Throughout at least the initial phases the learners meet one clearly delimited new element of the language at a time (SW-11). They feel that what they have done has moved them toward their long-term goal in an efficient way and that they have worked both well and thoroughly. The teacher is matter-of-fact both about the learners' successes and about their errors, but she always shows by her manner that she accepts the learners as persons.

The principle of clear delimitation of objectives applies also to the *kind* of vocabulary met in the early lessons. It consists of just the bare bones that will enable the teacher to present the sounds and basic structures of the language: the noun for "rod," colors, numbers, a few verb forms, prepositions, and the like. The words that would be needed for telling interesting stories or sharing personal experiences are considered "luxury" vocabulary, and are firmly postponed.

The teacher generally exercises "control" (as I used that word in Chapter 3) and in the early stages may also exert much of the "initiative" in deciding which syllables or words which learner will work on at any given moment, or which rod structure will be built. Within her initiative, however, she provides frequent situations in which the learners have more than one correct response available to them. Students are engaged in a constant series of trial-and-error approximations to the language.

When the learners respond correctly to the teacher's initiative, the teacher usually does not react with any overt confirmation that what they did was right. To do so would transform the activity from a gamelike but matter-of-fact exploration of new realities, and turn it back into the traditional "Now-try-to-do-this-so-I-can-tell-you-how-you-did" relationship. If a learner's response is wrong, on the other hand, the teacher indicates that the learner needs to do further work on the word or phrase; if she thinks it necessary she actually shows the learner exactly where the additional work is to be done. Sometimes points that have not been completely mastered are left to clarify themselves overnight.

There is no memorization, no translation, and no repetition for its own sake in the absence of meaning. Students frequently help one another and learn from overhearing one another. A final detail: The teacher uses a collapsible metal pointer to guide the learners' attention to the charts or rods, even when those objects are within easy reach of her hand. One purpose of this is to minimize both the cognitive and the emotional effects of the teacher's presence, and so to avoid diluting the learners' attention to the succession of new combinations of meanings and linguistic forms.

TECHNIQUES INCORPORATING FEATURES OF THE SILENT WAY

A one-hour demonstration

EWS: In a lecture course on teaching methods, I conducted a one-hour experience with beginning Turkish for a class of six volunteers. The volunteers were seated facing me on three sides of a totally empty table top.

- I started by writing a set of words on the board including the words for the numbers 1-6 and for three colors. Among the pronunciation points that would have been unfamiliar to monolingual speakers of English were two front rounded vowels, a contrast of vowel duration in an unstressed syllable, and a stressed high back unrounded vowel (spelled ı) that does not occur in English stressed syllables. There were also three points at which familiar sounds were spelled in unfamiliar ways.

altı	iki	turuncu	dört
beş	kırmızı	üç	çubuk
bir	mavi	yeşil	

- I then spread my hands, palms up, and raised my eyebrows to convey the question, "What now?"

- After a few seconds, someone read aloud one of the words from the board. I pointed to the word matter-of-factly and *without conveying approval or even pleasure.*

- We continued in this way until all of the words had been read correctly. When a learner's pronunciation would have been unacceptable in Turkish, I pointed to the letter where work needed to be done and continued to do so until the pronunciation was acceptable. Then *without conveying approval or even pleasure* I stepped back from the board to await the next learner. This readily took care of all matters of pronunciation except for the final *-r*.

- I let the group continue in this way for a few minutes, until the pronunciation-spelling linkages seemed to have become established at least in Holding Memory (Chapter 1).

- Next, with some flourish, I placed on the table top first one orange rod, then near it but separated from it, a pair of orange rods. I chose the orange rods both because they are the longest and because of their bright and conspicuous color. Again I stepped back and waited.

- Almost immediately people began guessing words. I ignored what they said except for the words for "one" and "two." When they pronounced either of these words, without conveying approval or even pleasure, I simply used my collapsible pointer to indicate the appropriate number of rods. We continued in this way, adding a larger configuration each time, until the volunteers had among them identified all the numbers from one through six.

- In a similar way the volunteers taught themselves and one another the words for all three colors.

- Finally, I silently invited them to describe configurations such as "two green rods."

During the entire demonstration I had said nothing at all either in Turkish or in English. If a learner had trouble at some point, I didn't act perplexed or disapproving. Instead I went on around the circle as though forgetting about the learner's difficulty, but making sure that the necessary information was present in what I had asked the second or third learner to do. This hour was the best I had conducted, both with regard to the amount learned (by spectators as well as by the six participants) and with regard to the comments afterward.

---

1 *In what details of overt technique does this account differ from the description in the preceding section?*

- Where does the gamelike atmosphere (SW-10) show up in this account?

- At how many points can you find expressions of allowing—requiring—learners to be active rather than passive (SW-1)?

- Which of the other 18 points about the Silent Way (pages 123f.) are evident here?

---

2 *Describe a successful technique you have used based on some other approach.*

- To what extent did it exemplify one or more of the 18 points?

- How might it have been modified to reflect Gattegno's ideas more closely?

- Do you think those modifications would have improved it for your students? Why, or why not?

From a six-hour demonstration

I conducted 6-hour experiences with Silent Way Turkish for two groups of secondary school language teachers in Bellingham, Washington, in the summer of 1976. Each experience consisted of four sessions. There were twelve people in the first group, sixteen in the second.

What we did was clearly billed as "an experience, not a demonstration." That is, with exceptions that I will describe below, the actual procedures I followed were similar to what I had used in my "demonstrations." The longer time, however, allowed us to go much farther into Turkish. We were able to do a fair amount with reading and writing. With regard to grammar, I even led the participants straight into and through what may be the worst thicket in Turkish structure: three sets of noun endings involving two separate types of vowel harmony. As one part of the final session, we experimented with learning a short dialog of the type found in the textbooks that the participants themselves were teaching from, using a technique derived from the Silent Way. A number of features of the Bellingham experience deserve comment.

> Twelve people were too many for me to deal with around the table at one time. I knew from the demonstrations that spectators can learn along with active participants. My first thought, therefore, was to have two teams, or "shifts," of six learners each, who would alternate between the active and observing roles. I decided, however, to have each of the spectators stand behind one of the people who was seated at the tables. I mentioned the possibility that this "support person" might want to place his hand lightly on the shoulder of the person and to give any assistance requested by the person at the table. In the beginning, I directed the teams to exchange places about every ten minutes. Later, when I saw that learners had a feel for these two roles, I allowed individuals to trade back and forth as they felt the need.

3 *In what ways if any was this episode consistent with my description of the Silent Way?*

In what ways does what I did here show influence from my training in Counseling-Learning (Chapters 5 and 6)?

In what ways if any might the presence of Counseling-Learning features make this supposed experience with the Silent Way less authentic? Less effective?

This feature of the experience was warmly received, and was the subject of much favorable comment. For one thing, it contributed to the security of the learner in two ways. The person in the "support," or "backup," role was sure of not being called on by me. Perhaps for this reason, the support person was frequently better able to produce the phrase I was calling for than was the person I was directly "teaching" at the table. At the same time, the person at the table had the security of knowing that there was always someone to fall back on when needed. The only difficulty that we encountered in this relationship was that sometimes the support person would give help before it was requested. In doing so, she or he deprived the other person of the opportunity to work through things for her or himself. If the course had continued, I think this wrinkle could easily have been ironed out.

---

4 *If you had been in this class, which position would have been more congenial for you?*

- To what extent is the elicitation of correct words and phrases from secure, happy learners consistent with the *practice* of the Silent Way?

- To what extent is it consistent with the *goals* of the Silent Way?

Although this innovation was apparently successful, it may have run counter to the spirit of the Silent Way. If the essence of the Silent Way is to affirm the individual learner in his self-contained independence—one might almost say, in his existential aloneness—and to guide him through work that he must do on himself, then whatever dulls that awareness of self-contained independence may distract, delay, or even defeat the deeper kind of learning. An atmosphere of too much support and solicitude may therefore be inappropriate from this point of view, even if it does, in the short run at least, produce more right answers more comfortably. This is an issue that I myself need to explore further.

At any rate, I have on this and other occasions found it easy to teach in this way, one at a time, all of the grammatical endings of the Turkish noun. After doing so, and after the students have met several nouns, I then use the rods in a quite different way. The long orange rod stands for the noun, while other rods stand for the endings. In Turkish, a noun may have a plural ending, plus one of a series of endings that show the person and number of its possessor, plus one of another series of endings that carry other grammatical meanings. So the orange rod is followed by three columns of rods lying on the table.

I begin with just the noun plus the rod that stands for "plural." The students must choose between two forms of this ending, according to the last vowel of the noun stem. When I tap the orange rod with the pointer, a student gives a noun. When I tap the "plural" rod, the same student gives the same noun with the appropriate form of the plural ending. If there is an error, I wait, or tap the "plural" rod again. We go around the class rapidly in this way. The steady rhythm, the visual effect of gazing at the rods, and the gentle, non-demanding tapping of the pointer combine, I think, to make relaxed concentration easier for the students.

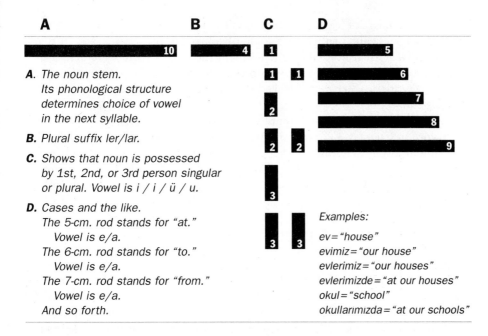

A   **B**   **C**   **D**

A. *The noun stem.*
Its phonological structure
determines choice of vowel
in the next syllable.

B. *Plural suffix ler/lar.*

C. *Shows that noun is possessed*
by 1st, 2nd, or 3rd person singular
or plural. Vowel is i / ı / ü / u.

D. *Cases and the like.*
The 5-cm. rod stands for "at."
   Vowel is e/a.
The 6-cm. rod stands for "to."
   Vowel is e/a.
The 7-cm. rod stands for "from."
   Vowel is e/a.
And so forth.

Examples:

ev = "house"
evimiz = "our house"
evlerimiz = "our houses"
evlerimizde = "at our houses"
okul = "school"
okullarımızda = "at our schools"

As the activity continues, I add one suffix at a time (there are eleven altogether), identifying each by a word (e.g., "to," "from") if necessary. Each suffix has from two to sixteen forms, depending on what precedes and/or follows it. I direct each student in producing about three forms of his chosen noun. Just which forms these are depends on what I think the student needs to work on at the moment. Mistakes are dealt with in a way calculated to allow the student to do as much of the work as possible without disrupting the shared sense of moving ahead together in a way that gives learning in exchange for the time spent. So if I think the student will catch an error himself, I give no indication that one has been made. If that is not sufficient I lift my hand, usually from the wrist and not form the elbow or the shoulder. The purpose here is to convey the necessary information with minimal emotional impact. If I think more information is needed, I tap again the rod—or the part of a rod—that shows where the error is located. Only if that is insufficient do I bring my hands and face into the picture. The total elapsed time for one of these "repair" activities is only a few seconds.

I think I am learning not to ask another student to provide a correct form for a student who still cannot come up with the desired form. To do so inevitably carries the impact of comparison, and comparison leads to an atmosphere of relative evaluation. When all students give and receive this kind of help with about equal frequency, this leads to a beneficial sense of community. But a student who feels that she is always or almost always on the receiving end may become discouraged. She may then decide that she lacks the ability for this kind of thing. She may also conclude—usually wrongly but sometimes rightly—that the other students are impatient with her for "holding them back."

Another reason for not having students supply each other with correct responses in this activity is that to do so allows them to fall back on their ability at producing sounds by mere mimicry, and to miss out on the mental work that is at the heart of learning by the Silent Way.

This way of dealing with errors could of course be cumbersome and turn into a prohibitively great burden on the teacher's memory if there were many times when students were unable to come up with the desired form on their first turn. This is why the teacher must "learn" the students as he is "teaching" them the language (SW-17).

In this activity, I maintain complete "control," in the sense in which I used that word in Chapter 3. That is to say, I tell the student what to do at all times, and how to do it; in addition, I keep them informed as to the relation between their answers and the language as established speakers use it. Besides "controlling" the activity, I assume part of the "initiative" when I specify which endings a student is to add to her or his noun. If I were also the one who decided which noun each student was to work with, I would be exerting 100 percent of the "initiative," as well as 100 percent of the "control."

For reasons that we need not go into here, some Turkish nouns are easier to add endings to than others are. An argument in favor my exerting 100 percent of the "initiative" in this way is that if the students are left to themselves, they may shy away from the more difficult nouns. An argument against full teacher "initiative" is that when the students put even a small bit of themselves into a drill, the drill is less likely to go dead on them. This second argument assumes that when people feel reasonably safe, they will not simply stagnate in the easiest options but will reach out and explore further. When they do so, they know more precisely than even the most sensitive teacher can know just what they are ready for at any given moment. Here is an additional reason for sharing the "initiative" in this particular procedure.

As a variation, I sometimes allow the students to choose their own suffixes, as well as the noun itself. This is of course a further sharing of "initiative," but still completely under the teacher's "control." It seems to work best when the students use their fingers or the pointer to actually touch the rods as they pronounce the endings.

This way of using the rods has drawn a large amount of student comment, virtually all of it favorable. The only class that did not enjoy it consisted of people whose concept of grammatical abstractions such as "second person singular" was not strong and clear. It seems to be especially appreciated by those students who find it hard to work with "just words." Such students have often said how thankful they are that they can have something to work with that they can see and touch and move around for themselves, to correspond to the grammatical noises they are learning. One is reminded of Gattegno's dictum: "There is no truth in words."

There are several ways in which the teacher can keep this procedure from working well. One is to overuse it and run it into the ground. I have already said I think the sharing of a little "initiative" may lengthen the students' attention span. A second way of sabotaging the procedure is to give the students their individual tasks according to some plan or schedule that does not require the teacher to be constantly "learning" the students. This will produce tasks that are frequently inappropriate—too hard or too easy. A third way is to act patient with a student who is having more difficulty than the others. It's all right to *be* patient, but the teacher who *acts* patient may cause some of the same anxieties as the teacher who acts *im*patient. A fourth way is to remain silent while presenting the task but to become "helpfully" vocal as soon as the student hits a snag. If the tasks have been chosen by a teacher who both knows the language and is continuously "learning" the students, these snags will not destroy the forward momentum of the class. On the contrary, they are invaluable occasions for real learning, which the vocal teacher spoils.

In the brief "demonstrations," I had not bothered with reading and writing at all. In Bellingham, I wrote the first words on the board as soon as the learners were able to pronounce them. Later, when the learners had met all of the features of Turkish spelling that were unfamiliar to them, I had them do the writing.

I felt that this was consistent with the principle of making people aware of what resources they had inside themselves, and of not doing for learners what the learners can do for themselves. This part of the work went smoothly, and people seemed to enjoy it.

Beginning with the second session, I set aside a few minutes now and then for the learners to write out their own phrases in Turkish and correct them among themselves. They were able to do so with an occasional silent indication from me that something was still amiss.

As a part of the last session, I wrote on the board a brief greeting dialog in Turkish. The format was one that is well known in many published courses: individual words followed by full sentences, with a translation in a parallel column. The first step was to have the learners read the Turkish aloud. They seemed pleased with themselves to discover that among them they could do so fairly readily. Again, the only help from me was a occasional silent indicator that they needed to take another look at one letter or another.

As the second step, I erased the first word (*gün*) from the board. Since that word happened to have one syllable, I set a one-centimeter rod on the table, pointed to the rod, motioned to them to speak, and they said *gün*. The second word (*aydin*) had two syllables, so I next replaced it with a two-centimeter rod on the table. Using the pointer, I had the learners "read" first one rod and then the other until they were comfortable with them. In this way, we gradually replaced the entire five-line dialog with rods whose lengths corresponded to the number of syllables in the words. I also spent a little time jumping back and forth at random among the wooden "words" and found that this seemed to pose no particular difficulty for the students.

---

5 *How consistent and how inconsistent is this fragment with what you know of the Silent Way?*

- Although this bit of technique worked rather well with these learners, certain serious theoretical objections could be raised against it. What are some of them?

- What answers might be given to some of those objections?

The third and last step consisted of having the learners, as a group, copy the dialog from the rods back onto the board. The discovery that they were in fact able to do so was exciting to all of us, though I pretended not to heave a sigh of relief.

6 *Relate the "reading and writing from rods" part of this episode to concepts from Chapter 1: "clutter," the contrast between holding memory and permanent memory, learners' purposes, and any other concepts that you find applicable.*

- To what extent do you think this technique would be suited to you as a learner? What would be its strengths and its weaknesses in this respect?

- Would it or some adaptation of it be suitable for your students? Why, or why not?

THE SILENT WAY AND CHAPTERS 1-3

Let us now take a final look at the Silent Way from the point of view of Chapters 1-3.

The godlike characteristics of the learner are conspicuous in Gattegno's thinking: the ability to make infinite use of finite resources, and the ability to transcend one's animal nature by seeing oneself as seeing, seeing oneself as seeing that one sees, and so on. The mortality of the learner is equally clear in the urgency Gattegno feels for efficiency in learning—for being sure that we "exchange time for experience"—rather than wasting it. And the picture of the Self creating itself even from the moment of conception, on physical as well as intellectual levels, certainly affirms the heroic aloneness of a Self at the center of its own universe.

Going on now to Chapter 3, the Silent Way is anything but a power vacuum, and it emphatically rejects any idea of trying to protect the learner from making errors. In the short run at least, it looks much closer to the Evaluative Paradigm: "Now try to do this so I can tell you how you did." It differs, however, in three important ways from most teaching that is conducted on that basis. First, there is very little "positive feedback" from the teacher in the sense of telling learners (in words or silently) that their responses were "right" or "very good." Second, although the teacher's overt reactions are mainly to mistakes, they are given in a totally matter-of-fact way. The learner is supposed to feel that her wrong response (or her *right* response!) is *not being "corrected" or even "affirmed," but is being accepted and worked with.* Third, the teacher learns the learner at the same time that the learner is learning the language. This means that the teacher does not merely present the learner with a prefabricated series of challenges, but also provides new challenges as he sees they are needed,

No one who has read Gattegno's *The Mind Teaches the Brain* (1975) can doubt that he has taken a deep and very steady look inside the learner. The people in his classes are whole, complex persons, and not simple few-dimensional simplifications. In his two books directed especially to language teachers, he is very clear about the learner's need to feel secure in three areas: in knowing what is being asked of her or him at any given moment; in knowing how her or his performance compares with what is expected; and in being accepted as a person without regard to any linguistic difficulties she or he may have.

On the other hand it is not clear to me how much importance Gattegno attaches to the kinds of resistance, conflict, and alienation that we sketched in

Chapter 1; to the learner's attitudes toward speakers of the target language; or to the learner's reactions to being "ignorant, powerless, and constantly evaluated"; or to his or her reactions to pleasant or unpleasant experiences with fellow learners. Gattegno's position may be that if the teaching is done well enough those factors will fade from the picture of their own accord.

The Silent Way certainly provides clear, firm and continuous "control" of the learning process in the sense in which we have been using that term. Within this control it is possible to leave room for an exciting amount of "initiative," even creativity, on the part of the learners. I have seen two Silent Way teachers who vigorously exploited the opportunities to give initiative to the learners even while they (the teachers) maintained tight control over what was going on. The other teachers I have seen have given much less initiative to the learners, at least in the early stages.

In its emphasis on the ways in which learners learn by listening to one another's efforts, the Silent Way not only allows interdependence but even requires it. There are also endless opportunities for cooperation among the learners, under the close monitoring and control of the teacher. But I am uncertain, just as I am unclear concerning "initiative," about exactly how far the Silent Way teacher is supposed to follow up on those opportunities.

As far as I am aware Gattegno said nothing to language teachers about "vibes." I believe however that "good vibes"—an air of the teacher's competence and of confidence in herself and her learners—are important for success in using the Silent Way just as they are in using any method.

The Silent Way does not provide for the teacher to lay aside the Teacher mask and replace it with an Ordinary Person mask. It may at least allow such an exchange as long as "control" (in my sense) is not lost; I am not certain.

A Silent Way teacher sets short-term goals for her learners and lets them know when "the ball lands outside the court." She does this in an alert, matter-of-fact way, without either praising the learners or reproaching them. She thus acts the way Self 1 (the Conscious, Critical Self) ought to act. In doing so, she often finds herself in conflict with the learners' own Self 1's. The Self 1's of most learners are in the habit of dealing in praise and reproach, and of having teachers who provide a continuous supply of one or both. For this reason learners sometimes experience conflict and anxiety at the beginning of instruction by the Silent Way. Once they adjust to the new style and begin to let their own Self 1's work *the way the teacher is working,* they frequently have a feeling of elation, and their learning rate leaps to a level that they would not have thought possible.

Between activities or between sessions, the Silent Way teacher from time to time allows learners to ask questions or to talk about the experience in their native language. At these times the teacher does not remain silent, but in other respects remains true to the principles of the Silent Way. Thus, when she is asked a question she may choose to avoid giving a direct answer. Instead of a direct answer she may say something that directs the questioner's own mind toward work that may enable him to find the answer for himself, within himself. In the same way, if a learner expresses confusion or discomfort, the teacher may try to reply in a way that will give the learner a hint at where or how to work within himself rather than giving him the kind of supportive understanding that we talked about in Chapter 2. In their first experiences with the Silent Way, learners and other people sometimes regard this kind of reply as ill-mannered.

Perhaps the following chart will be useful in relating the work of the learner and the work of the teacher to a few of the terms I have used.

Principle	Learner	Teacher
Learning is work for the purpose of adjusting to the outside world	In meeting a new challenge,	The teacher provides the challenges
Independence	I use resources from within myself	relative to the student's present resources,
Responsibility	in order to decide for myself	but remains silent, noninterfering,
Autonomy	among the choices	while the student works to choose
Independence again	offered by the resources within myself (for no other resources are available to me).	among the resources that we have guided him or her in developing.
Remembering/ Learning	The result of this work	This kind of teaching
Retention/ Acquisition	may become a new part of myself.	frees the student.

7 *Examine this firsthand account by EWS:*

One time when Gattegno had come to the Foreign Service Institute to conduct two days of training for members of the language staff, I invited him to our home for dinner along with four or five teachers who had expressed an interest in his work. Also present were my teenage son and his girlfriend.

I had hoped that the time before the meal would be a period in which the teachers could socialize a bit with Gattegno and perhaps ask him a few informal questions. Such was not to be, however. His manner during the opening session that afternoon had been so uncompromising and so out of keeping with commonly accepted ideas of politeness, that my guests were tongue-tied. There was a deafening silence about the Silent Way.

Into this silence stepped my son. He had heard that Gattegno had a doctorate in mathematics, and since math was one of his own favorite subjects, he began asking questions. It soon became apparent to me that my son's attitude toward the subject and Gattegno's attitude were quite different. For my son, math was something he had always been good at, something he enjoyed, and something he might someday get a job at. Gattegno's view of the subject was of course subtler, deeper, and founded on the place of math in total education. As the conversation continued between them, however, I became aware that my son's vision of math was noticeably expanding, becoming less instrumental and more humane.

The following morning, I told Gattegno what I thought I had observed and remarked that although Gattegno had been anything but silent in talking with my son, he had nevertheless been providing a series of minimal challenges that had led to my son's developing his own thinking. This, I ventured, was an example of the Silent Way without silence.

Gattegno said nothing.

- In terms of the 18 principles listed in Chapter 5, what might have been my basis for wondering whether Gattegno's very verbal interaction with my son was an example of the "Silent" Way?

- Think of at least three different meanings that Gattegno's lack of overt response might have been intended to carry. Which do you think he did intend?

---

8 *Here, in no particular order, is a partial list of features in which the Silent Way differs at least in degree from other approaches. Add other differences you have noticed.*

- silence of the teacher

- use of cuisenaire rods

- subordination of teaching to learning

- working "pinpointedly"

- _____

If possible in discussion with colleagues, order the completed list according to each of the following yardsticks:

- Degree of novelty or "strangeness" relative to the more familiar approaches.

- Degree to which it might have been nice if your own language teachers had incorporated this feature into their work with you (or the degree to which you're just as glad they didn't).

- Demands on you as teacher if you tried to take it seriously.

- Ease with which teachers following other approaches could profit from the feature even if they did not try to adopt the Silent Way as a whole.

10

A Third Way: Suggestopedia

Why this chapter?

In the preceding chapters I have capitalized Counseling-Learning and the Silent Way, while in this chapter I write suggestopedia in lower case. In all three instances I am attempting to conform to usage.

The third "way" I discussed in 1980 was suggestopedia. Suggestopedia began as an educational application of the psychological theories of a Bulgarian psychiatrist, Dr. Georgi Lozanov, and was developed through close collaboration between him and the late Dr. Evelyna Gateva, a teacher of Italian and Spanish language and literature, a student of the arts, and in her own right a professional classical singer and voice teacher. At that time (1980) I warned readers that I wasn't in a position to offer them an authoritative account of this approach, and the same is true today. Why, then, include it at all? For the same reasons as in 1980: (1) The ideas behind suggestopedia fit in with and in fact contributed to the ideas I have talked about in earlier chapters, and shed on the question "What's at stake?" their own distinctive light. (2) Reading about suggestopedia set me to doing some things that I'm glad I did even though they themselves could never be called examples of suggestopedia. (3) Reading about suggestopedia has helped me to make sense of certain things that have happened to me as a student, teacher, or supervisor of teachers in language classrooms.

Because it's sometimes hard to separate principles from practice when they are presented together, let me begin with a non-academic example.

Suggestopedic Principles in Something That's Not Suggestopedia

Episode 1.

Gerry and the nursery song–1: The scene is a grassy lawn on a warm summer night. Two young parents are sitting in a swing with their first child Gerry, fourteen months old, between them. The sky is full of stars. One of the parents turns to Gerry, points to the sky and exclaims, "Oh, look, Gerry! Just look at all the stars! Stars! (*Pointing again*) Stars! Stars!"

The other parent puts an arm around Gerry and sings softly,

Twinkle, twinkle, little star!
How I wonder what you are!
Up above the world so high,
Like a diamond in the sky.

The parents repeat the song several times, both in unison and individually.

1 *Some of what Gerry carried away from this encounter was in the form of what we would normally refer to as "conscious." Other changes in Gerry's inner resources were not in the usual sense "conscious." Leaving aside that distinction for the moment, let's suppose Gerry already had some understanding of "I," "you," "little," and "sky," and gets some of the meaning of "star" and "up above" from the parents' gestures. What else may Gerry have picked up from this exchange?*

Some of what Gerry got from listening was probably linguistic:

- The song has four parts (we adults think of them as "lines"), separated by pauses. Gerry of course can't count using numbers, but that is not the point.

- Each of those parts has seven smaller parts (what we call "syllables").

- Some of these smaller parts are louder than others. (We commonly call these "accented" syllables.)

- It's possible to guess accurately when a louder or softer syllable is coming. (There's a regular "meter.")

- The last syllable in a line rhymes with the last syllable of either the preceding or the following line. So Gerry discovers the ability to make successful predictions here too.

2 *A person Gerry's age can hardly put into words any conclusions drawn from this experience,* but what are a few of the ideas that may have been formed or strengthened by it concerning how people interact in the world?

Other conclusions that Gerry may have come away with were psychological:

Gerry 1: This experience was with my parents, whose ability to deal with the world I have come to trust.

Gerry 2: My parents took responsibility for initiating and guiding the experience.

Gerry 3: My mind can make linguistic predictions as to number of syllables, occurrence of stressed syllables, and the like.

Gerry 4: My mind's predictions have been confirmed as I listened to my parents just now.

Gerry 5: I've been exposed to some new language in a setting where I feel loved and welcomed.

It's also worth noting some of the things that Gerry did not come away with:

Gerry 6: My parents didn't ask me to repeat the song or in any other way seem concerned with how I responded to it (though they seemed delighted when I made a gurgle that they interpreted as me joining in).

Gerry 7: They didn't mention words like "trochaic tetrameter."

Gerry 8: They didn't give me a vocabulary quiz before I could have my bedtime feeding.

Let me emphasize that the above is not intended as an example of any kind of suggestopedic teaching or learning. It does however illustrate some essential features of suggestopedia:

Gerry 9: The text is *connected and interesting, and has cultural significance.*

Gerry 10: In its length and complexity it is *beyond what learners at Gerry's stage are conventionally expected to be able to handle.*

Gerry 11: The presentation of the text is *introduced with at least a little explanation of meaning.*

Gerry 12: On the other hand, the parents *don't systematically direct Gerry's attention to each word equally* just because it is in the text.

Gerry 13: The text and parts of it *come up in one way or another in subsequent days.*

Gerry 14: The interpersonal atmosphere is one of *joy and easiness,* rather than of earnestness and challenge.

Gerry 15: The words are associated with music (though, as we will see, in a way quite different from how words and music work together in suggestopedia) so that there is *an artistic side to the linguistic exposure.*

Gerry and the nursery song–2: The time is ten years later. Gerry is now in the sixth grade. One day while reading Lewis Carroll, Gerry's class runs across the following text:

> *Twinkle, twinkle, little bat!*
> *How I wonder what you're at!*
> *Up above the world so high,*
> *Like a tea tray in the sky.*

The students are first mystified, then amused. They have discovered parody.

A few minutes later, Gerry says aloud, "Twinkle, twinkle, little fish." The teacher laughs and says "Yes?" in a way that invites Gerry and the rest to play with this new parody.

This sequel illustrates one further characteristic of suggestopedia. Notice what the teacher did *not* do with the students' discovery of parody. Most obviously, the teacher didn't respond to Gerry by saying, "But now let's get back to my lesson plan" or something to that effect. But the teacher *also did not* take the discovery itself as an occasion to assign the class to come up with new parodies of their own (Gerry 14). Instead, the teacher was *alert for any attempt at spontaneity on the part of the students, encouraged it, and was ready to work with it.* (This is **Gerry 16**).

SUGGESTOPEDIA

At the beginning of Chapter 7 I pointed out that there is fairly widespread recognition of the existence of various degrees of psychological difficulty among the population in general and among language students in particular, but that there is much less agreement concerning the sources of those difficulties and concerning what can or should be done about them in an educational context. As a psychiatrist, Lozanov is of course quite aware of the whole range of well-known difficulties, whether emotional depression or depressed ability of the immune system to fight off the common cold or whatever.

The difficulty that receives Lozanov's central attention is however one that is seldom even mentioned by others. It is the fact that language students never, or only very infrequently, learn at a rate even close to what has been attained in classes conducted by his method, or with as little effort and fatigue. We continue to produce, modify, improve, reject and replace methods that bring our students achievement ranging from merely "high"-by-conventional-standards, to mediocre, to disastrous by any standards. Proponents of suggestopedia offer release from this labor of Sisyphus.

In Lozanov's view, this erratic and unsatisfactory outcome is caused by failure of students to use more than a tiny fraction of the powers they were born with—powers that influence concentration, creativity, volume of material retained per unit time, and duration of retention, for example. This failure is in turn due to (1) absence of conditions that would activate students' "reserve powers," and (2) continual subtle messages ("suggestions") from all around them that such reserve powers do not exist—that language study is by its very nature hard and tiring ("No pain, no gain!") and certainly not for everyone. The young parents should have placed Gerry in a little chair opposite them instead of between them in the swing, and Gerry should have made at least a little effort to mimic the material as they presented it.

Lozanov's prescription fits his diagnosis: (1) Establish and maintain conditions that will activate the students' reserve powers, and (2) replace society's negative suggestions with positive ones from the teacher and the course at large so that those powers can take effect. To fill this prescription he and Gateva have devised a whole pharmacopoeia of materials and techniques along with rigorous training for teachers who propose to use them.

I will not even attempt in this book to give a full how-to description of those techniques or of the construction of the materials. To do so would almost certainly be both inadequate and worse, misleading. And since my purpose is not advocacy, detailed recipes are in any case unnecessary. Instead I will first give a brief overview of the format of suggestopedic instruction, followed by some thoughts that what I've read, seen and heard have stimulated in me.

What you would meet in a suggestopedic course

Let's begin with an actual experience narrated by Barbara Fujiwara and some comments by Jennifer Deacon.

> **Barbara Fujiwara:** How can one capture the multifaceted richness and depth of the suggestopedic learning experience in a brief or even long description? In Dr. Gateva's Italian class, I felt we were immersed in the rich beauty of the

Italian culture and language. We were seeing the art and the landscapes of Italy in the posters and pictures adorning our classroom and textbook, we were hearing the language, sometimes to the majestic background of classical music, we were speaking it, and we were singing it. Everywhere we looked in our classroom, we saw Italian vocabulary, Italian grammar, Italian realia, Italian toys and every day our classroom was different.

But perhaps most significant to me was the richness and depth of my own learning experience, the excitement, involvement and creativity, and the opportunity to develop different parts of my personality. If I begin to recreate that course in my memory, many scenes appear in my mind but here I'll recount just one.

Every day, Dr. Gateva would start off by asking us for our news. I looked forward to hearing the latest episode in the continuing dramatic sagas of the other members of the cast. Had Santino won his soccer match? What new ineptitudes was Dottore Orsini's young wife displaying? What was happening with Agnese's eight puppies? What about Carlo's endless problems with his six wives? We groaned and laughed at each new installment in the adventures of our newly created identities.

I was inordinately fond of my own new persona. It was a relief to take a rest from being Barbara Fujiwara, English teacher, and be Dottore Chiara de Felice whose hospital in Assisi combined the best of Western and Eastern medicine. One morning I was eager to tell my news. I was off to China to investigate the use of ki energy in healing. The night before I had seen a Japanese documentary on a Chinese ki doctor who in an experiment had demonstrated that he could send his ki to a patient across the room and affect the patient's brain waves. Looking back, I am amazed that I was ready to explain this in my beginning Italian. What inspired me to attempt such a feat? Partly it was the class atmosphere in which we teased and bantered each other about the tall tales we were telling. But the most important factor was the steady stream of belief flowing from Dr. Gateva. "You can understand!" was the message we got when she was telling stories. "You can do it!" was the message we got when we were telling stories. Her belief overcame the limitations imposed by the social norms that Dr. Lozanov discusses and even more importantly, the limitations I had imposed on myself. That day her belief seemed as strong and transforming as the ki from the Chinese doctor. Words popped up from the large store of vocabulary; most memorably, "onda," from the placid waves in the canzone "Santa Lucia."

3 *Which features of this account are already familiar to you from other approaches to language teaching?*

- Which features are not?
- Which features seem most important to the writer?

Jennifer Deacon: After [my training with Drs. Lozanov and Gateva] I taught a few first-level suggestopedic courses here in Ottawa. Even though I didn't have the full-colour art work to go with the text, the learners responded enthusiastically to the method. They liked the variety of activities as much as anything. However, what I learned from Dr. L. and Dr. G. is that the key to a good suggestopedic course is the presentation of the concert session.

The teacher controls the input of language, inasmuch as she highlights some phrases or emphasizes certain sounds or coordinates the rhythm of the language with the music, imparting a sense of dignity or joy or lightheartedness or whatever. I knew when I had succeeded—it felt very natural.

A suggestopedia course consists of ten units of study, each of which takes exactly six hours of class time and (by some accounts) a little student time just before bedtime and just after getting up in the morning. The day's study consists of four 45-minute periods. Each unit consists of a long dialog, a bit of explanation, and many activities that draw on ("elaborate") what was in the dialog. The dialog itself is introduced during the third period of one day. During the fourth period of that day, the teacher reads the dialog aloud twice to the students as they sit back and listen to music (the "concert" session). The whole of the next day and the first half of the third day are devoted to activities of many other kinds.

The course is built around a long, rambling story told mainly as a series of conversations involving a large number of engaging characters. The conversations in successive lessons are connected to one another, so that there is an emerging plot. Each conversation is in effect an act in a developing playscript. This makes it possible for the students to generate mental images having more richness and depth than with the usual free-standing dialogs involving just two or three characters, such as we are accustomed to from some other courses. The length of the conversations serves the practical purpose of introducing students to a large hunk of new vocabulary (hundreds of words) and the psychological purpose of implying ("suggesting") confidence in their ability to handle the task. (This is reminiscent of Gerry 10.)

The activities based on this document fall into three general categories. First there is an introductory phase in which the meanings are conveyed to the students through a full range of media including translation where that is needed, and essential grammatical points are explained or put across through demonstration of one kind or another (Compare Gerry 11.)

The third phase, called "elaboration," contains a wide variety of activities including games (Gerry 13).

Some key concepts in suggestopedia

SP 1: Some of these activities are emotionally and artistically designed for introducing various points of meaning, pronunciation, or grammar.

SP 2: Others bear a superficial resemblance to activities long used by good language teachers in other traditions, but the criteria for designing them and selecting among them are unique to suggestopedia: not relief or respite or amusement, but a psychosocial confidence and security that will unlock reserve powers of the students' minds, and open up opportunities to see and rejoice in the amount of material they have mastered.

The final phase consists of activities in which with increasing spontaneity, students contribute their own real or imaginary content.

As Deacon indicates, however, the crucial phase is the second, which consists of the widely publicized "concert sessions." Fujiwara's account gives us some idea of how all three phases are permeated by careful management of the physical environment and by subtle expressions of confidence.

SP 3: Suggestion. In everyday life we are constantly receiving "suggestions." Suggestions vary greatly not only in their content but also in how overt they are. "Don't walk, run to your nearest supermarket and get yourself a bottle of Wizzo!" is pretty direct. Less direct but still overt is "Wizzo has been shown to significantly reduce the risk of smudging on furniture finished with some forms of polyurethane." Other suggestions however come in at or outside the fringes of awareness: a bottle of Wizzo simply sitting on a shelf in the well-appointed home of a glamorous character in a television drama. Suggestions enter the brain along with all other stimuli and participate in shaping the networks of long-term memory. These networks in turn are the source of our ideas—our conscious or not-so-conscious ideas—about what can be done and how to go about trying to do it. In general, the less we are aware of a suggestion the harder it is for us to resist it or change it. I would guess that among the most powerful suggestions are conclusions we draw for ourselves, and that among those the most powerful are the ones we haven't put or can't put into words. Lozanov's overall strategy is to conduct instruction in such a way that students will draw for themselves a new set of unconscious or even conscious conclusions that will open up to them possibilities far beyond what they had even dreamed of before.

SP 4: Reserve powers. The suggestions with which suggestopedia is most concerned have to do with learning: how slow or rapid it may be, how easy it may be or how painful it must be, how long its results can be expected to last, and how learning may be undertaken. Lozanov and Gateva tell us that we and our students have built-in powers that in the past have been used only by a few individuals, and even by them usually for just a moment at a time. If all the students in a class use such powers and use them consistently in an organized and well-orchestrated manner, they say, learning may be many times more rapid than we have known hitherto, it will be easy and even restful, and its results may last indefinitely. The approach called suggestopedia is Lozanov and Gateva's proposal for how to accomplish this.

We commonly fail to employ our reserve powers for either or both of two reasons: (1) conditions are not right for activating our full powers; (2) to use newly activated powers would violate norms we have internalized earlier.

SP 5: Barriers. Because suggestions can be so powerful and so insidious, mental and emotional health require that we build and maintain barriers against them. According to Lozanov, we have three such barriers.

- We resist suggestions that don't make sense to us in terms of what we already know. ("The ice on that pond looks solid, but it's only been frozen over for a day or two, so I won't venture out on it." "It's obviously impossible for me to learn 800 or even 100 new words a day, for in the past I've had trouble holding on to even ten!")

- We resist suggestions that undermine our feelings of confidence and security. ("Everyone else is jumping off the high diving board, but I'm afraid of what might happen to me when I hit the water." "Why should I sit back and close my eyes while the teacher reads the conversation along with the music?")

- We resist suggestions that we do something we think is morally or ethically wrong. ("I won't play the lottery because trying to get something for nothing is wrong." "We shouldn't be playing all these games in class—we should be working!")

Lozanov recognizes that without these three barriers to protect it, any personality would very quickly be torn apart by all the disorganized and conflicting suggestions that constantly strike it from outside. So he does not set out to destroy these barriers, or even to attack them directly, for that would lead to more trouble, not less. He seeks only to circumvent them, to sneak around them, or to pass through them by blending with them.

SP 6: Placebos. The trick is to lead the student to forget about or to ignore the limitations that society has suggested in the past. But before she can allow herself to do so, the student needs some excuse, some justification for venturing outside of the old fence even after the gate has been opened. A doctor sometimes sees that a patient's body could cure itself except that the patient is convinced that his illness requires help from a professional. So the doctor gives the patient a prescription that costs money, and that has a scientific-sounding name, but that is made of nothing but sugar or cornstarch. The patient gets well after taking these pills not because of any chemical action, but because the person has now used his own powers—powers he didn't know he had or was afraid to use—to cure himself. A medicine of this kind is called a "placebo."

Suggestopedia makes much use of pedagogical placebos in order to "desuggest" the undesirably restrictive social norms and to leave the student open to other, positive suggestions. In fact, every element in a suggestopedic course that is noticeably different from previous language instruction can have, in addition to its other effects, also a "placebo" effect.

SP 7: Conditions for using the full range of powers. But when can and will a student actually take advantage of these wonderful "full powers of learning"? Suggestopedia calls for the simultaneous and continuous maintenance of a number of conditions, of which I will mention six of the most conspicuous. Two are found in the printed materials: in their content and in their structure; two are artistic: music and pictures; the other two are psychological: authority and an atmosphere of "joy and easiness." Only when the didactic, artistic, and psychological aspects are well synchronized will suggestopedia be fully effective, and then it may even produce desirable biochemical effects. Some training in the use of the voice and of the body is therefore part of the preparation of a suggestopedic teacher.

SP 8: Structure of materials. The conversations around which the lessons are built are in many ways unlike the basic dialogs of the familiar audiolingual format. Perhaps the most striking difference is with regard to length. A suggestopedic conversation is several times as long as the 25-line limit we used to observe where I worked, and as I said earlier the conversations of the entire course comprise a rambling but connected whole with cultural as well as practical significance (cf. Gerry 9).

SP 9: Another distinctive feature of a suggestopedic conversation is that the native language glosses or translations are printed on separate pieces of paper so that they can be withdrawn after the students have pretty much "deciphered" the meaning of the conversation as a whole.

SP 10: The location of grammatical paradigms and other such information is also unique to suggestopedia. In the book they are located near where the student is likely to need them, but grammatical information also shows up on posters somewhere in the classroom.

SP 11: Contents of the conversations. Like the dialogs of some other styles of teaching, suggestopedic conversations involve likable people of various ages doing things the students may someday want to do.

SP 12: In their style, however, they are more likely to be positive in their content and to be upbeat, light, even whimsical in their tone. (This point is related to Gerry 9 and 14.)

SP 13: Another quality of a good suggestopedic conversation is that as the study progresses the conversation in the book will prove to be a suitable basis for students to draw on in the fourth phase, when they are telling stories of their own.

What is the *least* valuable way of using music in a language class?

SP 14: In the eyes of the popular press, the key to successful suggestopedia lies in the second of its three phases—the concert sessions. For once the press seems to have things right. Gateva and Lozanov are quite clear about the importance of the concerts. As Deacon's account attests (p. 146), this comes across clearly to students in their courses as well.

During a concert, the students listen as the teacher reads the conversation against a background of classical music. (This is comparable to, though quite different from Gerry 15.) There are two concerts in each unit, one "active" and the other "passive," which differ with regard to their purpose, the type of music they employ, and the way in which the teacher does the reading. In other approaches to teaching, the reason for the music might be simply to make the course more pleasant, or to provide "relief" from the supposed "drudgery" of language study. Neither of these is true for suggestopedia, however.

SP 15: The purpose of the music is to provide auditory input which, through its artistic qualities and through its integration of emotion and logic, will stimulate the mind to operate in new and much more powerful ways. The goal is not just some general physical relaxation, but a "concentrated psychorelaxation." That is something quite different, perhaps akin to what Goleman and others call "flow." And because the various aspects of instruction are carefully intermingled and coordinated with one another, the student doesn't really have to choose which aspect to focus on at any given moment.

SP 16: Pictures. Analogously, the pictures and other art objects visible either in the textbook or in the classroom are selected or designed with an eye to their effect on releasing the reserve powers of the students' minds: perhaps through their proportions or their colors, or through their value as representations of the culture.

SP 17: The Golden Mean. A subtle but apparently very powerful element in suggestopedic materials is a concept from ancient geometry known variously as the

Golden Proportion, the Golden Section, or the Golden Mean. Imagine a straight line connecting Point A to Point C. Now imagine a bead B able to slide along the line. Try to slide B to exactly that point, closer to A than to C, at which the distance from A to B (AB) divided by the distance from B to C (BC) is the same as the distance from B to C (BC) divided by the total length of the line (AC). When you have done so, you will have created a "golden section," or reached the "golden proportion." (The numerical value of this "golden mean" turns out to be approximately 1.62.) That ratio may be found not only with beads on strings, but also between the dimension of a rectangle (hence the proportions of many picture frames). More interesting is the fact that it often shows up in art (e.g., the Parthenon) and in nature (e.g., certain proportions of the human figure, and the curvature of the shell of the chambered nautilus). In fact, this abstract relationship is so widely encountered that some thinkers down through the centuries have seen in it a symbol of the creative process in general, or as the key to the physics of the cosmos, or at least an essential component of beauty. Whatever may be the truth of these beliefs, one thing emerges as very likely: that *there is indeed something in the human nervous system that responds to and works in accordance with this ratio.* If through graphic arts or verbal text or even through music one can somehow insinuate this abstract ratio into a student's nervous system and activate it there, perhaps we can hope this activation will spread and enhance the functioning of the other parts of the brain as well. Suggestopedia makes deliberate and frequent use of this principle.

Incidentally, the connection between the mathematical relationships among the parts of verbal texts and the mathematical relationships present in graphic material that accompanies them has a longer history than had been realized until recently. The very no-nonsense author of a recent study of *The Earliest Irish and English Bookarts,* writing about manuscripts of the seventh to tenth centuries, emphasizes "the shared concepts of form that underlie both the literary arts and the decorative arts" for books of that day. "Much," he says, "can be learned about formal plans of poems from studying the pictures [that accompany them], and studying the divisions of verse texts can lead to a better understanding of the layout of many of the portrait or symbol pages." From this he infers "a common philosophical and esthetic basis" for "endeavors of art in different media." The Golden Mean is in fact one of the relationships to which he gives most attention.

R. Stevick
1994

SP 18: Authority. The most important background element, though, is not paint for the walls of the room, or any special furniture, or any other tangible piece of equipment. It is what Lozanov calls the "authority" of the teacher. By "authority," Lozanov means much more than the ability to issue instructions that will be carried out. The central element in "authority" is the teacher's apparent competence—his competence in the eyes of his students—plus his reputation for being able to produce amazing results. Gerry's parents (Gerry 1) possessed this kind of authority in Gerry's eyes. People will not trust themselves even to a strong bridge if it looks flimsy, but if they do not set foot on it they will never arrive at the place to which it leads. Suggestopedia differs from other methods in that it considers the authority of the teacher and of the school, and even of suggestopedia in general, to be an integral part of the method, and not just desirable extras.

We have seen this same principle at work to some extent in the history of language teaching outside of suggestopedia. At least a portion of the early successes that swept audiolingualism to a dominant position in some parts of the world in the 1950s must have come from the well-publicized exploits of the linguistic scientists in organizing training in seldom-taught languages during World War II. And at least some part of the success of programmed instruction and of its current successor, computer-assisted instruction, must rest on what people have read about those pigeons who were taught to appear to play Ping-Pong. This is not to belittle either of these methods or the sources of their success. But the same kind of "authority" that these methods have profited from generally and in haphazard fashion is in suggestopedia developed consciously and painstakingly, and used with great efficiency.

SP 19: Suggestopedia employs a broad spectrum of means for establishing and maintaining authority in the special sense of the previous two paragraphs, all the way from using the academic titles of its practitioners, to details of the teacher's dress, posture and voice, to the fact that the parts of the day—even the 7-minute "pauses" between sessions—begin and end exactly on schedule. It is largely to this end also that the teacher is required to start each day with a detailed written plan. Suggestopedia recognizes that as the day goes on the teacher will inevitably improvise on that plan and depart from it, but as she does so she is unlikely to give off the subtle signals of momentary uncertainty that would immediately undermine her authority. Authority is enhanced every time something goes well in the class, especially when the students' minds associate success with a feature of the course that they perceive to be unlike methods they have encountered in the past.

It is also partly for the sake of maintaining authority that there is no informal teacher-student contact between classes, and that students are not invited to express their reactions except in a written questionnaire at the end of the course. This restriction also has the effect of encouraging the students to focus on the stress-free and cheerful content of the materials rather than on themselves.

SP 20: Joy and easiness. Suggestopedia overlooks no detail in promoting a sense of "joy and easiness" within and among its students. The most general and most essential contributor to this sense is the students' feeling that their teacher—their authoritative teacher—is enjoying them and believes in them (Gerry 5; Fujiwara). Other sources of joy are the thrill of discovery in figuring out the text, the language, and what the teacher is saying (Gerry 3, 4); the greater thrill of discovering, observing, and verifying one's own mental powers; the fun of exercising opportunities for creativity; and the pleasure of finding oneself surrounded by beauty.

SP 21: One specific device that contributes to "joy and easiness" is that at the beginning of the course students adopt fictional names and occupations around which new identities are created. They will keep these identities and develop them in their own ways day by day to the end of the course.

SP 22: One function of the new identities is to stimulate mental imagery that will be as vivid as possible and that will snowball as the days and weeks go on. To this end, each of the occupations is prestigious or interesting in some way, and may even be glamorous. Since the student's "real" identity is entirely excluded from the classroom, he receives from and creates within this new surrogate identity—largely on the unconscious plane—a number of positive, pleasant associations that go with that occupation. He will thus feel good about this fictitious Self, and in that Self will be more ready to enter into whatever is happening on the conscious level. In this character, he may take roles in conversations involving a whole new set of characters that are being played temporarily not by his real Self, but by his surrogate Self.

SP 23: But the space afforded by the surrogate identity is not merely a pleasant nook in which the student—perhaps in daily life a serious manager or accountant or language teacher—can enjoy a bit of play. As Barbara Fujiwara's account shows us, it is also a space in which the student can feel secure: "If a mistake is noticed, it was made not by me but by Dottore Chiara de Felice." This is another way in which such a simple and time-honored device as fictional identities can contribute toward "joy and easiness."

SP 24: Let me give just three more examples, notable because each by itself seems so small, of suggestopedia's vigilance in maintaining a sense of joy and easiness. (1) In the psychological realm, what most people would call "breaks" —short intervals between class sessions—are called "pauses." The word "break" carries for many people the idea of relief from something that one needs relief from—something hard, tiring, or otherwise onerous. Such terminology and such implications are diligently excluded from every aspect of suggestopedic instruction. (2) In the purely physical realm I'm sure no method would advocate classrooms full of stale air, but suggestopedia is the only one I've seen that repeatedly specifies that during each "pause" the room is to be "reaired." (3) In the aesthetic realm, there are to be fresh flowers in the classroom every day.

One sure way to *destroy* joy and easiness very quickly would be to put students on the spot. Gerry's parents avoided this mistake (Gerry 6, 8).

SP 25: Suggestopedic teachers are trained to relate to students in ways that don't imply confrontation, or at least don't provoke confrontation of the academic variety. For example, in activities that need recall from the hundreds of words presented in earlier parts of the course, recall is not by individuals but by the group. What most students don't come up with, at least one student will, and the needed word can then be recognized and used by everyone. Another example is the treatment of student errors, which is done casually and conversationally just as if the teacher were simply clarifying his understanding aloud.

On the other hand, Fujiwara recounts an incident during her suggestopedic training when she was engaging her students in short, simple exchanges within what she was accustomed to thinking of as the limitations of their present level. At that point, she reports, "Dr. L broke in and began to engage the students (a few were true beginners!) in a discussion of Nazism. I was amazed. Afterwards, he told me that the exchanges seemed to be suggesting to them that that was all they could do (probably just what I was thinking) and that it was important to get them to talk about topics that they would get emotional about." Here the confrontation was not over their academic mastery of the language, but over an issue on which they had probably communicated many times in the past through the medium of their native language. The emotional involvement would have at least two effects. Certainly it would lead to richer and more vivid mental imagery to be stored along with the words they were hearing and using. But as I learned during two or three years when I was writing poems from time to time, strong feelings of various kinds can cause the resources within one's long-term memory to become more fully, more sharply and more readily available. (I'm making no claims as to the literary quality of the product!) In this incident Lozanov, operating (as I suppose) through what in Chapter 3 I called an "Ordinary Person" mask, was expressing confidence that the students' true abilities were far beyond what they had been displaying.

Another way to interfere with joy and easiness would be to have students engage in activities that had no relationship to any of their needs or motivations except some very general occupational need to learn the language, or the equally general academic desire to do well in the course (Gerry 6).

SP 26: Through interesting content and carefully designed games, as well as through the famous "concerts," instruction consists of a series of activities each of which carries within it one or more kinds of inherent payoff: pleasant physical stimuli or social interaction, discovery, self-expression, and the like.

Interrelations among these elements of suggestopedia

One might trace out a self-perpetuating cycle among all of these elements of suggestopedia:

- Authority in the suggestopedic sense of the word contributes directly not only toward enlisting the initial cooperation of the students, but also toward maintaining the "placebo effect" of many aspects of the course.

- The placebo effect helps to desuggest limitations and reservations, and so to release the reserve powers of the mind that are called into operation by the artistic aspects of the course.

- These activated and released powers make learning easier and therefore more joyful.

- The rising sense of joy and easiness validates the method in the eyes of the students and so enhances its authority and the authority of the teacher. And so back to the beginning of the cycle.

Of course the interrelationships among the various aspects of a suggestopedic course are more numerous, more complex and more subtle than this attractively unilinear "cycle" makes them sound. The cycle does however indicate how suggestopedia's all-embracing concern for the actual and perceived authority of the teacher is not an end in itself. This is because the cycle does not operate on a flat surface.

SP 27: As students progress through the course and their reserve powers begin to operate on the subject matter, and an atmosphere of joy and easiness continues to encourage them, their ability quickly rises and they begin to display spontaneity. This is exactly what the teacher has been waiting for. (Remember Gerry 16!) The teacher is careful to work with this student-generated material, for out of it the best learning will grow. Now is a time when the teacher can create open-ended situations and invite the students to participate in them. Though in the beginning the teacher directs and controls the students' activity in great detail (Gerry 2), some of this control gradually relaxes. Spontaneous exchanges among students are, however, not allowed within the course without the monitoring and eventual control of the teacher.

In summary, then, the overall sequence in suggestopedia is not authority-conformity-retention as in some approaches, but authority-cooperation-autonomy. Similarly the central strategy of the approach is not to teach a course employing a particular set of esoteric techniques; rather it is to believe in the full learning powers of the students and to convey this belief to them continuously in countless mutually-harmonizing ways, and to confirm it by what the students see they are doing.

WHY DOES SUGGESTOPEDIA WORK?

In 1979, Betty Edwards published a wonderful book for the artistically ungifted, titled *Drawing on the Right Side of the Brain*. Edwards' method of teaching drawing—or better, her method for bringing out drawing ability—is of course not to be confused with suggestopedia. What they have in common is a reasoned and effective approach to drawing on innate resources that too often are lying dormant. One teacher familiar with both is Kristin Newton.

> **Kristin Newton:** I teach both Suggestopedia and Drawing on the Right Side of the Brain seminars, and I've found that the students in each experience have very similar reactions. First, they generally don't believe they have any ability to learn a foreign language or draw, but they are longing to do so; second, they gradually become conscious of, and more accepting of, how their brain processes information, which varies from individual to individual; third, they struggle as they realize that their preconditioned responses don't work anymore, they need to let go but are afraid to do so; fourth, as they begin to let go of the old ways of perceiving and thinking, they make major breakthroughs, which they sometimes don't realize until weeks, or sometimes months, later; fifth, they experience other benefits in addition to learning a language, or drawing, such as increased confidence, reduction of stress, etc.

Teachers' Voices

I must report that my own experiences with Edwards' book shortly after it came out were quite consistent with Newton's five points. Even when the reasoning behind these methods or any other is subjected to challenges from the scientific community, their efficacy is an independent question.

Frameworks

Turning back now to suggestopedia, can we—should we—must we—take it seriously? If suggestopedia has really worked as well as many witnesses credible to me have reported, then we're dealing with a fact, and all relevant facts deserve our careful attention. Under these circumstances the answer to this question has to be a clear Yes.

But *why* does suggestopedia work? The answer to this question is much less clear. I suspect even Lozanov will never cease studying and researching the details. I certainly don't have the answer. The remainder of this section will consist of my own speculations in terms of the contents of Chapters 1-3. I can see many points of affinity.

■ *The general goal in any educational undertaking is to make appropriate changes in the resources of the learners' long-term memory.*

I mean this as a truism, though I recognize that suggestopedia would phrase it differently.

The numbers SP 1... identify points listed on pp. 143-144. They will be referred to later by those same numbers.

■ *Those resources are made up of networks.*

The "network" terminology is metaphorical on the psychological level, but is probably a literal description on the neurological level. This terminology is more suited than most others to representing the subtleties and complexities with which suggestopedia works.

■ *Networks are made up of many kinds of items.*

Suggestopedia of course provides the usual range of verbal and sensory items. But it also points out the existence of "barriers," which I think of as combinations of items derived from past experiences and modifiable by experiences in the course (SP-5).

■ *Some of these items are relatively abstract.*

In addition to "barriers" [above], some of the distinctive contributions of suggestopedia are emphases on joy (SP-20), confidence (SP-2), integration of logic with emotion (SP-15), and the Golden Mean (SP-17), all of which are quite abstract.

■ *The key items in a network are often affective.*

A term used in suggestopedia is "double planeness." If I understand this term correctly it stands for an insistence that every activity in the course be viewed as taking place simultaneously on both the surface level of overt content and the deeper level of personal significance. This would mean that students would never have to attempt to "internalize" material just for its own sake—just because "it may come in handy some day." Similar thinking is evident in the requirement that each of the "elaboration" activities in the third phase carry with it payoffs beyond the standard practical and academic ones. (SP-26).

One side of "affect" has to do with what we commonly call needs, purposes, motivations or drives. Some of these are very general. One such goal is to meet some practical need for the language, whether for current employment or for future travel or for something else.

Suggestopedia's response to this need includes an exceptionally large vocabulary for the amount of time spent, and relatively high level of readiness to interact in the language. The degree of accuracy is less clearly documented. Another point is that the model conversations in suggestopedia are designed with an eye to their serviceability as bases for personally interesting and significant improvisation by students (SP-13). (This latter feature is of course found in some non-suggestopedic materials as well.)

- *A second very general desire is to perform well academically.*

More than most methods, suggestopedia is designed so as to maintain not only the feeling of doing well but also the reality, at least when "doing well" is defined from a suggestopedic point of view. Some have raised the question of how well the graduates of a beginning course would fit into a second course taught by another method, particularly an accuracy-oriented one. I don't know.

- *Other general needs are physical. One of these is for physical movement.*

Not all of suggestopedia ever did take place in the much-advertised easy chairs, which I understand are in any case no longer considered necessary. Many of the elaboration activities in the third phase of each lesson involve the major muscles of the arms and legs. Perhaps this becomes more animated as the course progresses and the students' spontaneity increases.

- *Another general physical need is for fresh air.*

I couldn't help noticing suggestopedia's explicit concern for this and other physical needs that most other approaches seem to take for granted (SP-24).

- *Yet another general need is for beauty.*

I'm not aware of another approach that pays so much attention to having beautiful things around, whether pictures and artifacts (SP-16) or music (SP-15). Culturally authentic articles help to create a French or Japanese or other world for the students. The effects of beauty—the abstract memory items that flow from it—probably cover a wide range. Socially, it's a sign that someone powerful cares. Physically it is reassurance that I need not prepare to defend myself. Emotionally it may dispose the student to look on the bright side of things. There are probably other aspects that I haven't thought of.

- *One of the greatest of the general social needs is for confidence in the person in power—the teacher.*

This of course is the reason for the emphasis on "authority" (SP-18), as well as for the aspects of the approach that support the authority of the teacher: "joy and easiness" (SP-20), careful construction of the materials, and all the rest.

- *Also essential is the students' confidence in themselves.*

Implicit here are "joy and easiness" (SP-20) again, the liberating use of self-created identities (SP-21), careful design, selection, and management of the elaboration activities (SP-25), and avoidance of negative suggestions (SP-19, 26).

- *But confidence in the teacher without a feeling of being accepted by him or her could still severely limit access to and use of the student's full powers.*

Fujiwara's account of her reaction to her teacher's "steady stream of belief" provides an excellent example here. (See also SP-2).

- *A feeling of being accepted by one's peers is also freeing.*

This is a further value of the protection afforded by the continuing fictional identity (SP 21). The consistent avoidance of confrontation and expressions of stress both in the materials (SP 20) and in the conduct of the class (SP 19) also contributes to this feeling.

■ *Within this atmosphere of confidence and acceptance, students need lots of interaction, whether in cooperation with one another or in playful competition.*

This is one of the criteria for designing the elaboration activities (SP 26) and for selecting among them as the class session progresses.

■ *Besides needs, purposes, etc., affect also includes the student's own feelings and emotions and those of his or her classmates.*

In addition to its systematic cultivation of joy and easiness, (SP 20) suggestopedia makes sure that the content of the model conversation is lively and upbeat (SP 12).

■ *In my view of the learning/memory process, new sensory inputs go directly to relevant sites in the brain, rather than passing first through "short-term memory" or the like.*

Such an idea supports, and is supported by, suggestopedia's emphasis on the importance of peripheral stimuli that a student has never noticed consciously and may not understand at the time (SP 3). This is certainly true for many aspects of the fine arts component of the course, both musical (SP 15) and visual (SP 16).

■ *These new inputs interact with the existing configurations of existing networks in long-term memory.*

Here I believe suggestopedia is unique in its recognition that these networks generally include "barriers"—judgments and expectations about what is proper or what is possible, or both (SP 5).

■ *We are not clear about the inner dynamics of this interaction.*

Perhaps it is in this *terra incognita* that some of the "reserve powers" lie (SP 4). Under these circumstances I think we can welcome Dr. Gateva's experimentation with unverbalized factors such as the aesthetics of music (SP 15) and visual or tactile art (SP 16). This is an area where her training and expertise far exceeded the resources of most of us word-driven language teachers.

■ *Whatever those inner dynamics may be, they lead to new patterns of activation within long-term memory, and this in turn sends new images to the "worktable" of working memory. The results of what is done more or less consciously on the worktable now become input back to long-term memory.*

The progressive unfolding of a single story line throughout the model conversations (SP 8, 11-13), plus the continuous development of a set of new identities by the students themselves (SP 21), plus the emphasis on encouraging and working with spontaneity (SP 27), should ensure that the meanings attached to the linguistic forms will be relatively rich, complex, and vivid.

■ *How long, and how readily, the results of new combinations will remain available from long-term memory varies. In general, if a new combination of items is complex, rich, and affectively strong, its availability will be easier and longer lasting ("permanent memory"). If on the other hand the combination is simple, impoverished, and affectively weak, its availability will be more difficult and will last only a short time ("holding memory"). But if we can get material into holding memory, and if, while it is still there, we can work it into further experiences that are affectively strong, then it will become more permanent.*

Some of the techniques of suggestopedia seem clearly designed to get lots of new material into holding memory: the printed translations and the grammar tables, for example. The same may be true of the powerful and centrally important concert sessions. The task of converting this temporarily-held material into more permanent status is what the elaboration activities (SP 26), and especially the spontaneity (SP 27) are for. At least that's my guess.

SUMMARY

In Chapter 1, I listed five ways in which affect participates in the learning/memory process.

On the basis of what I have read and heard about suggestopedia, the approach seems to fit the ideas in Chapter 1 rather well. First of all, suggestopedia provides, as input to the networks of long-term memory, a strong flow of affective data that are both plentiful and appropriate. Since these data are overwhelmingly pleasant and in several ways non-threatening, they should give rise to a minimum of "clutter on the worktable," and the rich, complex, and vivid mental images that the combination generates should thus become well-integrated with the verbal material in the networks of long-term memory. As for involuntary auditory playback ("the din in the head"), I would not be surprised if the concert format turns out to be one of the circumstances that activate this potentially valuable mental activity. *External* affective feedback is quite clearly of a quality that will sustain enthusiastic participation by the students both in giving attention to others and in speaking out themselves. I can however imagine with regard to *internal* affective feedback that the linguistic norms of the non-native peer group may have their typical result in the fossilization of various imprecisions of language.

The special status of music in the workings of the mind appears with particular clarity in certain neuropathologies. Some interesting case histories can be found in Sachs (1985) Chapters 1 and 15.

WHY ISN'T SUGGESTOPEDIA MORE WIDELY USED?

As I reread the preceding section of this chapter, its picture of suggestopedia looks highly favorable. Certainly in terms of my own understanding as I expressed it in *Memory, Meaning & Method, Second Edition* and in the first chapter of this book, the approach stacks up very well on almost every point. Readers may therefore quite properly ask, "If suggestopedia's so good, why is it not used more widely?" True, suggestopedic classes may be found in dozens of countries around the world, but I would be surprised if in even one country the number of language classes conducted by this approach exceeds 1% of the total. Again the question, "Why not?"

From an outsider's point of view, certain superficial matters spring to mind. The 12-student class size and the size and furnishings of the classroom seem luxurious by the standards of most school systems. Teachers need special voice training both for singing and for speaking, and possibly also in such matters as the basic theory of music, dramatic arts, choreography, and painting. Most language teachers lack these abilities, and schools seldom hire with such qualifications in mind. Even the requirement for daily fresh flowers in the classroom might be seen as budgetarily onerous.

Another part of the answer may lie in the relation between parts and whole. I've just said that suggestopedia "stacks up well" against a list of individual features, each of which seems to me to be desirable in an approach. But Lozanov and Gateva tell us, both as promise and as warning, that (to use a mathematical metaphor) in suggestopedia the whole outcome is the product of the parts, not just their sum. The intricacy and delicacy of interdependence among all the elements of suggestopedia may be a factor in its limited adoption. If furthermore well-meaning but inexpert admirers of the work of Lozanov and Gateva use some approximation of the method and label it suggestopedia, then any inferior results they produce will reflect badly on the name of the method, thus reducing the confidence and lowering the expectations of students who come to authentic suggestopedia later.

But we need not listen only to outsiders. The originators of suggestopedia have themselves been refreshingly ready to shed light on the difficulties that would be encountered in any large-scale adoption of suggestopedic foreign language teaching. In his introduction to their 1988 *Handbook,* Lozanov points out that any teacher qualified to implement the approach needs a solid understanding of such matters as its global nature, the theory of reserve capacities, and the nature of "concentrated psychorelaxation," and he reports that progress in establishing these qualifications can be slow. He further says that teachers too easily allow their principal goal to shift gradually from "inspiring" their students to merely "amusing" them. Or they too often introduce some of the elaboration activities in a formal and confrontational way rather than indirectly and in harmony with the spontaneity of the students. Teachers sometimes forget to search for their students' reserve capacities; on the other hand, if the reserves are released to too high a degree, that may itself lead to unpleasant complications.

In one of her contributions to the *Proceedings of the International Conference on Suggestopedia* (1990), Gateva lays out some of the difficulties of suggestopedia in teaching foreign languages, especially for beginners. The fundamental and biggest difficulty, she finds, lies in the area of teacher training. An effective suggestopedic teacher needs thorough grounding in technique, and even some undeniably artistic, versatile, and intelligent teachers somehow can't manage to synchronize the artistic and didactic sides of the method. But technique is not enough. The teacher also needs deep within himself the basic understandings mentioned by Lozanov [see above]. A teacher who lacks full confidence in the method and in himself can hardly inspire in his students the self-confidence that is essential to their success in suggestopedia.

Gateva goes on to say that a second basic difficulty lies in the selection of students. In the real world, within any new group we will find certain degrees of clique formation, intolerance, and other interpersonal pressures. (Grethe Hooper Hansen, an experienced user and clear exponent of suggestopedia concedes that like all methods, suggestopedia favors some learning styles over others.) Unless the teacher can get all this under control from the beginning, Gateva warns, the whole process faces failure. She lists a number of other more detailed difficulties, such as over-reliance on repetition in the elaboration phase, or the timing and manner of giving praise. Numerous and serious as some of these difficulties may be, however, she believes that they are not impossible to overcome, and that the first step toward overcoming them is to face them squarely.

Under these circumstances the reaction of some might be, "What if this new approach does lead to the kind of results they claim for it? It's still like an expensive racing car, delicate in its many adjustments and demanding on its driver. It might be nice, but we simply can't afford such a wonderful device just for routine trips to the market for a loaf of bread or a few fish and the like. We can get results at the high end of the range we're now accustomed to by merely applying more fully and more ingeniously what we already know. So let's just forget about suggestopedia."

I can understand that kind of reaction, but I think it would be unfortunate. In the automotive metaphor, even the designers of family sedans and utilitarian pick-up trucks study newer and more sophisticated vehicles in order to learn from them and improve their own products. But to leave that metaphor, maybe the difference is between those who strive to teach more language and teach it better within the expectations of our existing society, and those who dream of developing themselves personally and professionally so that they can accept and meet the challenge of helping their students to achieve their full human potential and thus to lift society itself to a higher level. Lozanov and Gateva have been working from backgrounds and assumptions quite different from Gattegno's, and have arrived at a method that contrasts with his in almost every respect. Yet once again I seem to hear echoes of that same humanistic vision we found in the Clifford Bax poem on page 125.

A REMINDER

Needless to say, a teacher who wishes to use suggestopedia should have some live, face-to-face training in it. As I indicated in the Prologue and in Chapter 1, the descriptions in this book are intended to illustrate certain general principles, rather than to teach readers how to use the approaches for themselves. Meanwhile, the reader may wish to consult what other writers on methodology such as Larsen-Freeman (1986), Richards and Rodgers (1986), Blair (1982), and Oller and Richard-Amato (1983), have said about the Silent Way.

During the period when I was working on the suggestopedia chapter for the 1980 version of A Way and Ways, I was in charge of Turkish instruction at the Foreign Service Institute. A student who was having to leave for Turkey halfway through the course was sounding distressed because she had not yet come to the passive forms of verbs. I doubt that such situations ever arise in Dr. Lozanov's courses, and I don't know what he would do if they did.

■ What assumptions based on accumulated suggestions from earlier years would you guess this student was working from?

■ Describe more than one way in which you or I might have responded to her at this point.

The thought struck me that this student's ignorance about the passive voice was really a small matter. What was of great urgency (and here I think Lozanov was whispering in my ear) was her idea that the passive was some mysterious forest, or some treacherous bed of quicksand, through which she could pass safely only with the help of a licensed guide and an officially published chart.

- To what extent do you think this idea of the student's was actually realistic or accurate?

- What would have been the probable effects of my answering the student in a way consistent with that?

To have answered the student's question as I used to answer such questions would have been a service to her in the short run. In the long run, however, it would have been a disservice, because I would have implied—"suggested"—to her once again that her own powers were very weak.

Instead, I said to the student in Turkish, "Oh, it's not all that difficult." Then, turning to a Turk who was with us, I said, as if I were uncertain, *Vermek. . . ver-ilmek?*" ("to give"..."to be given"?). After another example or two of this kind, all without English translation, the student saw for herself what we were doing, and began to contribute examples of her own, complete with correct vowel harmonies in the suffixes. I had been right in guessing that she would be able to do this.

- Did the student's success here surprise you? Why, or why not?

- What risks did I assume in acting on this guess?

If I had not been right, I would have had to change my technique quickly, and without her noticing that I had changed it. Otherwise, I could have ended up having conveyed the ideas that (1) she was as limited in her ability to deal with these things as she had thought she was, and that (2) she was in the hands of an incompetent teacher.

Once I saw that the student was playing happily with the kind of passive that I had introduced her to, I gave her the other essential fact about Turkish passives: "It's not all that simple." Then as we had done earlier, we gave her a few examples of another passive-like suffix and let her play with it. Finally I said in English, "So you do have to know which verbs form the passive in which way. But from what we've done here you can recognize passives when you run into them from now on, and you also know that no one way of forming passives is harder than the others."

- What if I had given the student the information in the last sentence at the beginning rather than at the end of my response to her expressed concern?

In earlier days, I would have responded to the student's question quite differently. First, I am sure, I would have picked up the nearest piece of chalk and made for the blackboard. Once arrived there, I would have outlined what I knew on the topic as simply and clearly as I was able. My central purpose would have been to prepare the student for understanding and producing correct passive forms in her future encounters with the language. If I did the kind of job I was trying to do, I would leave her feeling that she now understood Turkish passive verbs, and feeling relieved from her earlier anxiety on the subject, and grateful to me for having relieved her from her anxiety by putting this new knowledge into her mind. As I gave the explanation, I would have been aiming for exactly this kind of result, and so my facial expression, my tone of voice, and all the rest would have automatically begun to convey earnest messages like, "Now always remember. . . !" and "Are you sure you understand. . . ?" And when someday, as was almost inevitable, she failed to apply her new knowledge correctly, she would say to herself (or she would hear me saying), "You've forgotten. . . !" We would be back to the chain, as old as the Garden of Eden, in which knowledge leads to responsibility, responsibility leads to guilt, and guilt means that one can get no good thing except by the sweat of one's brow.

This anecdote makes a nice story that has a happy ending at least for the time being, and vindicates some of the principles of suggestopedia. But:

- How do you think the effects of this (suggestopedic) treatment on the student's linguistic and personal competence six months down the line would have compared with the effects of a more conventional response to her concern?

- In any case, how feasible in everyday language teaching is the kind of response I gave?

---

4 *When you were growing up:*

- How many of the people you saw frequently spoke more than one language? All? Most? Some? Just a few? None?

- What were the attitudes of those who did not control more than one language toward those who did?

- What were the expectations about children of your generation concerning languages? "They will speak at least some of the official language"? "They will study some language, but never have much use from it"? "They probably won't even study one"? Other?

- What did people seem to think about the ease or difficulty of gaining practical control of a new language? "No big deal"? "Like anything else, it takes work"? "Only for the gifted few"? Other?

Compare your answers with those of colleagues. Where and how did your culture suggest or desuggest "joy and easiness"? limits? What is and is not a proper way to approach language study?

As well as you are able, try to answer the above questions as they might apply to the homes of your students.

---

5 *Use of foreign languages sometimes shows up in various ways in dreams. For example, Barbara Fujiwara tells of a woman studying German who had a dream in which she had three buckets—masculine, feminine, and neuter—and she was putting words into the appropriate buckets.*

- Supply some adverb ending in *-ly* between the words "was" and "putting" in Fujiwara's description. Then compare your word with those supplied by others. What might these answers indicate about the subtle suggestions you may be giving to your students?

6 *Have you ever dreamt about using some specific words or phrases in a foreign language?*

- What was the occasion? What did you actually say or hear?

- How did the other person or people in your dream seem to react? How did you yourself feel about it?

11
THE STAKES

As may be evident from the Prologue and Chapter 1, the subtitle of this book took me by surprise. At first, of course, we all assumed the book would be simply TeacherSource: A Way and Ways *(or because of its reduced length, perhaps* A Way and Ways Lite*). But that sounded like what its original had come too close to being: a promotional document for certain unconventional approaches that in 1980 were still obscure.*

Someone suggested just plain TeacherSource: Methodology. *No, I said, writing toward that word would require a more comprehensive and more encyclopedic treatment than I was offering. So we were still without a working title.*

"Then what do I want to write toward?" I asked myself. "Something that will keep you reminded of how your 'way' of looking at your work has changed or stayed the same since 1980," came my reply, "something focused not on why everyone should try these three 'ways,' but on what everyday foreign language teachers can learn from three methods that they themselves don't use. Something too that will retain what other teachers say they found new or most helpful in A Way and Ways.*" This answer brought with it almost immediately the phrase "What's at Stake," and then in question form, "What's at Stake?" Now, after four chapters about my "way" of seeing and six about three "ways" of teaching, it's time to pull together what I said there and turn to the question we (the editors and I) have chosen as our subtitle.*

QUESTIONS ASKED BY COURSE-PLANNERS

Frequently asked questions

In designing a course, language teachers routinely ask themselves certain questions. Three of the most common are:

1. WHAT is this course supposed to teach (which language, level, skills, styles and registers, etc.)?

2. FOR WHOM are we designing it (which age, cultural and educational backgrounds, size of class, etc.)?

3. WHY are we designing it (to serve which practical or academic purposes)?

On this basis we ask and answer a fourth question:

4. HOW shall we go about it (which approach, method(s), techniques)?

Less frequently asked questions

But there are other questions that language teachers *don't* routinely ask themselves. One of them lies close to what this book is about:

5. Is this course to serve any DEEPER AIMS in addition to the teaching of language?

"Deeper aims"? asks the reader. What I mean by "deeper aims" shows up in Tim Murphey's message to students on the inside front cover of his book *Language Hungry*:

> "The information in this book can *change your life* when you *choose to use it and improve yourself.* You will learn to *enjoy learning even more passionately* than you do now. You will *welcome new opportunities* around you and willingly *take healthy risks* that will challenge and thrill your mind and body. It's up to you, though, to *choose to use the information, to experiment with it, to risk finding more joy in learning.* For finally, *you are your own best teacher.*" [italics in 1996 edition]

The key phrase here is "change your life," as contrasted with just "add to your language capabilities." Donald N. Larson, a veteran language teacher and trainer of both learners and teachers, speaks of a difference between learning a new language as development of a new organ, contrasted with doing it simply as the addition of a new tool. We see here a concern for pursuing new "life goals," not just for reaching certain "language goals." This concern shows up in all three of the "ways" I have discussed. Its clearest and most dramatic statements are probably Gattegno's:

> "*Fully developed awareness,* and nothing else, can prove to be a leap that can generate the next layer of evolution for man. . ." Two thousand six hundred years [after Socrates] the West [still needs] to make the [evolutionary] leap represented by *that new awareness*. . . Today we are witnessing [such a] leap. That leap, if the race can make it, will lead to the dawn of *a new age.*"

Curran, by profession a clinical psychologist, often spoke of the learner in CLL as developing a "new language self," and considered the learner's progress through the five stages of Counseling-Learning to be an instance of personal maturing from the womb to responsible adulthood, and even an instance of healing in a therapeutic sense.

Fujiwara quotes Gateva's statement that

> "The entire suggestopedic process from the beginning to the end is pointed at the creation of high and long-lasting motivation to learn and *to achieve perfection* not only in the material learned, but *in general.*"

Fujiwara's own comment is:

> "Suggestopedia offers us as educators a rich and deep understanding of the process of human learning and growth. It proposes that we develop ourselves personally and professionally so that we can

accept and carry out *the challenge to help our students achieve their full human potential.*" [emphasis added]

I don't think there *is* one universally correct reply to this fifth question, but anyone who answers it with "yes" must face one more question:

6. WHICH DEEPER AIMS? Building awareness, as in the Silent Way? Activating the learner's full range of reserve powers, as in suggestopedia? Emotional maturity in community with others, as in Counseling-Learning? Or something else?

With this question in mind, let's take a final look at "the three ways" described in the earlier chapters.

---

1 *For thought, comparison, and discussion: In preparation for this task, take a few minutes individually to recall your comparison materials. Better yet, go take a look at them.*

- What appear to have been the authors' answers to Questions 1-3 above?

- What were their main answers to Question 4?

- What, if any, consideration do the authors of that textbook or course seem to have given to Questions 5 and 6? How is it evidenced?

- Regardless of the authors' conscious intentions, what deeper aims might this course serve best?

COMPARISONS OF "THE THREE WAYS"

I'll begin by saying in as few words as possible how these three ways look to me, and then go on to guess at how each might look to practitioners of the others.

A few one-liners

Metaphorically, I see the Silent Way as a brook, its waters crystal clear with a few carefully chosen aquatic plants prospering in its depths. In the same metaphor, Counseling-Learning is a lush field, but sometimes full of weeds. Suggestopedia is then a garden that is rich and intensively cultivated, but subject to blights and small variations in climate.

If I were asked to choose an object or a picture to stand for the Silent Way, I would think first of the collapsible pointer. My corresponding icon for Counseling-Learning would be the conversational circle, and for suggestopedia the concert session.

If the Silent Way were a musical instrument it would be a piccolo, minimal and precise, lively and portable. Counseling-Learning would be a guitar, capable of harmony and suited to promoting feelings of intimacy within groups. Suggestopedia would be a pipe organ, more complex and perhaps more powerful than the others, but not so easily transportable.

Each of these approaches recognizes one or another cardinal virtue: a virtue on which all other virtues hinge. For the Silent Way that virtue is surely awareness, for Counseling-Learning it is understanding, and for suggestopedia it appears to be "concentrated psychorelaxation."

2 *For thought, comparison and discussion: Just for fun, try your hand at devising brief characterizations for your comparison materials. What metaphors, icons, musical instruments, cardinal virtues, or other "one-liners" can you come up with?*

From death to life

In the early part of this book I suggested that some things language learners and teachers do may be at least in part attempts to "deny physical or symbolic death." Now let me remind readers that language learning can also be exactly the opposite of that. In fact, each of the three approaches we have considered is in its own way a fresh and hopeful affirmation of life.

The Silent Way, for example, sees the Self of the learner as isolated and independent. It also sees the splendid power that that Self can have—that it can develop—when it comes to know itself and so to shape itself. The Self of Gattegno's Science of Education is the "Invictus" of William Ernest Henley's well-known poem, who thanked "whatever gods may be/for my unconquerable soul," and who in defiance cried out to the world that "I am the master of my fate!" As this finally and fiercely lonely Self develops, it may come to give something of its own to the world in which it finds itself and *to* some of the other Selves around it, while at the same time learning to learn *from* those Selves. Among them, a group of such Selves may attain a degree of "community."

The life-affirmation of Counseling-Learning is in some respects exactly the reverse of the Silent Way's. It too sees the individual as alone. But where the Silent Way affirms the aloneness of the learner and pushes him or her to come face to face with that aloneness and to live through it and beyond it, Counseling-Learning begins by reducing aloneness through the warm, total, womblike support of the counselor-teacher. In addition, the lonely Self of each learner receives support as it finds its place in a developing community of other learning Selves. As a Self progresses through the five "stages" of Counseling-Learning, however, it becomes less and less dependent—more and more self-standing, particularly if it succeeds in making the crucial transition between Stages 3 and 4. Both in Counseling-Learning and in the Silent Way, the path that the learner follows runs between independence and community, but it runs in opposite directions.

These two approaches differ also in what they see as interfering with the learner's progress along that path. The Silent Way focuses mainly on the cognitive work—the cognitive adventures—that meet the learning Self. Counseling-Learning gives more explicit attention to interpersonal and intrapersonal forces of all kinds. By doing so, it was able to help me to make sense of two intensive weekends I spent in Silent Way courses that were similar to each other in class size, student type, overt techniques, and degree of linguistic challenge, but totally unlike in their handling of the intra- and interpersonal factors—and in their outcomes.

I have less to say about suggestopedia because my experience with it has been so small. Apparently, however, suggestopedia makes explicit to the teacher many details of peripheral communication, an area in which Counseling-Learning has only a little to say, and which the Silent Way seems to ignore altogether. It sets the individual down right in the middle of the community-individuality path I was talking about above. The community (at least in the beginning) is prefabricated and totally synthetic. As the days pass, however, and as spontaneity begins to show itself, suggestopedia brings this plaster image of a community to life. It hopes that the real people who have lived in this community will leave the course better prepared for coping with the world outside, even without the elaborate packaging that had been provided by the suggestopedic course.

---

3 *For thought, comparison and discussion:*

- In what respects, if any, could your comparison materials be called "life-affirming"?

- In what respects, if any, might they be considered "life-depleting"?

How the three "ways" might look to one another

A practitioner of the Silent Way might appreciate the detailed control and the constant initiative that the suggestopedic teacher exercises in the first hours of each unit of study. He might also find compatible with his own outlook the absolute faith in the reserve powers of the student, and the effort to release the powers in ways that will produce extraordinary learning. On the other hand, he would not be comfortable with the fact that in suggestopedia the learner is neither required nor even allowed to work out for herself the kinds of things to which the Silent Way devotes so much time and attention.

The suggestopedic teacher, in turn, might note that the Silent Way teacher is making only partial and haphazard use of peripheral communication. She might also be alarmed at the way the Silent Way student is so often thrown on his own resources in working with new material—a situation where struggle is likely to suggest inadequacy and self-doubt, at least in the short run. In place of "joy and easiness" we have earnestness and the acceptance of occasional temporary frustration. Another striking difference between the Silent Way and suggestopedia is the contrast between the minutely meticulous presentation of one point at a time in the former, and the deluge of new material in any suggestopedic conversation. Here is another replacement: specific insights and cognitive awarenesses instead of general confidence in global reserve powers.

The Silent Way teacher would note that the student in Community Language Learning, far from being forced to be as independent as possible, is allowed to remain as dependent as she likes for as long as she thinks she needs to be. Whatever conversations the students originate in the first step of the "classical" procedure (Chapter 5) are certain to present them with new "challenges" that the Silent Way teacher (or any other kind of teacher who is concerned over the careful grading and sequencing of structures) would find inappropriate for them at the time. Moreover, the students interact with one another as persons and not just as language learners; this interaction exposes them to unnecessary distractions and anxieties. Finally, the large amount of "luxury" vocabulary (Chapter 9) even in the earliest conversations diverts energy from the learning of the more basic parts of the language. She would therefore see CLL as an inefficient way of deploying the learner's limited amount of available time and energy in the quest for awareness.

The Counselor-Teacher, from his point of view, might feel that the Silent Way demands of the learner an openness and a fortitude that many will find impossible at least at the beginning. It is as though the learner is being commanded to start out in Counseling-Learning's "Stage 4" (Chapter 5). The Counselor-Teacher might also be uncomfortable with the degree to which his Silent Way counterpart holds on to the "initiative," and with the lack of warmth that some Silent Way teachers show. Finally, he might feel that at least in the beginning stages the Silent Way is overly cerebral.

The suggestopedic teacher would remark that Counseling-Learning's counterpart of joy and easiness is security and acceptance, and that spontaneity is being allowed to learners—almost required of them—too early. This same suggestopedic teacher might feel that the Counseling-Learning teacher is making better use of peripheral communication than the Silent Way teacher is, but that he is still largely unaware of what he is doing in this respect and so can hardly hope to use it efficiently. Two features of Community Language Learning—the opportunities for students to talk about their reactions to the course and the lack of fixed and connected materials—would appear undesirable because they would waste time, interfere with concentration, and (worst of all) undermine the all-important authority of the course and the teacher. The lack of obvious structure and even (which is not the same thing!) the flexibility of the teacher, may in some learners create new anxieties as stubborn and as destructive as the anxieties that Community Language Learning is so good at reducing.

Looking in turn at suggestopedia, the Counseling-Learning teacher might question whether suggestopedia's decision not to give explicit attention to students' ongoing psychological reactions may be part of the reason for the method's reported vulnerability to the effects of "clique formation, intolerance, and other interpersonal pressures." Similarly the Counseling-Learning teacher would concede that the fast-moving and highly structured suggestopedic atmosphere can temporarily anesthetize or neutralize some of the student's personal anxieties, but he might go on to wonder whether it has not thereby limited the total scope of the learning experience.

Investigations

4 *For thought, comparison and discussion:*

- What positive points might the author(s) of your comparison materials have found in each of the three unconventional "ways" discussed in this book?

- What negative points, or what doubts, might they have raised?

- What are a few suggestions that a user of Counseling-Learning, the Silent Way, or suggestopedia might make for revising or adapting various parts of your comparison materials?

(If you put some time and thought into your answers here, this may prove to have been the most useful Investigations task in this book!)

HOW THE THREE "WAYS" LOOK TO ME

As for me, I see the excitement and the potential in each of these three approaches, but I also see a few dangers. I see dangers, but also the possibilities for more life and better learning. I see the Silent Way as elegant but austere. I see "CL/CLL" as warmly human but sometimes hard to control. I see suggestopedia as powerful but also complex and demanding. Each of these three ways runs askew of the best-trodden paths we know.

To produce satisfactory results always requires a certain degree of craftsmanship even when one is following a conventional textbook in which everything is spelled out, and even when one is trying for nothing more than high test scores for one's students. I think all three of the "ways" we have looked at would agree that sticking entirely to preexisting materials limits the depth of goals at which one can aim, and that this shallowness in turn limits both the quality and the quantity of learning. But as we move away from ready-made materials the demands on the teacher increase, and it is also true that as we aim for deeper goals, the demands on the teacher increase. Any of these methods at which we have been looking therefore asks of the teacher a level of craftsmanship that must be unusually high, and that must be maintained day after day.

As I continue my own development in teaching, I find certain areas in which I would like to learn more from each of these methods. I am strongly attracted to the lean, logical elegance of Silent Way teaching, but I am also attracted to the rich interpersonal experiences of Counseling-Learning. Certainly I could be more useful to my students if I had more of the discipline of the Silent Way; and if I had more skill at making Lozanov's two "planes" support each other through orchestration of physical, verbal, and aesthetic elements; and if I had fuller, quicker insight into what from minute to minute my learner-clients are showing me.

Insight, technical skill, discipline. The fully ready teacher has all three. For me, though, insight is first. Without it, how can the teacher choose the method, the material, the technique that fits? These choices, coupled with the skillful use of what is chosen, then come second. But without self-discipline, skill is only virtuosity—a show that enthralls students rather than setting them free. It is just here, *in working toward the student's freedom alongside and intertwined with his or her learning of language skills,* that the three "ways" of this book find their common goal. The light they share is knowledge that of these two—the freedom and the learning—each can make the other stronger.

WHAT'S AT STAKE?

Because this learning takes place in the human mind, and because this freedom is the freedom of human personhood, the possibilities for good are breathtaking, but so are the risks of ill. This must be truer in the field of education than in any other field. Now what exactly *is* at stake?

At stake first of all are the time, the energy, and the trust of the students, as well as the financial costs of instructing them. All these resources are limited and they are precious, because whatever we commit to one purpose is going to be lost forever to other purposes. We cannot at the same time give *primary* attention and *top* priority both to accuracy and to fluency, for example, or both to building the learner's confidence in her ability to succeed by taking one small thing at a time and to building her confidence in her ability to succeed by responding in a largely unanalytical manner to a flood of verbal and nonverbal material. We must therefore make some high-stake decisions.

Most obviously, we pick one or more methods to follow. In making those choices we ask ourselves questions like, "Will this approach actually work *at all* to build language skills in the kind of students I'm responsible for?" "If it will at least work, will it do *all* it claims it will do for my students' language skills: develop in them amazing accuracy, amazing fluency, amazing vocabulary, or amazing something else?" "Even if it will do all those things, how *efficient* will it be relative to its competitors?" Like professional guides in a desert, we say to ourselves,

> *"If that's really a lake over there, then I can safely lead my caravan in that direction, thus saving them many long hours of unnecessary tramping over the hot, dry sands. If it's a mirage, though, I would not only be wasting their time and energy, I might even endanger the final outcome of the expedition."*

But we also face choices of deeper goals. Most generally we decide—and we must decide, either deliberately or by default—whether or not to say with Tim Murphey (1998) that "What my students will find in this course can not only give them certain language skills; it can also change their lives when they choose to use it and improve themselves." We may act as if this choice didn't exist, but it does. In the desert metaphor, our question is,

> *"Am I guiding my caravan just to some city on the plain, where they can sell and buy and do all they came there to do? Or do I hope also to lead them up the mountain beyond the town to a spot where they can look down and glimpse the city, glimpse themselves and one another from an angle that's somehow new, and in that glimpse become new themselves, and in this newness return to that same city on the plain and live there in some new way?" (Of course if enough of them do this, the city itself might even be transformed!)*

A different statement of approximately the same answer is to be found in the last half of Chapter 5 of *Humanism in Language Teaching* (Stevick 1990).

If we do decide to include deeper life-goals along with the language-goals, the next choice that faces us is "Which life-goal?" Of course we may pursue more than one life-goal within the same program, but I do think *we need to decide which goal we believe is, in the nature of things, central to the rest:* Activation of one's full powers, perhaps? Developing skills at constructive interaction with others? Self-awareness? Self-understanding? Self-fulfillment? Something else? In Chapter 12 I will offer my own reply to this question.

One final point:

Arnold Irwin was my teacher for 9th grade Latin, which was my first exposure to any foreign language. Mr. Irwin's area was social science, but someone had to teach the Latin class, so he did. I, on the other hand, was sitting there with all the aptitudes and predispositions that would later take me through an enjoyable career tinkering with languages from around the world. It's hardly surprising, therefore, that I occasionally noticed an error in Mr. Irwin's own Latin. Whenever I did, I pointed it out immediately and publicly. Mr. Irwin could have reacted with embarrassment or with annoyance or with some kind of indirect retaliation, but he never did. The man's grace at those times made an impression on me even then, and has for over sixty years served me, I hope, as a model. I doubt all this was part of some consciously selected "life goal" that Mr. Irwin was working on in us. It was just the man.

We can consciously choose or not choose one or another set of "life goals" that we want to help our students work on. We can pursue those chosen goals openly and intentionally or indirectly and covertly or not at all. But whether we are consciously working on such matters or just on language skills, the "life-goals" that will be affected most in our students are not necessarily the ones we think we are putting across. They are the goals—the values—that our students find built into us and into how we teach them, our fellow human beings, day by day.

---

5 *For thought, comparison and discussion: Think back on the teachers or other people who taught you some of a foreign language.*

- What assumptions did you pick up from them about language? About learning? About yourself as a learner?
- Was there ever a "Mr. Irwin" in your life?

12

THE LANGUAGE TEACHER AND DOSTOYEVSKY'S "GRAND INQUISITOR"

In the other chapters of this book I have recorded what went on in certain classes, and we have looked together at certain theories. I hope that what happened in those classes has lent color to the theories; at the same time I hope that the theories have made out of my narratives more than anecdotes.

But an event is just one foothold in the rock; a theory is a thin cable that ties events together—that lets us climb from one foothold to another with less risk of falling off the mountain. Theories do not tell us where the trail leads, or why one should try to climb it, or anything about the ethics of being a guide to those who climb. The answers to these latter questions come not from observations of events, and not from theories. A TV commercial tells us that "without chemicals, life itself would be impossible." It is certainly true that any form of life as we know it has its chemical side—it uses chemicals. But it is also true that human life would be impossible without myth, and without metaphor. It is to these that we must turn unless we have decided to ignore issues that have lain just beneath the surface throughout much of this book.

On the basis of reactions of many readers since 1980, I have concluded that the flow of this chapter need not and should not be broken by any further "Voice" or "Task" material.

THE GRAND INQUISITOR AND THE PRISONER

Into *The Brothers Karamazov*, which was his final novel, Dostoyevsky placed one chapter that had no direct relation to his main story. It was about a long poem that Ivan, one of the brothers, had written or claimed to have written, and that he was paraphrasing for his brother Alyosha. The action of the poem takes place in Spain, in Seville, at the height of the Inquisition, a period when heretics were being sought out and tried and imprisoned, and many of them burned at the stake. At this time, according to the poem, the Son of God has heard the prayers of thousands who were begging him to come to earth again and he decides to visit his people, not in the long-prophesied and final Second Coming, but for a moment only. So he appears in the streets of Seville as an ordinary citizen, but people recognize him without naming him, and they are drawn to him, and he heals their sick, and raises from the dead a little girl whose coffin is being borne into the church. But as he does so, the Cardinal, the Grand Inquisitor, sees him. And the Cardinal sends guards, and has him seized and taken to an old prison, and there they lock him in. At night, in deepest darkness, the Grand

Inquisitor enters the cell and the door closes behind him. The rest of the "poem" is a monolog addressed by this old priest to his Prisoner.

The Grand Inquisitor reproaches the Prisoner, even scolds him. The Prisoner had set out to give the whole human race something to live by, but also something to die by, something that would link, in meaning, the beginnings and ends of existence. But, says the Inquisitor, the Prisoner had botched the job—botched it so badly that after some centuries a team of priests, acting in the Prisoner's name, had to assume control, and so replaced the Prisoner's work with their own.

What the Prisoner had hoped, says the Inquisitor, is first that all mankind would come to see the world—to see life—for themselves rather than letting someone else deliver them a simplified and printed map of it. Once they began to see for themselves, he hoped that they would then direct their own footsteps and choose their own paths, rather than waiting to be led like sheep. In doing so, each would become himself rather than being a carbon copy of someone else. More, they would respect each other—see one another "whole against the sky," love one another even to the point, at times, that one would give up, to benefit another, what he himself most cherished. One more point: if this way is not to contradict itself—if it is not to lead to nowhere—then whoever follows it must choose it without bribery and without threat—must (as the Grand Inquisitor put it) be "great enough and strong enough" to choose it by his own free will.

Miracle, mystery and authority

"Are people truly like this?" asks the Grand Inquisitor, and answers, "No!" One in a million maybe, but for the rest in offering this freedom you have only added to their burden of anxiety and pain. They are in fact—except your very few—not strong but weak, not great but worthless, vicious, and rebellious. They crave two things and two things only: to go on living, and to find someone into whose hands they may entrust their consciences. Even while they rebel, they long to be controlled. So says the Grand Inquisitor. And this is the heavy task that the Inquisitor and those with him have taken on themselves: to bear responsibility for convoying, even with lies and trickery, their blind and frightened fellow humans from birth until the grave. The tools by which they will accomplish this, he says, are three in number: first "miracle," then "mystery," and then "authority." Mystery is the substitute for independent thought; authority is what imposes and enforces mystery; miracle is what assures the follower that he or she has in fact trusted his or her destiny into the right hands.

Language teachers live in this same world that Dostoyevsky was writing about. We too sometimes control our students (and even other teachers) through mystification: when we explain to them more than they are ready to receive; when our explanation use words that are ours, not theirs; when we tell them directly or indirectly that "Life is too short to learn German," or English, or Korean, or whatever; but most of all when we make them permanently our dependents by doing for them what they could do for themselves.

In our reliance on miracle we are not very different from the missionaries who won converts through their use of Western pharmaceuticals among the people of Africa and Asia: as linguists we have used minimal pairs of words (*beat* vs. *bit* in English, high tone *bá* vs. falling tone *bâ* in a tonal language) to show those who have hitherto been baffled where to concentrate their efforts in pronunciation; we have awakened teachers to "the furious sleep of green ideas," and we have explained to anyone who would listen the reason why "the love of a good woman (or man)" is ambiguous. As methodologists we have put our wares into the hands of gifted teachers who have conducted brilliant demonstration lessons that left onlookers convinced that they and their previous methods were inferior. I am not denying the validity of minimal pairs or the usefulness of transformational-generative understanding of how sentences are related to one another, and I am quite ready to admit that some methods may be inferior to others. Certainly I would not quarrel with having demonstration lessons taught by good teachers.

What I am saying, however, is that through our apparently miraculous ability to juggle minimal pairs or whatever, we have made converts to our own set of mysteries and enticed people aboard our own methodological bandwagons; and that these miracles have often been as relevant to the real needs of teacher and pupil as aspirin and antimalarials are to real spiritual needs. And that through climbing the administrative ladder, or through gaining control over funds, or through personal prestige or charisma, we have gained authority, and have used that authority to support and perpetuate our own brand of mystery.

The three "ways" about which I have said so much in this book certainly have not shrunk from the use of miracle. "Hypermnesia" as it was reported in the Sunday supplements once performed this function for suggestopedia (probably contrary to the originators' desires). So did Lozanov's success in using suggestion as the sole anesthetic for a patient during major surgery. Curran's ability to listen to a client in such a way that after only 5 or 10 minutes the client came out with important new insights, or with release from long-standing anxieties such as fear of flying, had the effect of "miracle." The first experience as a student in the Classical Community Language Learning format often produces such a blessed feeling of well-being and relief that people are disposed to accept uncritically whatever theory the demonstrator-teacher then proceeds to lay on them. Similarly, the first experience of watching as a flood of student language pours out in the presence of teacher silence sometimes leads onlookers to regard the teacher-demonstrator of the Silent Way as something of a miracle-worker. And so on. I suspect that every method that has been widely used secured its first foothold in the attention of the profession through the efforts of talented snake-oil vendors who really believed in it.

Each method uses "miracles" to claim for itself, in the name of its originator or guiding figures, the territory that it proposes to civilize by subjugating that territory to its own particular "mystery"—to its own intellectual model of learning and teaching, or to its own insights and discoveries about language, or to its own "state-of-the-art" hardware and software—and sets out to make the local inhabitants fluent in the jargon that its initiates use for the Siamese-twin purposes of expounding the model and making the model difficult to challenge.

I do not mean to say that there is no place for "miracle, mystery, and authority." It seems clear that Dostoyevsky would not have said so either. After all, the Prisoner himself is reported to have made deliberate use of miracles; the religion that he left behind—indeed any religion—has its own essential mysteries; and it was said of him that he taught his hearers as one who had authority. The issue, then, is not "whether" miracle, mystery, and authority; it is rather "what kind of" miracle, mystery, and authority, or it is the place of miracle, mystery, and authority in education. It is this issue that I am trying to get at in this final chapter. I do not expect to settle the issue, but I do hope to open it for thinking and for discussion.

Two kinds of "authority"

The word "authority" as we hear it every day has two meanings. One of these meanings carries with it the use of coercion; the second implies a relationship in which both parties believe that one of the parties is competent to direct, guide, or instruct the other. When Lozanov makes a great point of the importance of "authority" in suggestopedia, he is pretty clearly talking about the second type. This second type of "authority" is what we have in mind when we say, "She's an authority on such-and-such a subject." I believe it lies, unspoken but implied, behind the successful use of all other methods as well. The Grand Inquisitor with his police and prisons and *autos-da-fé* seems to have been talking about the first—the coercive—meaning of "authority." Yet how easily a taste of recognition as "an authority" can lead to an appetite for widening that recognition and, more pernicious, for perpetuating it. Here is where the benign authority of well-deserved recognition may develop into the malignant use of whatever control we have over our students or our colleagues: to cut the troublesome ones off from a chance to be heard, and from those who do not give confirmation to our own brand of mystery, to withhold the grades, tenure, money, status, or whatever symbols of recognition they must have to live.

Two kinds of "mystery"

I have just distinguished between two kinds of "authority." I think there may also be two kinds of "mystery." Some mysteries are made by human hands and human brains, formed to enhance the standing of their makers and maintained in order to keep their makers and their custodians one-up on those around them. Other mysteries are natural mysteries. Some natural mysteries lie in areas that we will someday understand but are still exploring: how people express and recognize interrogation or remonstrance, for example, or what rules account for the choice of high tone or low tone on a given syllable of a given verb in Shona (the first Bantu language I worked on). Other natural mysteries are those we may explore but will never completely understand: how a particular learner's mind works, for example, or what it is that some people find so exciting in Elizabethan drama, or in the landscape of modern Spain, or in the discovery of rules that govern conversation in a particular culture. Natural mysteries are mysteries we do not hold onto, but share with our students and with one another. But our theories—our tentative and partial maps *of* the natural mysteries—sometimes turn themselves too easily into artificial mysteries, and into weapons in a power struggle with those around us.

Two ways of using "miracles"

Let us turn now to "miracle." Surely in the task-oriented world of the foreign language classroom there must be place for some kind of "miracle," if only because students need to believe in what they are doing and in the people who lead them in doing it. Perhaps the distinction that we need to make here is not between two kinds of miracle, but between two ways of using it. Miracle may be used on a continuing basis as a means of compounding mystery and perpetuating authority. Or it may be used as a means of getting people's attention and showing them where the natural mysteries lie.

The learner and the Grand Inquisitor

What I have been saying ties in with three often-stated goals of education in general: the goal of freedom, the goal of uniqueness, and the goal of tolerance. If education is to be a liberating or freeing experience, then it must enable students to see the world more clearly for themselves, so as to be able to choose how to use what energy they have, and let them act a little less impeded by blindness or by distorted images that do not correspond to reality. By choosing and acting more freely we become, each of us, closer to what only we can become, not pounded or squeezed (or inflated!) into the same shape as everyone else around us. This is the uniqueness. But my uniqueness will be unlike yours (we saw this in Chapter 5), and the two may not obviously fit together. Each of us must allow the other some of this uniqueness, and that is what I mean by "tolerance." Tolerance allows the pieces of this puzzle, the students in a classroom, the people in a society, to fly off, each in its own direction. Authority—the coercive kind certainly, but also the noncoercive kind we talked about—is a force that draws the pieces back together. But what will the pattern be, the pattern toward which these pieces will be drawn? This brings us back to the issue of "what kind of mystery?" The artificial, synthetic, made-by-people kind of mystery stifles "uniqueness"—tells each person what to see, and how to label what she sees, and how to run it through her mind. In choosing which manufactured mystery to follow, the miracle worker acts for the other person, and that is the end of "freedom." All of this brings to mind three other terms—Gattegno's—where he speaks of "independence," "autonomy," and "responsibility."

I have said that I see two kinds of "authority," though one kind sometimes corrupts itself into the other. I have said that there are at least two kinds of "mystery," though one of them may feed on exploration of the other. I have said that "miracle" lends itself to use in one way or another. And so it may appear that I have been leading up to some sort of recommendation, if not indeed to an exhortation: "Let us strive to cast out from our teaching any unnecessary mystification of our students, and forgo the power, security, and personal gratification that synthetic mysteries can put into our hands. Let us employ miracles sparingly, just enough to direct our students' attention to the natural mysteries, and to make possible a relationship of noncoercive authority that rests on the students' recognition of our genuine competence. Then we will guide them in a shared exploration of the realities of the language, and of the natural mysteries of the learning process. We will make it easier for the students to become more and more free, and for each to realize his or her own potential. In imitation of our example, the students will treat one another as we have treated them, and so tolerance, our third goal, will be realized."

This would, in the language classroom, have been not far distant from what the Grand Inquisitor said had been his Prisoner's dream. I have long felt myself drawn toward these goals, and I suppose I always will be. For just that reason,

I must be all the more careful not to slip at this point into mere exhortation or inspiration. In this chapter more than anywhere else in the book, I am trying to see things as they are and to write about them with objectivity.

But the Grand Inquisitor raises again that question of his, this time not in the dungeon in Seville, but in our neat, bright, well-ventilated classrooms now, more than a century after Dostoyevsky wrote. His question is, "Are students really like this? Will students really stand to be treated in this way?" His own answer—that only one in a million will accept this kind of freedom—is in my own experience too pessimistic for a language classroom. Yet, although he may have misplaced his decimal point, my own experiences in encouraging others to learn from or about the unconventional methodologies have led me to believe that he was at least partially right—that if he was not speaking the whole truth, he was at least speaking a half-truth, and this truth or half-truth he was speaking is one which some of us who have explored and committed ourselves to the so-called "humanistic" approaches to language teaching have largely ignored or brushed aside. Some of us have assumed that if we provide a warm supportive environment and the information that people cannot supply for themselves, and if we guide them by presenting them a series of tasks or challenges that are neither too great for them nor too trivial, then they will learn faster and more fully, and they will thank us for it. We have assumed that as they use powers they never knew they had, and as they watch their minds—their whole selves— unfolding, growing, they will exult in this thrilling, never-ending voyage of exploration, and in the discovery that they have it in themselves to discover, and to discover how to discover further, and so on forever.

Perhaps we were right in that estimate of students, and the Grand Inquisitor was wrong. But if people are like that, they are not in my observation obviously like that, except a few. I have sometimes seen students placed in a warm and accepting environment, given tasks that they were manifestly able to work out for themselves, and faced therefore with what was to all appearances a rich opportunity for all kinds of cognitive and personal growth, yet whose reaction was nothing but resistance and resentment. Like everyone else, I sometimes do things wrong, and some of this reaction may have been due to my own faulty techniques. But I am fairly sure that not all of it was. There remains, I am afraid, a residue—not universal but widespread—a residue of resistance and resentment against being given opportunities instead of rules and vocabulary lists—against being invited to explore one's own potential and to grow, rather than being immediately led to accrue some very specific communicative skills and repertoires for which one foresees a practical need. What most of us demand most urgently, it seems, is the means for meeting our most practical needs, and a leader whom we can follow without thinking, without wondering if we should have followed this one. From this point of view, the best leader is one who will keep us dazzled with miracles, who will guide us deftly but firmly to one concrete goal after another, and whose explanation of it all is both clear enough and vague enough so that we dare not question it. Here is the Grand Inquisitor with a vengeance!

The teacher and the Grand Inquisitor

But what of the teacher who does not follow the Grand Inquisitor? What of the teacher who, instead of offering (or claiming to offer) to the student exactly what he needs at the moment, offers instead to try to help him become able to get for himself five times as much? That teacher may be seen as undependable. What of the teacher who refuses to use the coercive kind of authority, who instead learns from her students what they can teach her, even as she invites them to learn what she knows but they do not? Such a teacher may provoke a feeling of uneasiness, for she is unlike the picture we have learned of what a teacher is. And what of the teacher who insists on telling his students that they have powers far beyond what they have dreamed about themselves? He will be punished for disturbing that safe dream, and for destabilizing a picture that had been assembled at the cost of so much pain.

How many students can thrive—or how many students can coexist—with a teacher who does not follow the Grand Inquisitor? The answer may very well be different for different ages and for different cultural backgrounds. Certainly more than Dostoyevsky's one in a million. Certainly more than one in a thousand, probably more than one in a hundred, and perhaps even more than one in ten. But the Grand Inquisitor is still someone for any would-be "humanistic" teacher to reckon with.

Anyone who sets out to be a "humanistic" teacher—who offers to his students freedom and growth in addition to accuracy and fluency—needs all of the technical skills of a teacher who is not trying to be "humanistic" in this sense. He also needs certain technical skills peculiar to one or more "humanistic" methods. In addition to all these skills, he needs greater flexibility in his use of them, for in making his choices and in determining his timing he will be taking into account much more than the students' accuracy and speed in mastering linguistic material. Most of all, however, he has to do without the Grand Inquisitor's "miracle, mystery, and authority" as means for controlling his students and for protecting himself against their attacks. All of this adds up to a tall order. It is no wonder that many teachers instinctively shy away from "humanistic" methods of all kinds. They see in their students, or in most of them, the human weakness and rebelliousness about which the Grand Inquisitor was so insistent.

We teachers, of course, are just as human as our students. This humanity can show itself in teacher-training courses and workshops. As proof of her qualifications for teaching the course or leading the workshop, the person in charge is expected to bring with her some miracles in the form of a suitably impressive list of her publications, offices held, etc., and to produce a steady stream of new miracles in the form of brilliant lectures and amazing demonstrations of new techniques. Woe unto any leader who refuses to stand on past miracles, who offers to his audience as miracle to be explored only their shared humanity. If, further, he refuses to cloak himself in mystery and conceal his own relevant weaknesses, but instead addresses himself to the mystery of the relevant uniqueness of everyone in the room, he may find that some of his audience will turn on him. If he uses authority only to organize the schedule and provide useful content, but holds himself back from posing as the all-sufficient director or answer-source, then some of his hearers may feel cheated and resentful. He then risks rejection and repudiation. Feeling thus rejected and repudiated, seeing his best efforts lost and his words ignored, he wonders whether his audience would not have been better off if he had yielded just a little—if he had given them just enough "miracle, mystery, and authority" to pacify their own craving. This dilemma is more poignant, and no less real, in a course or in a workshop whose purpose is to train teachers in "humanistic" methods. Here stands the Grand Inquisitor once more, just at the trainer's shoulder, certain that he, in the end, will win.

THE ARCADIAN MEETS THE UTOPIAN

Two characters

W. H. Auden once wrote two or three pages of free verse about a pair of characters who remind me a little of the Grand Inquisitor and his Prisoner. Two men pass each other at dusk on the edge of the city. One of them, the author, calls himself an Arcadian, and the other man a Utopian. As an Arcadian, the author inhabits an Eden where "one who dislikes Bellini has the good manners not to get born." Technology is represented only by saddle-tank locomotives, waterwheels, and other assorted "beautiful pieces of obsolete machinery." Since there is no technology, there are no mass media, so that the only source of political news is gossip. No one worries about a fixed code of behavior, but each observes his own compulsive rituals and superstitions.

The antitype of the Arcadian is the Utopian. He, the poet tells us, lives not in an Eden but in a New Jerusalem. There, "a person who dislikes work will be very sorry he was born." Technology plays a central role in the New Jerusalem: even *haute cuisine* has been mechanized, and the mass media provide the news in "simplified spelling for nonverbal types." There is no religion, but the behavior of everyone exemplifies "the rational virtues." Again, as in the Dostoyevsky myth, we find freedom, uniqueness, and patience with individual differences on the one hand contrasted with clarity, order, and progress on the other. Just as there was no two-way communication between the Inquisitor and the Prisoner, so the Arcadian remarks of his meeting with the citizen of the New Jerusalem that "Neither speaks," for "what experience could we possibly share?" But where Dostoyevsky left the relationship at that, Auden went on to wonder whether their meeting had indeed been, as it appeared, only a coincidence. Maybe, he speculated, this had been "also a rendezvous between accomplices who. . . cannot resist meeting," each "to remind the other of that half of [the truth] which he would most like to forget." They are anti-types, yes, Auden is saying. They are antipathetic and antithetical, yes. But they are also accomplices: neither can totally condemn the other without condemning himself for what he has omitted and yet depends on.

To carry out this observation one step further, Auden wrote in the first person as the Arcadian. But he could have not written this particular bit of verse if he had not caught with great precision the other point of view as well. In order to do that, he must have had within him at least a tiny bit of the Utopian. (I doubt, however, that a Utopian with only a trace of the Arcadian temperament could have written anything comparable to Auden's poem!)

What, then, are we to make of the confrontation between Inquisitor and Prisoner, or of the uneasy meeting between Arcadian and Utopian? Here is not only a gap. Here is a gap that bears on either side of it one or the other of two primal, opposed polarities, just as the earth and clouds gather their static charges that will become lightning and make the thunderstorm. In the electrostatic analogy, they provide a theoretical—a pencil-and-paper—short circuit across a gap that still bears its unseen but no less heavy charge.

We can say, as I said above, that the two points of view are just "accomplices," halves of a larger truth—a truth too large for one person to contain it fully. Or, as I also put it there, we may see the two halves residing side by side, in one proportion or another, within each person. Either of these views is partially right, of course. I believe, however, that they offer solutions that are too facile.

For a mythology that fits, I think we must concede that Auden was right in showing the Grand Inquisitor and his Prisoner, or the Utopian and the Arcadian, as separate persons. In the real world of the classroom and the faculty lounge we meet these issues in the give and take among flesh-and-blood people—in what goes on between us and those around us. And a part of what goes on between us turns on this issue: How much freedom shall we offer to our students, and how independent can we ask them to be?

In the practical, task-oriented, real world of the language classroom, we cannot allow ourselves to go to either extreme, of course. If the teacher maintains complete control and totally monopolizes initiative, then at best the students come out as automatons who go through their paces nicely on the exam, but then have trouble "transferring" their skills to the job or the taxi or the restaurant. To turn all of the control over to the students and to insist that they exercise all of the initiative, on the other hand, would almost surely be disastrous. To cut people totally adrift from structure and from guidance is irresponsible, whether done to salve the conscience or to inflate the ego of the teacher. (I know of no method that asks teachers to go to either of these extremes.) We must walk the fine line between too much latitude and too little. But that is a truism.

Two kinds of freedom

Here I think we need to draw yet another distinction, this final one between two kinds of "freedom." When we use this word we most often have in mind the absence of restrictions or limitations imposed by people or by conditions that are not really part of the person who is "free." So we talk about "freedom from" slavery, or from poverty, or from tooth decay, or from an officious or tyrannical teacher. In this first sense, "freedom" is indeed something we teachers may offer or withhold.

The second kind of "freedom" dwells within the person who is "free." When the moving parts of a mechanism get in each other's way, the mechanism begins to wobble, or slows down, or jams altogether. Then someone may go in and try to "free up" the parts where the trouble lies. In somewhat the same sense we sometimes say that an artist paints "with great freedom." This does not mean that the artist works carelessly or hastily. To be "free" in this sense requires both that one have considerable inner resources, and that these resources work harmoniously with each other. The raw material for an inner resource can come only from outside; that is why total external freedom would make further growth of internal freedom impossible.

This latter is a "freedom" that is not ours to offer. What we teachers do and what we don't do may make it easier or harder for this inner freedom to develop. But there is no simple formula either for implanting it or for converting one kind of freedom into the other. We may smother the internal kind by failing to allow enough of the external kind, of course. As I said in the preceding paragraph, we may also starve it by bestowing too much external freedom at the wrong time.

Mostly, though, our part of the enterprise is to watch for signs of internal freedom among those who have put themselves into our hands; and from our glimpses of it to guess what it is like in each class or in each student; and to remember where it was when last we sighted it; and to work with it as best we can.

But if we do succeed in catching sight of this internal freedom, and in guessing what it is like, and in remembering where it was, and if we go on to work with it, we then—by that very seeing and guessing and remembering and working—help it to grow. We find that our fingers—whether we intended them to or not—have touched what Buber called "the special connection between the unity of what [the student] is and the sequence of his actions and attitude." We may have started out to be "humanistic" teachers primarily because in that way we could get more language across to our students and make it stick longer. But now (again in Buber's words) we suddenly find ourselves engaged, willy nilly, in "education of character." Insofar as this is what we are doing, or insofar as this is what we appear to be doing, we may meet resistance that does not arise from any "weakness, viciousness, or rebelliousness" on the part of our students. The strongest among them and the most mature know already, from within themselves, that this undertaking is far from easy; that it is not accomplished overnight by some magical technique leading to a pat list of "desired outcomes" whose desirability has been only half thought out; that finding the right goal and finding a right way to it lie just at the farthest edge of human reaching. These "strong and wise" ones, far from begging for someone to lead them by the nose, absolutely refuse to let even the best-intentioned someone-else grant to them or instill in them—with "lighthanded paternalism," as Ann Diller called it—something that they know must come from within themselves.

Two reactions to freedom

We must also recognize that even those whom the Grand Inquisitor called "the few, the strong," who spend their lives alive in growth and in a search for inner freedom—even they have this searching and this growing as only one part of their daily cycle. Some of them will eagerly accept a "humanistic" language course as an arena, or as a medium, in which to find new adventures in discovering themselves and other people, and in which they can go on to become more than they had been before. Others of them, however, may decide that the language class is not a place where they choose to confront issues of alienation, or of personal values, or of restructuring cognitive strategies. They may just want to be taught subject matter well, by a method that they know already. We must respect this decision. Nevertheless, those issues still remain active in the classroom just as they are active everywhere, and they still continue to affect what goes on among and within the people in the classroom, to enhance or to reduce or to distort learning. So the "humanistic" teacher must face these issues whether or not students are ready to face them along with him—whether or not they are willing even to know that he is facing them.

The difference between the Grand Inquisitor and his Prisoner, between the Arcadian and the Utopian, and between those of us who take after one or another of them, does not lie simply in the giving or withholding of external freedom. The difference is not even in whether the amount of freedom is allowed to increase as time goes on. The difference lies in whether an internal freedom comes alive that grows not by some teacher's sufferance and schedule, but on its own. If that is to happen, then sometime, somewhere along the line, and likely early, the teacher offers to the learners, not more external freedom than they can handle, but more than they thought they could handle—more than they had a comfortable and well-tried way of dealing with. One of the marks of a fine teacher is exactly this ability to see the gap between the far-possible and the near-comfortable, and to be the kind of person in whose company many learners reach the far side of that gap. This is the teacher who is more like the Arcadian or the Prisoner than like their adversaries. And here is where this kind of teacher finds himself in trouble.

The risk: "death"

For remember that it is the Prisoner and his ilk that fall into the hands of the Inquisitors of this world, and not the other way around. Auden tells us that the Arcadian looking at the Utopian feels alarm, but the Utopian looking at the Arcadian feels contempt. The one dreads whatever brings sterility; the other is ready to destroy what leads toward instability. So a would-be "humanistic" teacher who offers freedom and demands independence beyond custom is the natural, predictable victim of punishment at the hands of those who guard custom and feel themselves guarded by it. (This in addition to whatever penalties she may have to pay for ordinary technical flaws in her teaching.) I have already mentioned some of the forms this punishment can take: resistance, resentment, rage, abandonment.

I think that here I am close to a point that Carolyn Hartl once made. She began by saying that the "humanistic approach to teaching is based on [more than] superficial sentimentality." I would agree, and I would add that repeating "humanistic" slogans and adopting an assortment of pedigreed "humanistic" techniques, or having students talk about their feelings, dreams, and preferences, does not guarantee that a teacher is not in the tradition of the Inquisitor or of the Utopian. Nor does the use of an ancient conventional textbook necessarily mean a non-"humanistic" teacher. The three "ways" that I have described in this book are "humanistic" in their intent and in their respective views of what goes on inside and among people; it is here, rather than in their techniques, that we may find hints for our own development as teachers.

What is necessary, says Hartl, over and above the theories and the techniques, is "the ability to model convincingly" in one's own person "the outcome" of this kind of teaching. To do so, she says, a teacher must be "willing and able to share the most important aspects of life, to give freely of self." Beyond that, if what I have been saying in this chapter is true, the teacher must be willing to become vulnerable, taking risks with the clear knowledge that "risk" by definition means occasional painful losses. Hartl suggests that this kind of teaching may or may not be for every teacher. I think she is right. We saw in Chapters 2 and 3 that "heavy-handed authoritarians" may be feared and disliked by their students, and that this may seriously limit their own effectiveness, but through using their "miracles, mysteries, and authority," they are usually able to keep any corrosive effects bottled up inside their students so that those effects do not spill out on them, the teachers.

Why then undertake a kind of teaching that is so demanding of skill and at the same time so risky? To risk and lose means among other things to die a little: to see one's ties with the outside world severed by just that much, and within to feel that Self out of which one's future messages to the world must rise called into question—called into question not only before others but before oneself, never being quite sure where this loss, this particular failure, came from, whether merely from some error of technique, or from having guessed wrong about what this particular student truly could have done, or from having opened for the student a door through which in fact he might have stepped but which he has slammed shut in our face. In addition, we meet the dying out of that echo from our colleagues that tells us, "Yes, you are on the right track. You are one of us." Not least, there is also the basic physical loss in slipping, by the amount of any failure, that much closer to unemployment—to economic death. Remember Eric Berne's way of putting it: that when we don't get the strokes we need, "our spinal cords shrivel up."

Once more, then, why not avoid this deadly risk? Perhaps the answer to this question is one of the permanent natural mysteries. For some people, the answer lies in the nature of life itself. In earlier chapters I said that when we say that something—a person, an animal, a vegetable, a microorganism even—is "alive," we mean it is able to take into itself new things that it needs, and to use them, and to get rid of what it no longer needs, and to grow (in size or in other ways) into the world around it; and that in doing all these things it continues to be itself even as it changes. "Life" in this sense has not only length and breadth, but also depth. The same person who is physically sound and economically prosperous may on other levels have stopped taking in the new, and letting go of what no longer fits, and changing: may, for the sake of hanging onto the Self that is, have given up knowledge of, and further unfolding of that very Self. This grinding to a halt, this digging into a permanent position, this inflexibility is a loss of life, therefore a kind of death on the one level—the symbolic level—that is available only to human beings and not to animals or plants.

The reward: "life"

This is what the would-be "humanistic" teacher sees. But the very seeing of it is an act—or better, it is a process—that is going on continuously at the deepest, most uniquely human level, inside the teacher. Therefore to withhold what flows out of this insight—that is, to fail to offer more and deeper "life" to her students, would for this teacher be a contradiction of her own life process, and a denial of it: therefore a termination of it. So the teacher risks one kind of death for the hope of a different kind of life within herself as well as in her students.

What this kind of teacher tries to do—exchanging life on one level for life on another by helping her students to find in themselves a freedom that will be their own, an understanding and a self-understanding that will go on growing of itself—this is impossible. Yet it does take place.

So it is because she has seen the impossible event take place—because she knows that the process, incredible as it is, can still continue—it is out of this knowledge, this experience, that this kind of teacher takes up her authority with not a little reverence, and bears it with a natural humility, handling with courage the mystery-behind-mystery, playing out her part in simple, daily miracle.

References

Abbs, B. & M. Sexton. 1977. *Student's Book for Challenges*. London: Longman.

Alexander, L. G. 1968. *For and Against*. Langenscheidt-Longman.

Allard, Fusako & Roslyn Young. 1990. The Silent Way. *The Language Teacher* 14.6: 27–29.

Allibone, S. Austin. 1876. *Prose Quotations from Socrates to Macaulay*. Philadelphia: Lippincott.

Arnold, Jane (Ed.) forthcoming. *Affect in Language Learning*. Cambridge: Cambridge University Press.

Atkinson, R. C. & R. M. Shiffrin. 1968. Human memory: a proposed system and its central processes. In K. W. & J. T. Spence (Eds.) *The Psychology of Learning and Motivation. Vol. II*. New York: Academic Press.

Auden, W. H. 1957. Their lonely betters. *Selected Poetry of W. H. Auden*. New York: Random House.

Becker, Ernest. 1973. *The Denial of Death*. New York: Free Press.

Berne, E. 1964. *Games People Play*. New York: Grove Press.

Blair, Robert W. (Ed.). 1982. *Innovative Approaches to Language Teaching*. Rowley, MA: Newbury House.

Bloomfield, Leonard. 1933. *Language*. New York: Henry Holt.

Blot, David & Phyllis Berman Sher. 1978. *Getting Into It: An Unfinished Book*. New York: Language Innovations, Inc.

Bodman, Jean & Michael Lanzano. 1975. *No Hot Water Tonight*. New York: Collier-Macmillan.

Buber, Martin. 1924. Essays on "Education" and "The Education of Character." In *Between Man and Man*. Macmillan.

Corey's Golden Geometry Page http://gemini.tntech.edu/~cc18823.

Curran, Charles A. 1972. *Counseling-Learning: A Whole-Person Model for Education*. New York: Grune and Stratton.

Curran, Charles A. 1976. *Counseling-Learning in Second Languages*. 230 Edgewater Rd., Cliffside Park, NJ 07010: Counseling-Learning Institutes.

Curran, Charles A. 1978. *Understanding: A Necessary Ingredient in Human Belonging*. 230 Edgewater Rd., Cliffside Park, NJ 07010: Counseling-Learning Institutes.

Damasio, Antonio. 1994. *Descartes' Error: Emotion, Reason, and the Human Brain*. New York: Avon.

de Bot, Kees. 1996. The psycholinguistics of the Output Hypothesis. *Language Learning* 46.3, 529-555.

Dostoyevsky, Feodor. 1880. *The Brothers Karamazov*. New York: Modern Library.

Edwards, Betty. 1979. *Drawing on the Right Side of the Brain*. Los Angeles: Tarcher.

Ehrman, Madeline E. 1996. *Understanding Second Language Learning Difficulties.* Thousand Oaks, CA: Sage.

Freire, Paulo & Donaldo P. Macedo. 1995. *A Dialogue: Culture, Language, and Race.* Harvard Educational Review 65.3 377–402.

Fujiwara, Barbara. 1993. The richness and depth of suggestopedic education. *Japanese Journal of Suggestopedia*, 1.1, pp. 1–12.

Gallwey, W. Timothy. 1974. *The Inner Game of Tennis.* New York: Random House.

Gateva, Evelyna. 1990. Development of the Potential Creative Talents of the Personality through Suggestopedia. In *Proceedings of the International Conference on Suggestopedia*, Salzburg, 1990, 51–71.

Gateva, Evelyna. 1990. Some Difficult Moments in the Suggestopedic Teaching of Foreign Languages. In *Proceedings of the International Conference on Suggestopedia*, Salzburg, 1990, 91–99.

Gattegno, Caleb. 1973. *The Mind Teaches the Brain.* New York: Educational Solutions, Inc.

Gattegno, Caleb. 1976. *The Common Sense of Teaching Foreign Languages.* New York: Educational Solutions, Inc.

Gattegno, Caleb. 1977. *Evolution and Memory.* New York: Educational Solutions, Inc.

Goleman, Daniel. 1995. *Emotional Intelligence.* New York: Bantam.

Halgren, Eric. 1994. Physiological integration of the declarative memory system. In Delacour, J. (Ed.) *Memory Systems of the Brain.* New York: World. pp. 69–152.

Hamilton, Vernon. 1983. *The cognitive structures and processes of human motivation and personality.* Chichester: John Wiley and Sons.

Harris, Thomas A. 1967. *I'm OK — You're OK.* New York: Harper and Row.

Hartl, Carolyn. 1979. *Modern Language Journal.* 63:4, pp.228f.

Hooper Hansen, Grethe. 1996. Lozanov in Uppsala. *Seal Journal*, Summer 1996, pp. 25–27.

Hooper Hansen, Grethe (forthcoming). Emotions and language learning: A Lozanov perspective. In Arnold (Ed.) *Affect in Language Learning.* Cambridge: Cambridge University Press.

Iki, Setsuko. 1993. Interview: Georgi Lozanov and Evelyna Gateva. *The Language Teacher.* 17.7 3–17.

Jakobovits, Leon & Barbara Gordon. 1974. *The Context of Foreign Language Teaching.* Rowley, MA: Newbury House.

Larsen-Freeman, Diane. 1986. *Techniques and Principles in Language Teaching.* New York: Oxford University Press.

Lazare, Françoise. 1997. Words in Colour in an inner-city neighborhood. *Questions,* vol. 15 p. 29.

Lightbown, Patsy M. & Nina Spada. 1993. *How Languages are Learned.* Oxford: Oxford University Press.

(Lozanov) No editor. 1990. *Proceedings of the International Conference on Suggestopedia*, Salzburg, 1990. Tierp. Sweden: Stiftelsen Pedagogisk Utveckling.

Lozanov, Georgi. 1990. Suggestopedia and Some Aspects of the Psychophysiology of the Potential Abilities (Reserves) of Personality. In *Proceedings of the International Conference on Suggestopedia*, Salzburg, 1990, 9–16.

Lozanov, Georgi & Evalina Gateva. 1988. *The Foreign Language Teacher's Suggestopedic Manual*. New York: Gordon and Breach.

Maley, Alan & Alan Duff. 1978. *Drama Techniques in Language Learning*. Cambridge: Cambridge University Press.

McCarthy, Gregory. 1995. Functional neuroimaging of memory. *The Neuroscientist*, 1.3 pp. 155–163.

Mick, Alice. 1974. From two high school teachers. *Educational Solutions Inc. Newsletter*. 3.4 7–9.

More, Thomas. 1516. Utopia. Vol. 36 in the *Harvard Classics*. New York: Collier.

Murphey, Tim. 1996. *Language Hungry!* Nagoya: South Mountain Press.

Murphey, Tim. 1998. *Language Hungry!* Tokyo: Macmillan Languagehouse.

Oller, John W., Jr. & Patricia Richard-Amato (Eds.). 1983. *Methods That Work*. Rowley, MA: Newbury House.

Postman, Leo & Charles Weingartner. 1969. *Teaching as a Subversive Activity*. New York: Dell.

Rabinowitz, Jan. 1990. Effects of repetition of mental operations on memory for occurrence and origin. *Memory & Cognition* 118(1), 72–82.

Richards, Jack C. & Theodore S. Rodgers. 1986. *Approaches and Methods in Language Teaching: A Description and Analysis*. New York: Cambridge University Press.

Sachs, Oliver. 1985. *The Man Who Mistook His Wife for a Hat, and Other Clinical Tales*. New York: Summit.

Stevick, Earl W. 1971. *Adapting and Writing Language Lessons*. Washington, D. C.: Superintendent of Documents.

Stevick, Earl W. 1980. *Teaching Languages: A Way and Ways*. Rowley, MA: Newbury House.

Stevick, Earl W. 1989. *Success with Foreign Languages*. Hemel Hempstead: Prentice Hall.

Stevick, Earl W. 1990. *Humanism in Language Teaching*. Oxford: Oxford University Press.

Stevick, Earl W. 1996. *Memory, Meaning & Method: A View of Language Teaching*. Second edition. Boston: Heinle & Heinle.

Stevick, Earl W. (forthcoming). The role of affect in memory. In Arnold, Jane (Ed.), *Affect in Language Learning*. Cambridge: Cambridge University Press.

Stevick, Robert D. 1994. *The Earliest Irish and English Bookarts: Visual and Poetic Forms Before A.D. 1000*. Philadelphia: University of Pennsylvania Press.

Swartz, Ted. 1977. Untitled. *Educational Solutions, Inc. Newsletter* 6.2-3, Dec 1996-Feb 1977 14–16.

White, Alan. 1974. From a district administrator. *Educational Solutions Inc. Newsletter*. 3.4 2–3.

Index